SUSTAINABILITY
THE CHALLENGE

SUSTAINABILITY
THE CHALLENGE

People, Power, and the Environment

L. Anders Sandberg, Sverker Sörlin
editors

BLACK ROSE BOOKS

Montréal/New York
London

Black Rose Books No. BB265
Hardcover ISBN: 1-55164-121-6 (bound)
Paperback ISBN: 1-55164-120-8 (pbk.)
Library of Congress Catalog Card Number: 98-71028

This is a book in the Northern Studies Book Series of CERUM,
the Centre for Regional Science at Umeå University, Sweden.

Canadian Cataloguing in Publication Data

L. Anders Sandberg, Sverker Sörlin, editors
Sustainability–the challenge: people, power and the environment

Includes bibliographical references and index.
Hardcover ISBN: 1-55164-121-6(bound)
Paperback ISBN: 1-55164-120-8 (pbk.)

1. Sustainable development. I. Sandberg, L. Anders, 1953- II. Sörlin, Sverker

HC79. E5S88 1998   333.7   C98-900279-9

Cover design: David Cassels, U-EDIT

BLACK ROSE BOOKS

C.P. 1258	250 Sonwil Drive	99 Wallis Road
Succ. Place du Parc	Buffalo, New York	London, E9 5LN
Montréal, H2W 2R3	14225	England
Canada	USA	UK

To order books in North America: (phone) 1-800-565-9523 (fax) 1-800-221-9985
In Europe: (phone) 0181-986-4854 (fax) 0181-533-5821

Our Web Site address: http://www.web.net/blackrosebooks

A publication of the Institute of Policy Alternatives of Montréal (IPAM)
Printed in Canada

Le Conseil des Arts du Canada depuis 1957 | The Canada Council for the Arts since 1957

Table of Contents

Part III Voices from the Margin

Tables And Figures

NOTES ON CONTRIBUTORS

Kurt Viking Abrahamsson is an Associate Professor of physical geography at Umeå University, Sweden. He is currently working as Senior Scientist at the Spatial Modelling Centre in Kiruna in northern Sweden. His research interest have focussed on land use problems in northern areas, and on physical planning in coastal areas. More recently he is focusing on human ecology, natural resources, sustainable development and environmental problems.

David V. J. Bell is Director of the York Centre for Applied Sustainability, Chair of the Ontario Learning for Sustainability Partnership, and former Dean of the Faculty of Environmental Studies at York University. He is currently completing a set of 12 one hour radio broadcasts for the "Open College" on "Sustainability: Canadian Perspectives on a Global Challenge." He is the author of *The Roots of Disunity: A Study of Canadian Political Culture* (Don Mills, Ont.: Oxford University Press, 1992) and co-editor of *Local Places in the Age of the Global City* (Montreal: Black Rose Books, 1996) and *Political Ecology: Global and Local* (London: Routledge, 1998).

Joanna M. Beyers is a doctoral candidate in the Faculty of Environmental Studies at York University. She is an earth scientist concerned primarily with the human relationship to nature. Her dissertation focuses on Canada's Model Forest Program and National Forest Strategy, using various analytical tools from the fields of resource policy, science, political science, and the history of ideas.

Eivor Bucht is a Professor in the Department of Landscape Planning, Swedish University of Agricultural Sciences in Alnarp near Lund. She has a PhD (Agr. Dr.) in landscape architecture and her dissertation focused on public parks in Sweden from 1860 to 1960. She was previously Associate Professor in the Department of Architecture at the KTH (Royal Technical High School) in Stockholm and the founder and head of the Secretariat for Open Space Planning, Movium, in Alnarp. Her research interest comprises different aspects of open space, such as design, history, and ecology. Her recent research focuses on the same aspects for transportation infrastructure.

Lars Carlsson is an Associate Professor in the Division of Political Science at Luleå University of Technology in Sweden. In 1995/96, he was a visiting scholar at Indiana University, U.S. In September 1997 Lars Carlsson joined the Sustainable Boreal Forest Resources Project at the International Institute for Applied Systems Analysis (IIASA) in Austria, where he holds a postdoctoral scholarship from the Swedish Council for Planning and Co-ordination of Research (FRN). At IIASA, he is researching the institutional aspects of the Russian forest sector. Dr. Carlsson received his doctorate in political science from Umeå University, Sweden, in 1993. His dissertation dealt with issues related to policy implementation in local economic development.

Peter Clancy is an Associate Professor of political science at St. Francis Xavier University in Antigonish, Nova Scotia. His recent works on forest policy and industry politics have appeared in *Acadiensis, Business Strategy and the Environment, Journal of Canadian Studies, Trouble in the Woods,* and *New Maritimes.* He is presently working on questions of sustainable forest management in Canada and is preparing, with L. Anders Sandberg, a book on forestry science, professionalism, and politics in Nova Scotia.

Thomas Dunk is an Associate Professor in the Department of Sociology, Lakehead University. He is the author of *It's a Working Man's Town: Male Working-Class Culture in Northwestern Ontario* (Montreal: McGill-Queen's University Press, 1991) and editor of *Social Relations in Resource Hinterlands* (Thunder Bay: Lakehead University, Centre for Northern Studies, 1991) and (with Stephen McBride and Randle W. Nelson) *The Training Trap: Ideology, Training, and the Labour Market* (Winnipeg: Society for Socialist Studies, 1996). His current research focuses on the intersection of culture, identity and social inequality.

Katarina Eckerberg is an Associate Professor in the Department of Political Science at Umeå University with an additional background in forestry and environmental studies. She is the author of *Environmental Protection in Swedish Forestry* (Aldershot: Avebury, 1990), co-author of *Comparing Nordic and Baltic Countries: Environmental Problems and Policy in Agriculture and Forestry* (Copenhagen: Nordisk Ministerråd, 1994), *Process and Policy Evaluation in Structure Planning* (Stockholm: Swedish Council for Building Research, 1993) and author of numerous articles on environmental policy implementation in Sweden and the Nordic-Baltic area. Recent research includes national and local responses to sustainable development and Agenda 21 in an international and comparative perspective. She is also on the Steering Committee of the new Umeå School of Environmental Studies, which is an interdisciplinary collaboration between Umeå University and the Swedish University of Agricultural Sciences in Umeå, strengthening education and research on environmental issues in Umeå.

Anna Gibson is a graduate student in the Faculty of Environmental Studies at York University. Her position as the Coordinator of the Haliburton Highlands Bioregional Atlas Project began during her undergraduate degree at Trent University and continues to be a focus in her work at York. Her primary interests focus on bioregionalism, sustainable communities, and bioregional community mapping as a means of knowledge production and empowerment.

Peter Harries-Jones received his first degrees in anthropology from Rhodes University, South Africa and the University of Oxford, UK. Subsequent resesearch in Zambia resulted in several publications on the politics of independence. His more recent work at York University has been on the joint themes of communication, epistemology of social movements and the environmental movement in particular. His most recent books include *Making Knowledge Count: Advocacy and Social Science* (Montreal: McGill-Queen's University Press, 1991); and *A Recursive Vision: Ecological Understanding and Gregory Bateson* (Toronto: University of Toronto Press, 1995). The latter, which is based on archival research of unpublished letters and manuscripts, presents the matrix of ideas from which Bateson drew his holistic perspective or "ecology of mind."

Alf Hornborg is a Professor of Human Ecology, Lund University. He has previously worked in the anthropology departments of Uppsala University and Gothenburg University. His recent research interests focus on an attempt to integrate world systems theory and ecological economics in order to reconceptualize industrial technology in the light of an ecological theory of unequal exchange. He has also published articles on modernity, identity and power. He has conducted fieldwork in Peru and in Nova Scotia. Previous research interests include indigenous Amazonian social organization and Andean ethnoarchaeology.

Russell Janzen is a PhD student in Political Science and the former Project Coordinator of the Centre for Research on Work and Society, both at York University. He has been a trade union activist and is currently a member of the Green Work Alliance and the Toronto editorial group of *Capitalism, Nature, Socialism*.

Ella Johansson is an Assistant Professor at the Department of Ethnology at Umeå University, Sweden. She is the author of the book *Skogarnas Fria Söner* [The Free Sons of the Forest] (Stockholm: Nordiska Museets Förlag, 1994) on masculinity and modernity among loggers during the industrialization of Sweden. She is leading the planning of a cross-disciplinary project entitled "Flexibility as tradition," which deals with culture, social relations and economic adaptation in peripheral regions over the long term. Her recent research focuses on epistemology in the social sciences and on personhood, masculinity and popular conceptions of socio-economic relations.

Jamie Lawson is completing his PhD dissertation on the forest-use conflicts in the Temagami and Algonquin Park areas at York University's Graduate Program in Political Science. His particular interests are the inter-civilizational tensions exhibited in the environmentalist/First Nation relationship, as both movements seek changes to forest practices.

Anna-Lisa Lindén is a Professor of Sociology at Lund University in Sweden. She is a member of The Swedish Panel on Climate Change and The Swedish Council for Forestry and Agricultural Research. Her publications focus on urban and environmental sociology, values, attitudes, lifestyles, and the globalization of lifestyles and consumption patterns.

Laurel Sefton MacDowell is an Associate Professor in the Department of History at Erindale College, University of Toronto. She teaches and writes in the areas of Canadian working class and environmental history. She is an active member of the North Toronto Green Community.

Peter J. Murphy is Professor Emeritus in forestry at the University of Alberta, and previously Associate Dean for forestry in the Faculty of Agriculture and Forestry. He is past-president of the Canadian Institute of Forestry and past president of the Forest History Society, Inc. of Durham NC. Among his published works is *History of Forest and Prairie Fire Control Policy in Alberta* (Edmonton: Alberta Energy and Natural Resources, 1985).

L. Anders Sandberg teaches in the Faculty of Environmental Studies at York University. He is the editor of *Trouble in the Woods: Forest Policy and Social Conflict in Nova Scotia and New Brunswick* (Fredericton: Acadiensis Press, 1992). His recent work on forest-related issues have appeared in *Acadiensis, Journal of Canadian Studies, Environmental History,* and *Economic and Industrial Democracy*.

Klas Sandell holds a position as a lecturer in human geography, Department of Social Science, University of Örebro, Sweden and is associated with environmental history, Department of History of Science and Ideas, Umeå University. With a PhD background in 1988, from Tema on Water and Environmental Studies, Linköping University, he focused on human ecology, attitudes towards nature and development strategies. His current research include out-of-doors and environmental history in 20th century Sweden, and outdoor life as a research area and an academic subject for the Department of Physical Education and Health, University of Örebro.

Bo Sundin is a Professor in the Department of the History of Science and Ideas at Umeå University, Sweden. His research interests focus on the history of technology, the intellectual history of popular movements in Sweden and ideological aspects of environmental protection and the preservation of cultural heritage. He is currently conducting a project on "The Cultural Heritage and the Future" financed by the Swedish Institute for Future Studies.

Sverker Sörlin is a Professor of environmental history in the Department of History of Science and Ideas at Umeå University, Sweden. His interests encompass history of science, environmental history, research policy, human ecology, and third world issues. He has published numerous scientific papers and books, essays and journalistic accounts in Swedish. He is co-editor of *Denationalizing Science: The Contexts of International Scientific Practice* (Dordrecht, Boston & London: Kluwer, 1993), and editor of *The Road to Sustainability: A Historical Perspective* (Uppsala: The Baltic University Programme, 1997).

John H. Wadland is an environmental historian who has been active in the field since he published his biography of *Ernest Thompson Seton: Man in Nature and the Progressive Era* (New York: Arno Press, 1978). He was for several years Editor of the *Journal of Canadian Studies*. Recently, after stepping down as Chair of the Canadian Studies Program, he became Director of the Frost Centre for Canadian Heritage and Development Studies at Trent University.

Anders Öckerman is a PhD student in environmental history in the Department of History of Science and Ideas at Umeå University, Sweden. His research is focused on Swedish forestry theory in the period 1860-1960. He teaches environmental history and ethics, and human ecology. He also has a degree in cultural anthropology and a M.Sc. in Forestry.

Lars Östlund is an Assistant Professor in forest history in the Department of Forest Vegetation Ecology at the Swedish University of Agricultural Sciences in Umeå. He presented a doctoral dissertation entitled "Exploitation and structural changes in the north Swedish boreal forest 1800-1992" in 1993. Present areas of research include interdisciplinary work in forest history regarding timber frontier development in Scandinavia and North America, pre-industrial forest use in Scandinavia, structural changes among key-stone tree-species in boreal Sweden and historical forest technology. He has taught forest history at most Swedish universities.

Foreword

In less than 24 months, we begin a new century and a new millennium. A thousand years seems like a long time, and in relation to human history, it is. But human beings are relative newcomers to the planet. If the history of the planet were compressed into a single week that began at midnight Sunday, human beings would not show up until a few seconds before midnight the following Saturday!

If the human species hopes to celebrate the birth of a further millennium, what must change; and what must be preserved? Obviously by posing this question, I am in effect begging it. My premise is that the status quo is unsustainable. At current rates of economic growth, fueled by over-consumption, population growth, and wasteful production, we will eventually exceed earth's carrying capacity.[1]

Figuring out how to change direction is the central concern of the next century, and the essence of the "challenge of sustainability" with which this book deals. Co-editors Anders Sandberg and Sverker Sörlin point out that this challenge will force us "to consider social and environmental aspects as intricately linked." This task is neither straightforward nor simple, particularly in countries like Sweden and Canada where the "master narrative of environmental discourse" views nature as an abundant source of raw materials and a convenient sink for wastes, with "experts" designated as sole arbiters of both types of human-nature interaction. This book offers a number of fresh visions and critical alternatives to the dominant "resourcist" discourse. Several of the contributors encourage us to reconsider both traditional and aboriginal perspectives as sources of insight. It is increasingly clear that we must somehow manage to adapt our lifestyle and system of economic production so that we learn to "walk softly on our sacred Mother, the Earth, for we walk on the faces of the unborn, those who have yet to rise and take up the challenges of existence."[2]

In 1992, leaders from 178 countries came together in Rio de Janeiro to map out a sustainability agenda for the twenty-first century. A comprehensive and ambitious document, the forty chapters of *Agenda 21* address most (but not all) of the key challenges that must be faced at the global, national and local level if we are to move to a more sustainable path. The chapter most closely related to the dominant concerns of this book is Chapter 11 ("Combating Deforestation").

In June of 1997, the United Nations convened a special session in New York to take stock of how far we have advanced toward implementing the recommendations of *Agenda 21*. The following conclusion sums up the major "unfulfilled expectations" and "obstacles to be overcome" in the forestry sector:

Although some corrective actions have been attempted to alleviate pressures exerted on forest resources, rapidly growing populations, poverty, unsuitable land use, adverse incentives, and the impact of human activities associated with production and consumption patterns have continued to damage forests.[3]

From the essays in this book, what lessons can we learn about sustainability? One of the fascinating properties of the theory and practice of sustainability is that virtually every issue recapitulates the whole struggle, just as each cell of an organism contains the DNA for the entire body. Though most of the contributions to this book on forestry and nature deal with micro issues, often very local in scope, together they touch on all the main themes of sustainability. From these authors we learn not only about the problems, but also about the kinds of actions that point toward solutions. The long march toward sustainability will consist of many small steps. We must begin somewhere, and we must at some point find our way through the forests without destroying them in the process. This book will serve as a useful guide.

As several contributors remind us, *Agenda 21* provides an impressive "blueprint" for the next century, but we have barely begun to construct the edifice of change it envisions. As we move from Agenda to Action, the issues discussed in this book will become urgent matters for debate and decision at all levels from the local to the global. Can we redefine economic development—particularly in the wealthy countries of the North like Sweden and Canada—so that it ceases to be a synonym for growth? Such a transformation will require what some have called a "second industrial revolution" to replace the resource-costly, fossil-driven technologies of the past with new technologies based on renewable energy, resource conservation, and labour intensity. The implications for the forestry sector include the need to reevaluate the labour-intensive sustainable forestry practices of the last century.

Conventional economics will dismiss this prospect as uneconomic and inefficient. After all, we live in a capitalist system embedded in a global economy. But conventional economics takes far too narrow an approach to defining capital, focusing almost exclusively on manufactured capital while ignoring the precious stock of natural, human and social capital we hold in trust for future generations. A new paradigm that embraces ecological thinking must replace the increasingly anachronistic mainstream approach.

As the ecological insight spreads through academic disciplines and popular culture, more and more people will develop a "new" sensibility about the relationship between humans and the environment in which we live; and understand better the importance of social equity to all forms of sustainability.

Much of what we need to learn has been present for a very long time in aboriginal and other cultures. "Modern" culture, by contrast, is tragically flawed. One of the attributes of the modern outlook that first emerged in the seventeenth century was the ascendancy among what Thomas Hobbes called "masterless men" of "the restless desire for thing after thing."[4] The eventual result can be described as a global lifestyle disease. Some have labeled this disease "affluenza," but it resembles more closely an addiction than a virus. In attempting to overcome it, we can learn more from counsellors than physicians.

Like recovering alcoholics, we need both wisdom and courage: wisdom to recognize those aspects of our natural and cultural heritage that must be preserved; and the courage to change the rest. Collectively, we must achieve the transition from an egocentric ethic (in which we care only about our own community or nation) to one of anthropocentrism (in which we care about all other humans) and ultimately to ecocentrism (in which we care about everything). At that point we might have a perspective of nature appropriate for the twentyfirst century.

Is this likely? Certainly not without a concerted effort to promote "education for sustainability" (as outlined in Chapter 36 of *Agenda 21*). Most assuredly little will change until we transform many of our structures and institutions; and until those who hold so much power, particularly in business and government, themselves become convinced of the wisdom of sustainability. This may never happen. It would arguably constitute the greatest cultural transformation in the (brief) history of humankind. But much is at stake. And the potential is there.

David V.J. Bell
Thornhill, Ontario
February 11, 1998

Notes

1. Of course "we" are not all equally culpable agents of the degradation of the natural environment. Residents of wealthy industrialized nations of the North (like Canada and Sweden) consume far more, on average, than those who live in the South. With less than twenty percent of the world's population, the North consumes over eighty percent of the world's resources. One formula that attempts to measure humans' impact on the natural environment views this impact as the product of population times affluence times technology. As the countries of the South become more populous and acquire more wealth and technology, environmental impacts and problems will grow proportionately.

2. "Prayer of Thanksgiving." Introduction to the first volume, "Looking Forward, Looking Back," *Report of the Royal Commission on Aboriginal Peoples* (Ottawa: Minister of Supply and Services Canada, 1996). The full passage from which the quotation was extracted is as follows:

Finally, we acknowledge one another, female and male. We give greetings and thanks that we have this opportunity to spend some time together. We turn our minds to our ancestors and our Elders. You are the carriers of knowledge, of our history. We acknowledge the adults among us. You represent the bridge between the past and the future. We also acknowledge our youth and children. It is to you that we will pass on the responsibilities we now carry. Soon, you will take our place in facing the challenges of life. Soon, you will carry the burden of your people. Do not forget the ways of the past as you move toward the future. Remember that we are to walk softly on our sacred Mother, the Earth, for we walk on the faces of the unborn, those who have yet to rise and take up the challenges of existence. We must consider the effects our actions will have on their ability to live a good life.

3. *Commission On Sustainable Development*, Fifth Session (April 7-25, 1997). "Overall progress achieved since the United Nations Conference on Environment and Development." Report of the Secretary-General. Addendum: "Combating Deforestation (chapter 11 of *Agenda 21*) and the Non-Legally Binding Authoritative Statement of Principles for a Global Consensus on the Management, Conservation and Sustainable Development of All Types of Forests" (New York: The United Nations Food and Agriculture Organization, 1997).

4. Thomas Hobbes, *Leviathan* (Menston: Scolar P., 1969 [1651]), Chapter 13.

PREFACE

On the 15th and 16th of May 1996, a group of Swedish and Canadian scholars assembled at York University for a conference entitled "The Challenge of Sustainability: Environmental Issues in Canada and Sweden," organized under the auspices of the Swedish-Canadian Academic Foundation (SCAF). Created in 1992, SCAF is a cooperative agreement between eight Canadian and Swedish universities to promote research, seminars and academic exchanges. Previous conferences have focused on the history of the welfare state, the position of Sweden and Canada in the European Union and the North American Free Trade Agreement, and labour and social policy.[1]

These conference themes reflect well the interests shared by Canada and Sweden in the past. Canadians in particular, have shared with others a fascination with Sweden's record on industrial strategy, resource use, and labour market and social policies. It has been less common to explore the impact of these activities on the physical environment. A conference on the environment therefore seemed timely and appropriate, given the shared heritage of Canada and Sweden, and the general urgency of environmental issues in the 1990s. The Faculty of Environmental Studies at York University took the initiative to organize and host the conference, while the Environmental History Section of the Department of History of Science and Ideas at Umeå University provided assistance.

During the conference and the process of putting together the chapters for this volume, it became increasingly apparent that sustainability is a rather ambiguous concept. Like the term development, sustainability is a concept that has been appropriated by many and even subverted by some. Most of the conference contributors suggested, either through powerful critiques of the status quo, or through exploration of alternatives rooted in the past or in the experiences of marginal groups, that sustainability and environmental issues need to be very carefully stated or articulated. Much of the present environmental discourse seems to revolve around the preservation of "wilderness areas" and parks, and this focus seems to provide a screen for the continued presence of highly manipulated environments. Both these environments are often exclusive, serving the wealthy's demand for recreation, solitude and "nature" experiences or the continued thirst for consumer goods. The contributors of this volume, we feel, speak for the rearticulation of an understanding and treatment of the environment. They look for a pluralist discourse of nature and environments in between (neither "[p]reserved" nor highly manipulated) where local people form an integral part of local ecosystems. The chapters that are included here do not, then, leave behind the concerns of previous conferences. The main message of the chapters is that social aspects are exceedingly important to the resolution of environmental problems.

As conference organizers, we would like to thank all the participants of the conference, and especially those that submitted essays for consideration for inclusion in this volume. We are grateful to Michael Stevenson, Vice President of Academic Affairs and Coordinator of the Swedish Canadian Academic Foundation, the former Dean of the Faculty of Environmental Studies David Bell, and Maria Cioni and Rosemary Nielsen of York International for providing continuous and generous support throughout the course of the planning and follow up work after the conference. We would also like to thank the Social Sciences and Humanities Research Council of Canada for a generous conference grant. Mary Bernard, Dianne Zecchino, and graduate student Lynna Landstreet of FES' External Relations shared in organizing the logistical support of the conference and its promotion. In Sweden, Anders Öckerman in Umeå took good care of all the Swedish participants.

As editors of this volume, we are grateful to Carina Hernandez, who oversaw the final preparations of the various chapters, and the York graduate students who assisted on the project, including Ken Ferguson, Marc McClean, Michelle Maxwell, and Jody Vandeputte.

David Cassels of U-EDIT designed the book cover, using his own art work. It symbolizes the nature or environment in between that forms the focus of this book, the nature that straddles the utilitarian and wilderness landscapes that dominate the environmental discourse currently. It also represents the view that nature is primarily culture, and that human actions and myths should not only be lamented for their negative impacts on nature, but also celebrated for their proper place in "nature."

We would also like to acknowledge the kind support of Umeå University's Centre for Regional Science, CERUM, whose Northern Studies Program has accepted the book in its Northern Studies Book Series.

The following private institutions gave generously in support of the conference, and the publication of the present book: Ericsson Communications Canada, the Swedish Women's Educational Association, Casco Nobel, Husqvarna Forest and Garden, the Embassy of Sweden, Avesta Sheffield Inc., Nobelpharma Canada Inc., and SKF Canada Limited.

There are three extra letters in the Swedish alphabet, å [aa], ä [ae], and ö [oe], which appear at the end of the alphabet. The index follows the way in which these letters appear in the Swedish alphabet.

L. Anders Sandberg and Sverker Sörlin
Toronto and Umeå
February 4, 1998

Notes
1. Two of the conferences have resulted in proceedings: Sune Åkerman and J.L. Granatstein, eds., *Welfare States in Trouble: Historical Perspectives on Canada and Sweden* (North York: Swedish-Canadian Academic Foundation, 1994)[also published as Umeå Studies in Humanities 124 (Umeå: Umeå University, 1995)] and Swedish-Canadian Academic Foundation, *The Entry into New Economic Communities: Swedish and Canadian Perspectives on the European Economic Community and the North American Free Trade Accord* (North York: Swedish-Canadian Academic Foundation, 1994).

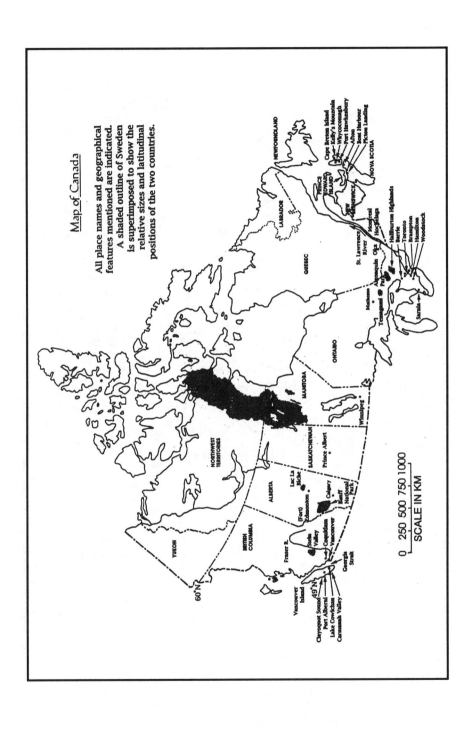

Map of Canada

All place names and geographical
features mentioned are indicated.
A shaded outline of Sweden
is superimposed to show the
relative sizes and latitudinal
positions of the two countries.

YUKON

NORTHWEST
TERRITORIES

BRITISH
COLUMBIA

ALBERTA

SASKATCHEWAN

MANITOBA

QUEBEC

ONTARIO

LABRADOR

NEWFOUNDLAND

60°N

Vancouver
Island

Chesnoqust Sound
Port Alberni
Lake Cowichan
Caramanah Valley

49° N

Georgia
Strait

Vancouver
Coquitlam
Sooke
Valley

Fraser R.

Edmonton
(Ford)

Lac La
Biche

Prince Albert

Calgary
Banff
National
Park

Winnipeg

Melbourne
Temagami
Oka
Park

St. Lawrence
River

Montreal
Montmagny
Haszeldega

Sarnia

Haliburton Highlands
Barrie
Toronto
Brampton
Hamilton
Woodstock

PRINCE
EDWARD
ISLAND

NEW BRUNSWICK

NOVA SCOTIA

Cape Breton Island
Kelly's Mountain
Whycocomagh
Port Hawkesbury
Afton
Boat Harbour
Pictou Landing

0   250 500 750 1000

SCALE IN KM

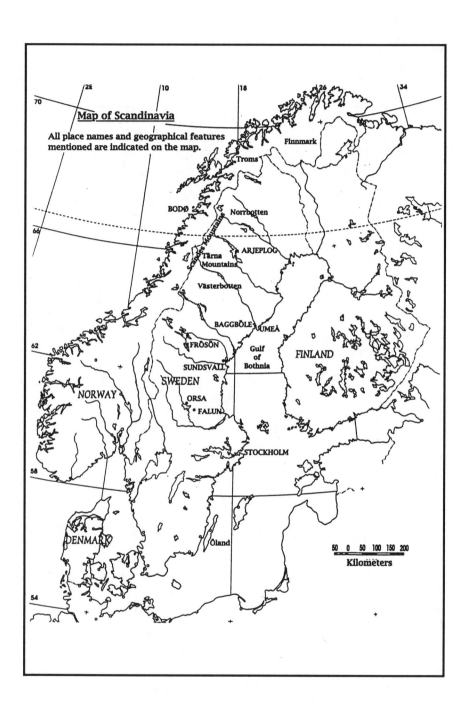

Map of Scandinavia

All place names and geographical features
mentioned are indicated on the map.

Chapter One

REARTICULATING THE ENVIRONMENT

Towards a Pluralist Vision of Natural Resource Use

L. Anders Sandberg, Sverker Sörlin

The concept of environmentalism has so many advocates and definitions as to be almost meaningless. Within the environmentalist movement, preservationists promote the protection of natural environments, or wild nature untouched by the human hand.[1] Biocentrists support the intrinsic value of nature, and question the anthropocentric and utilitarian focus on natural resource use.[2] The more mainstream environmentalists call for more or less stringent measures to curb general consumption levels and promote more environmentally-sensitive resource use and zero-level pollution.[3]

National governments and industry spokespeople, on the other hand, embrace the notion that industrial and economic growth can be compatible with environmental concerns. The Brundtland report is legendary here, combining the two concepts in the term sustainable development.[4] The sustainable development position stresses government intervention and the development of regulations to ensure prudent resource use and minimum pollution levels, or emphasizes voluntary measures and market incentives to steer business on a more sustainable path.[5]

Both the environmentalist and sustainable development positions have been criticized for several reasons. The environmentalist visions have been shown to overlook equity issues, such as those related to class, gender, generation, ethnicity and nation states. Wilderness preserves, be they in Sweden, Canada or the tropics, for example, while serving as repositories for biodiversity, refuges for endangered flora and fauna, carbon sinks and even sources of revenue from ecotourism, may also displace local people who previously gained a livelihood in these areas.[6] The focus on excessive consumption and waste similarly overlooks the growing number of poor within the industrialized countries and the vast majority in the Third World who do not enjoy an adequate standard of living.[7]

The sustainable development concept is equally problematic. Frequently called an oxymoron, a contradiction in terms, there are many examples which show that development (implying economic growth) cannot be sustainable, and that we need to confront the very growth mechanism of capitalist society in order to promote environmentalism.[8] National governments, for example, have been largely unsuccessful in cutting global carbon emissions. The greening of industry movement has similarly failed in many respects, revolving more around marketing savvy to appear green than any real environmental concern. A considerable backlash has in fact emerged against environmental concerns from various business and government organizations.[9]

We suggest that any act that purports to be sustainable must not only promote environmental integrity and biodiversity, but also human equity at the local, national, international and inter-generational scale. Sustainability thus refers to a condition that exists in the proverbial middleground between utilitarianism and biocentrism, and individualist and collectivist values. The challenge of sustainability is to consider social and environmental aspects as intricately linked.[10] Sustainability, in short, is about people and power, and the efforts to rearticulate environments towards a more pluralist and equitable form of natural resource use.

To rearticulate nature means first of all to accept as a given that nature is not only the nature "out there." Nature is also culture, and overlain by the signs and scars of resource use and human intervention. Nature is also culturally constituted in our minds, forming landscapes of different, and constantly changing, values. Fundamentally, it seems that the dualism between these double natures—to quote Kenneth Olwig's expression—[11] although probably unavoidable, has grown too deep. We should rather accept that the realm of human responsibility for nature goes far beyond that of creating designated reserved areas for protection and, at the same time, leaving other areas for uninhibited use. Nature has not only a past, but also a present and, not the least, a future. Rearticulation means to readdress that future, to enter human words and intentions into the ongoing process of moulding the material basis of our survival. In other words, the future of nature is a political issue.[12]

To widen the discourse of sustainability along these lines, it might be instructive to look at a number of real life cases that can anchor the concept in history and society. The contributions in this volume present empirical studies from two countries with many similarities, but also many differences. Sweden and Canada are northern countries with vast hinterlands and a long tradition as producers of export staples. They are also on the northern border of powerful economic neighbours, and share a focus, albeit within clearly different contexts, on socially responsible policies. On the other hand, Canada is extremely vast and, even compared to Sweden, sparsely populated. It is culturally diverse and harbours British and American political traditions that value the individual more highly than the collective.[13]

In the Swedish case, history goes a long way to explain its current policy of "realist sustainability." We should remember that the instrumentalist paradigm of unrestrained exploitation for human ends that sustainability seeks to at least redress, maybe even challenge, has had a long time to grow and become established. In Sweden, a tradition of political arithmetic—working with quantitative methods to identify and measure resources—gained ground already in the late seventeenth and early eighteenth centuries, that is well before the tradition of sustained yield that came to Sweden from the German states in the nineteenth century. The political arithmetic portrayed nature in this powerful Baltic nation as well-endowed and a divinely privileged repository of people (labour power), plants and animals. Industrialism in the nineteenth and twentieth centuries reinforced that tradition, placing particular pride in the fact that Sweden was rich in natural resources on which to build a new and glorious future.[14]

The often proclaimed sensitivity for nature and the mythological side of Nordic nature displayed in the arts was actually built alongside, or rather on top of, industrialized nature. It was the growth of the industrial economy and of an urban middle class with nationalist and aesthetic values that formed the sociological basis of the esteem for wilderness, and thus for preservationist and conservationist policies in the first decades of the twentieth century. However, these groups were also quite sensitive to the demands of industry, and responsibility for the productive capacity of the nation was sometimes used as an argument to sacrifice precious forests, waterfalls, or marshes, even among members of the Swedish Association for the Conservation of Nature, *Svenska Naturskyddsföreningen* (SNF). The role of nature as a national asset was a view that was almost universally accepted, and it should come as no surprise that the state had a marked presence in conservationist affairs as legislator but also provider of the ultimate ideology of nature: nature as the national common ground and the essential backbone of wealth on Europe's northern periphery, where the aboriginal Saami population was affected by centuries of territorial and judicial setbacks.[15]

After World War II, the environmental agenda was established fairly rapidly and with a remarkably focused political activity in the 1960s and 1970s, the state putting forth a comprehensive environmental legislation in 1969 and hosting the first United Nations Conference on the Environment in Stockholm in 1972.[16] This can be partly explained by the strong social position by scientists, advocating environmental concerns, through the nature protection committee the Royal Swedish Academy of Sciences, or through the SNF, where they were prominent. But at the very heart of the process lies probably—no substantial study exists to date—the strong position of the state. Environmentalism was implemented top-down, and was therefore both pragmatic and essentially instrumentalist in its approach. It can be argued that the relatively well organized response that the *Agenda 21* initiative has received in Sweden, with a host of activities especially on the organized grass root level, such as in schools, day cares, civil organizations and others, is to a large extent a manifestation of this tradition of a strong adherence to central authority. The gospel does not in all respects result in deed, however. If we look broadly at environmental indicators there is no reason to suggest that Sweden will come out significantly better than many other reasonably well-to-do industrial nations.

Sustainability is in that respect not something alien to the history of Swedish policies on nature, conservation, resource management, and the environment. Rather, the ambiguities of the concept and its predecessors has been there in the Swedish case throughout this century.[17] Even the more outspoken green stance being taken by the Social Democratic government that came into power in 1994 has followed essentially the same pattern. While it can be argued that no administration has done more to implement sustainability and *Agenda 21* principles into the everyday life of Swedish public institutions, it is still safe to say that the ideological underpinnings rest essentially on economic growth and defence of an efficient and productive society. Striking compromises with the official ideals, for example the lack of sufficient funding for forest reserves and a weak preservationist and biodiversity policy, might be explained by this. It is maybe telling that the current Prime Minister Göran Persson contributed to a social democratic party report in 1992 entitled "blue and yellow growth"—a message prompted by the accelerating economic crisis but at the same time well founded in the tradition of Swedish environmental policy.[18]

The country's environmental performance has, understandably, had its admirers. One is equally correct in pointing out that the bread and butter priorities have never been seriously threatened. What the critics will find, though, is that Sweden, probably alongside her Nordic neighbours, has operated within a conceptual universe of fundamental nature-culture dualism. Nature has been interpreted spiritually and manifested as the holy grail of national identity. On this side tradition has also put older agrarian landscapes. What has not been articulated, and definitely not advocated, is the partly used, partly bruised, fragmented and lamented, semi-urban, semi-rural, historic/contemporary chaotic-mosaic landscape that is the reality of ever increasing areas in many regions of the country. Why is it that these landscapes somehow have not qualified as either cultural heritage sites or nature reserves?[19]

The Canadian case also has important historical dimensions. In contrast to Sweden, Canada's heritage is colonial, and its resource and environmental policies were initially shaped by the demands of the mother country rather than a central national(ist) government. After Confederation in 1867 and the implementation of the National Policy Tariffs of 1879—which nurtured a secondary manufacturing base—the Canadian economy remained truncated, being largely supportive of the export staples economy and dependent on American capital and technology in the form of branch plants.[20]

The conservationist and preservationist movement that emerged was weakened by the Canadian staples tradition and the absence of a centralized state. The British North America Act of 1867 gave full jurisdiction of lands and natural resources to the provinces, which resulted in provincial governments and resource companies dominating the resource and environmental policy field. Provincial governments thus clamour for resource revenue and jobs in close collaboration with resource companies. The focus is on how to develop rather than to conserve, let alone preserve, natural resources. Even national and provincial parks have been much more open to resource use and commercial pursuits than their counterparts in the United States.

The Canadian federal government and science community have bowed to this history and jurisdictional split. Nature has been mathematized for the benefit of resource development, and the federal government and its research community have been at the forefront of that endeavour.[21] And just like in Sweden, the Canadian sensitivities and myths about nature in the arts, built on and supported the Canadian staples economy. The nationalist Group of Seven painters—who were inspired by Scandinavian art and pioneered the portrayal of Canadian wilderness (rather than bucolic domesticated scenes in the European tradition)—remained supportive of, and supported by, the industrial resource sector.[22] The provision of outdoor leisure and recreation also took on a colonial and elitist character.[23]

Nor did Canada, as Sweden, have a peasant economy based on husbandry and tradition to draw on. The mining of the soil, and the seemingly limitless settlement frontier, meant that agriculture was more of an extractive rather than renewable activity. Similarly, in Canadian resource towns, local populations and working people, have both been encouraged and pressured into supporting the staples colossus. All in all, Canadians appear to be plagued by an "environmental blind spot," much of it due to the over-dependence on polluting resource industries and, from time to time, a concern with the foreign domination of its economy.[24]

Yet, as elsewhere, a Canadian environmental revolution occurred amidst such events as the publication of Rachel Carson's *Silent Spring* in the early 1960s and Earth Day in 1970. But in contrast to Sweden, the state's reaction was less characterized by top-down initiatives; instead, the federal and provincial governments responded intermittently to the bottom-up pressures from the national and international environmentalist communities. Typically, the federal government tried to lead the way, but its efforts have been continually frustrated and/or resisted by the provinces. In oil and gas-rich Alberta, Bruce Doern writes, for example, that "environmental policy is energy policy."[25] But the efforts of the federal government have not been much better. The well-publicized green federal initiatives of the Mulroney Conservative government (1984-93) had more to do with maximizing electoral and bureaucratic standing than caring for the environment.[26] Since then, the spending on environmental matters by the present Liberal government and all provincial governments has decreased markedly. It is perhaps not strange, then, that *Agenda 21* of the Rio Conference on the Environment is unknown to most Canadians, and that Canada's commitment to reduce greenhouse gases has been an abysmal failure, though renewed commitments were made at the recent United Nations conference in Kyoto, Japan.

Yet the vastness of Canada and the relatively lateness of its "development" present some fascinating opportunities that are not present in Sweden. The remnants of old growth forests and pristine landscapes have allowed for a larger percentage of land being set aside for protected places than in Sweden, though it must be remembered that these areas are still not numerous or large enough to represent the uniqueness of all Canadian ecosystems. The areas set aside tend to be too small and/or confined to those landscapes that are the most remote and/or the least valuable for extractive use by humans.

Canada may also harbour a disproportionate number of marginal groups that do not fit, and who might provide alternatives, to the modern natural resource management scheme. Historically, Canada has constituted a haven for some of these groups, such as Ukrainians, Doukhobors, and Mennonites. As these lines are penned, Ontario Mennonites are helping eastern Ontario dairy farmers to hand-milk their cows—a long-forgotten and difficult task—because crippling rain storms have shut off the electrical power to the milking-machines. Perhaps the greatest prospect for change, however, lies in Canada's First Nations, whose legally-recognized rights to lands and its uses are now negotiated in and out of the courts. In some instances, public support, and political provisions, have resulted in some spectacular achievements, such as the social and environmental assessment report of Mr. Justice Thomas Berger, which halted the construction of the MacKenzie Valley Pipeline in 1977 before First Nations' land rights were settled in the area.[27]

Sweden and Canada thus present precisely the mixed cases that offer excellent opportunities to explore the varieties and contradictions of sustainability, just as the chapters in this volume do. Both countries still have a long way to go in order to rearticulate their national territories and environments, and to find in these spatial narratives new vistas and fresh balances between regions, sites and phenomena of the natural as well as the artificial.

In Part I, "Rearticulating Nature," the authors advance different theoretical perspectives on how to interpret environmental phenomena. All place themselves firmly in the middleground between culture and nature, recognizing the integral role of humans in ecosystems change.

Eivor Bucht and Bo Sundin suggest that modernist visions of the environment should not be disposed of too readily. Few environments have gone untouched by the human hand, and some of these need to be preserved and celebrated. Both authors provide powerful statements on what Swedish peasant and social democratic society may have in store in building sustainability.

Bucht looks at how third nature, the urban garden, used for utility and pleasure, has been neglected in the drive to develop and preserve the first and second natures, the rural utility landscapes and the wildernesses (the few that remain). The former, Bucht maintains, may have as important a role to play as the wheatfields and the wilderness parks in terms of providing food and biodiversity, as well as promoting an understanding of unique ecological processes.

Sundin's treatment of the concept of *hembygd* in Sweden, loosely translated as hometown, denotes people's attachments to local places over a long time. While such feelings are often conservative and nostalgic, Sundin also recognizes their importance in shaping a sense of personal well-being. Culture, in other words, is heritage. This is no less true in today's virtual world, where the individual's concept of place has expanded spatially while the time perspective has been shortened. In this situation, it may be important to preserve modernist notions of heritage, such as the welfare state, which is now so aggressively attacked by national governments in their efforts to overcome the flip side of globalization.

Anna-Lisa Lindén employs the social constructionist perspective to environmental behaviour at the individual and group level. Her point of departure is that environmental concern is seldom matched by remedial action, especially when these actions affect the western-based high consumer-oriented lifestyle. She nevertheless notes differences in the behaviour of younger and older generations and women and men.[28] She then develops a classification scheme of environmental values, suggesting four categories: the egoistic exploiter, the egoistic conserver, the collectivist exploiter and the collectivist conserver. Her findings suggest that Swedes, in spite of their nature-rooted culture and social democratic tradition, exhibit the traits of egoistic exploiters and conservers.

Lindén questions any claim that Sweden is qualitatively different in its pursuit of sustainability. If an environmental consciousness has emerged it is only different in degrees from other national contexts, and the historical and wider context of global capitalism continues to shape environmental policy.

Peter Harries-Jones provides a framework for envisioning a different society where a collectivist-conserver ethic prevails. Drawing on the dualism between left biocentrists and advocates of First Nations' land and resource rights, he advocates a science of holism, where the environmental concerns of the former are merged with the equity concerns of the latter. Drawing on Gregory Bateson's concept of "immanent spirituality," Harries-Jones argues for the inseparateness of the sacred and the material. This message echoes the concerns of the previous authors, which suggest that "reality has innumerable descriptions" and that there are alternative ways of thinking about and practising sustainability.

In Part II, "Common or Uncommon Ground?," various reflections on the possibilities and limitations of reformist environmental policies are illustrated by a number of chapters on forest-related issues in Canada and Sweden. There is much to be learnt from these accounts from a comparative perspective, the forest and the forest industry constituting a major source of cultural inspiration and economic revenue in both countries. The question of what constitutes common or uncommon ground—with respect to ecology, management, ownership, certification, and recreation—is addressed, and the conclusions confirm the importance of respect for diversity and a range of policy options.

Peter Murphy and Lars Östlund explore the nature of past forest environments, and point to the drastic anthropogenic forces that have changed the forest over time. Murphy points to the important relationship between the western boreal forest environment and fire. Rather than constituting a catastrophic event, which ought to be prevented through fire suppression, fires constitute an integral part of the boreal forest system. Murphy shows how the Aboriginal peoples understood this relationship, and lived in and treated the forest accordingly. He also shows the massive changes affecting the boreal forest under European settlement, including exploitative harvesting, clearings (for settlements and agriculture) and fire prevention. Murphy concludes by noting the recent emergence of ecosystems management, which concerns itself with more closely replicating the influences of fire or natural disturbances in forest harvesting in support of biodiversity, and re-introducing fire in other areas.

Östlund provides a picture of the important changes which have occurred in the northern Swedish boreal forest since the beginning of settlement and exploitation. His pioneering research attempts to reconstruct the nature of past forest environments, and the ensuing impact of human activities. His findings show that the much praised achievements of twentieth century Swedish forest management have had a high ecological price. Exploitative harvesting, the modern notion of keeping the forest "clean" of dying and dead trees, and fire suppression have changed the composition of the forest and associated forest ecosystems. Clearcuts have grown, old growth forests and trees have declined, single species even-aged forests have displaced more varied forests, and exotics have been introduced.

Anders Öckerman traces the apparent cyclical nature of the historical debate on and application of different silvicultural methods in Sweden. On the surface, preference for clearcuts prevailed in the nineteenth century, followed by selection cut methods in the early twentieth century, then a return to clearcuts in the 1950s, and finally a present preference for selection methods to support ecological forestry. Öckerman, however, suggests that there are more similarities and continuities between these methods than meet the eye. Both have contributed to the instrumentalist use of the Swedish forest—clearcuts actually persisting through the assumed selection cut periods—and its (as Östlund shows) ecological impoverishment. Öckerman is, however, hopeful that the current emphasis on ecosystem management, which uses the preservation of biodiversity rather than fibre production as a point of departure, might lead to a truly different kind of forestry.

Lars Carlsson describes the functioning of the forest commons in Sweden, a unique form of communal forest ownership based on a medieval form of land ownership. The forest commons have shown a remarkable ability to survive and adapt to urban industrialized society. Herein lie both their promises and limitations. Carlsson points out, for example, that in spite of increased company ownership of the forest commons, individual shareholders continue to control operations and their distribution of revenue. However, the forest companies have not conceded these powers for altruistic reasons: the forest commons work in close concert with state authorities to produce a reliable and constant supply of wood fibre from which the companies benefit.

Only the future will tell whether the corporatist relations that guide the operations of the forest commons for the mutual benefit of the producers of wood fibre will also be able to accommodate ecological values. On this point, Katarina Eckerberg provides a bleak picture of the Swedish record in promoting environmental sustainability in forestry. She notes that Sweden has few forest areas that have not been touched by human action. With respect to biodiversity, protected areas have been set aside in the northern parts of the country, where the state is a prominent landowner and land is less expensive. In the southern parts, where private lands dominate and where biodiversity is the most common, preserved areas are less frequent. Eckerberg suggests that in spite of recent legislation putting fibre production and biodiversity values at par, there is very little financial commitment to follow through at the enforcement level. She suggests that more regulations be put in place, more money committed, and more information on the consumer demands for sustainably produced wood be diffused, to preserve biodiversity.

Joanna Beyers and Anders Sandberg show how unsuccessful Canadian forest policy has been in promoting sustainable forestry. They show that the efforts of the Canadian federal government to promote sustainable forestry have been compromised by Canada's history as a producer of export staples; the ownership of natural resources by the provinces, which historically have pursued "development" at the expense of conservation; and the presence of a forestry science in support of instrumentalist and utilitarian values.

Peter Clancy explores another aspect of Canadian forest policy, the certification of sustainably managed forests. He argues that, despite its distinguishing features such as voluntarism and third-party validation, certification remains a politically contested process. This can be seen in both the origin and design of the Z808/809 system. It was formalized under the umbrella of the Canadian Standards Association, with a high degree of institutional collaboration between state forest agencies (at both national and provincial levels) and industry. The CSA approach centres upon the forest management system as a planning tool, and it is the application of the management system that is subject to certification, as opposed to the application of inherently sustainable practices on the ground. While this makes it attractive to forest industry interests, it may prove far less acceptable to the environmental public. Already many environmental organizations have eschewed the CSA process and looked elsewhere for a more rigorous approach. Perhaps the co-optation of sustainable forestry into managment systems logic represents a new "arithmetization" of sustainability?

Klas Sandell and Kurt Viking Abrahamsson show the broader environmental policy matters in Sweden. Sandell discusses the role of the Swedish *allemansrätt*, "the right of public access to nature," in outdoor recreation. The *allemansrätt* is the historical legacy and tradition that allows wide-ranging access to all public and private lands which are now under growing pressure because of the increased functional specialization of the landscape. He nevertheless argues that the *allemansrätt* provides a more sustainable alternative—which provides a public understanding for, and engagement in, environmental matters—in the face of the rapid growth of "factory"- and "museum"-based recreational activities.

Abrahamsson provides an example of the functional specialization of the landscape: the increased use of snowmobiles in the Swedish mountains. This has pitted local snowmobile users against outside recreation interests, prompting the question of who owns the soundscape of the mountains. Historically, snowmobile users have been favoured, but this may be changing as the recreational lobby is growing stronger. There also exist more restrictive precedents against snowmobile use in neighbouring Norway and Finland. Abrahamsson concludes by exploring the prospects of setting aside silent areas of the landscape for the enjoyment of people and wildlife.

The remaining chapters of the volume, in Part III, "Voices from the Margin," take still a different turn. They proceed to probe three different approaches in the pursuit of sustainability, all rooted in the histories of the labour movement, local bioregions, and First Nations of Canada and Sweden. They provide concrete examples of efforts to tread the middleground of instrumental and bio-centric, and individualist and collectivist values.

Ella Johansson, Russell Janzen, Thomas Dunk, and Laurel Sefton MacDowell provide insights into labour's position and potential role in environmental matters. They take issue with the jobs versus the environment debate, suggesting that workers' position in the environmental climate needs to be contextualized carefully, and that workers have had, and continue to have, a key role to play in improving human relationships with the environment.

Johansson provides a context to the emergence of the Swedish forest workers as a social class which provides insights into their environmental outlook. Rather than emerging as a lumpenproletariat, Swedish forest workers found the emerging forest industry of the nineteenth and early twentieth century an opportunity to escape from the poverty and humiliation suffered in the old peasant economy. In the international economy of logging and lumber exports, they were able to gain some wealth and status that contrasted with their lowly position in the hierarchical village society. In the process, the forest became an industrial forest of trees, trees that were cut into standardized logs with specific values.

This inhibited the development of any ecological thinking among the forest workers. One also wonders to what extent this backdrop provides the explanation for the ready implementation and acceptance of a sustained yield policy in Sweden, and the conception of trees as containing only instrumental value and utility.

Janzen provides a somewhat similar picture of the political, economic and ecological conditions that constrain and empower forest workers in British Columbia to act more environmentally. One constraint lies in the genealogy of work, the partial perspective of forest ecology that forest workers experience in the labour process. Another lies in the hegemony exerted by large integrated companies, the provincial governments, and the large forest workers' unions. In the past, a social contract of sustained yield has prevailed, based on increasingly large harvesting levels in return for revenue and well-paid jobs. Yet Janzen shows that workers have exerted some degree of control and independence, something which stems from the difficulty of turning the forest into a completely controlled work place. This may hold the potential for developing a more ecological forestry.

Dunk suggests that workers' environmental views might help unpack the complex question of what are natural processes. The current emphasis on favouring natural processes, such as letting "natural fires" range freely or reintroducing the wolf in national parks, may not be as natural as first contended. The North American environment has been deeply affected by human actions, including those from First Nations, which complicate the lofty goal of restoring nature to a "pre-European" state. Fuel build up from past fire suppression, for example, is likely to affect the impact of "natural" fires. It is in this context that forest workers, who are rarely the drones of the forest industry that environmentalists sometimes portray them as, may have a contribution to make in defining the middleground between natural and cultural processes.

Sefton MacDowell points to of the role factory workers have played in advancing the environmental agenda in the work place and in work place communities, though these efforts have been constrained in the Canadian situation by the resistance of resource companies and the state in promoting the growth of revenue-producing and job-creating staples exports.

John Wadland and Anna Gibson point to the importance of bioregionalism as a strategy to (re)build local communities in the face of globalization, showing how the university can play a role in that endeavour. They have been involved in a bioregional course and atlas project at Trent

University to document the environmental health of the Haliburton Highlands bioregion in Ontario. The project is ultimately aimed at empowering the local community to fight the forces of globalization.

In the final section, Jamie Lawson and Alf Hornborg examine lessons on environmentalism from First Nations communities. Here we see the forces of assimilation and resistance, and the search for reformist versus radically different alternatives at work.

Lawson tells two stories of First Nations struggles in the central parts of the province of Ontario. In Temagami, where a unique convergence of the First Nation and wilderness advocates took place, the First Nation sought to consolidate some continuity with a unique and traditional way of life: the seasonal occupancy of various parts of the land as well as the integrated use of the land centred around *nastawgan* trails and canoe routes. The struggle was over the jurisdiction of the whole territory rather than parts of it. Perhaps because of that, the group lost its struggle and now faces an insecure and uncertain position against a neoconservative provincial government bent on one-sidedly promoting resource development. In Algonquin Park, the First Nation fought a different battle. Here the Golden Lake Algonquins chose to fight their land claims by more conventional means. Backed by recent legal precedents, the Algonquins are presently seeking hunting and fishing rights in spatially defined areas within the boundaries of Algonquin Park, with hopes for a wider settlement.

Hornborg looks at the fight for land and cultural rights of the Mi'kmaq people in the province of Nova Scotia. He recognizes the prominent ways in which environmentalists have exploited the Mi'kmaq in their battles against the forest practices of the Swedish forest company Stora Forest Industries. He also acknowledges the Mi'kmaq's own ability to use their "First Nation's status" as a media tool. Yet Hornborg notes a qualitative change in recent Mi'kmaq environmentalism, a change that goes beyond a crass search for similar resource rights as prevailing in the dominant society, but an environmentalism rooted in "traditionalism," an authentic search for an alternative society based on traditional environmental values. With his chapter, we come full circle in our exploration. He provides a more empirical and concrete picture of the more theoretical elaborations in Part I. Here we see the spiritual and material merged in the aspiration of the Mi'kmaq people to build environmental sustainability.

One important insight of this volume is that there are many similarities between the state of the environment and the prospects for sustainability in Canada and Sweden. From one perspective, the differences between Canada and Sweden are not that significant. The epistemic figure of nature, the master narrative of the environmental discourse, remains the same: the natural environment is seen from an instrumentalist and utilitarian perspective, as a storehouse of resources where the prescriptions for sustainable resource use, be they the extraction of natural resources or the emission of pollutants and waste, are developed by experts. This is certainly the prevailing situation in Canada and Sweden, and the reforms that are currently pursued are constrained and compromised by that fact.

The promotion of economic growth by private firms constrain the prospect for a more environmentally sensitive society. The promotion of trade over-rides environmental concerns. Forests in both regions have been degraded, both in quality (Sweden and Canada) and quantity (Canada). Closed policy networks, consisting of businesses, and governments (and sometimes labour unions) control the environmental policy agenda at the exclusion of small producers and environmentalists. Monies for remediation are not forthcoming. The promotion of sustainable forestry is more rhetorical than real, and seems to have more to do with protecting markets than forest ecosystems. The functional specialization of the landscape into forest plantations, preserved wildernesses, and even "landscape corridors" for snowmobiles, is proceeding apace, while First Nations are pushed aside. This is an all too familiar story in all industrialized societies.

Another important lesson learnt from the chapters of this volume is that environmental issues are complex and certainly not a function of the dichotomies that are now often ascribed to them. The environment is not merely culture, as in silvi-, horti-, and agri-culture. Nor is it only about wild nature, the nature untouched by humans. The search for sustainability is primarily about finding alternatives between these extremes. It is about rearticulating what we mean by the environment, and finding a pluralist (not elitist) vision of natural resource use.

In this process of rearticulating, or reconstituting, the environment there is much to draw on in the contributions of this volume. Bucht, Sundin, and Lindén point to the relativity (or plurality) of environmental understanding, suggesting that there are more ways than one to seeing and perceiving reality. Harries-Jones advocates a combination of the material and the sacred. Lindén points to the older generation of Swedes, and Swedish women, as more conservation-minded and environmentally sensitive than the younger generation and their male segment (though the latter might be more aware and knowledgeable about environmental issues). Bucht writes about a "third nature," the "nature in between" promoted by urban gardeners who grow plants with a natural and utilitarian touch. Sundin reminds us of the importance of culture as heritage, not only as a nostalgic local history, but also as a celebration of the achievements of modernity. Sandell advocates an outdoor recreation based on the Swedish *allemansrätt*—providing broad access rights to public and private lands—rather than the capital- and energy-intensive reacreational activities supplied by private enterprise and the passive recreation provided by wilderness preserves and parks. Dunk, Janzen and Sefton MacDowell write about the different views that forest and industrial workers bring to the environment.

The chapters on First Nations societies remind us of yet other ways of perceiving nature. Sweden is perhaps not the place to look at, where the forces of domination and assimilation have been at work much longer and more thoroughly than in Canada. Lawson provides a qualified optimism. The efforts of First Nations in central Ontario have had mixed results. The attempts at building something uniquely complete, where the spiritual and material are combined in a comprehensive political and economic package, have been unsuccessful thus far at Temagami, whereas something more narrow, negotiated more squarely on the terms of the dominant society, has been more successful in Algonquin Park. Hornborg's final essay provides a sensitive account of what First Nations' struggles might contribute to the building of a new form of sustainability, taking account of both material and spiritual values.

The challenge of sustainability, then, is about imagining alternatives to the present dominant environmental discourse. These alternatives need not necessarily be invented, they are already amongst us, in the many alternatives that have been and are now posed in various forms of conflicts on how nature should be viewed and used. Canada and Sweden constitute two important examples where we can find such alternatives articulated.

Notes

1. These include both "radical" and "conservative" groups, such as Earth First and the Nature Conservancy (the real estate wing of the environmental movement).

2. See, for example, Arne Næss, *Ecology, Community, and Lifestyle: Outline of an Ecosophy*, translated and revised by David Rothenberg (Cambridge: Cambridge University Press, 1989).

3. See, for example, Doug MacDonald, *The Politics of Pollution* (Toronto: McClelland and Stewart, 1991).

4. World Commission on Environment and Development. *Our Common Future* (Oxford: Oxford University Press, 1987).

5. For a leading spokesperson of the greening of industry position, see Richard Welford, *Environmental Strategy and Sustainable Development: The Corporate Challenge of the 21st Century* (London: Routledge, 1995) and *Highjacking Environmentalism: Corporate Responses to Sustainable Development* (London: Earthscan, 1997). See also the journal *Business Strategy and the Environment* edited by Welford. Other accounts include John Elkington and Tom Burke, *The Green Capitalists: How to Make Money and Protect the Environment* (London: Victor Gollanz, 1989) and Francis Cairncross, *Costing the Earth: The Challenge for Governments, the Opportunities for Business* (Boston: Harvard Business School Press, 1991).

6. For an example in Canada, see Elizabeth May's celebratory account of the environmental movement's role in having a national park established on the Queen Charlotte Islands, *Paradise Won: The Struggle for South Moresby* (Toronto: McClelland and Stewart, 1990), and subsequent accounts of the limitations of that victory for the local population. Robert Matas, "In the Beginning There Was Moresby," *Globe and Mail*, November 13, 1993.

7. On this point, see Ted Schrecker, editor "Special Issue on Sustainability," *Journal of Canadian Studies* 31, No.1 (1996). On the way women have been affected, see, for example, Carolyn Merchant, *The Death of Nature: Women, Ecology and the Scientific Revolution* (San Francisco, 1980) and *Earthcare: Women and the Environment* (New York: Routledge, 1996); and Vandana Shiva, *Staying Alive: Women, Ecology and Development* (Atlantic Highlands, NJ: Zed Books, 1992); For the close connection, between some environmental groups and business, see Elaine Dewar, *Cloak of Green: The Links Between Key Environmental Groups, Government, and Big Business* (Toronto: James Lorimer, 1995).

8. See, for example, the powerful critiques in Wolfgang Sachs, editor, *Global Ecology: A New Arena of Political Conflict* (London: Zed, 1993).

9. Andrew Rowell, *Green Backlash: Global Subversion of the Environmental Movement* (London: Routledge, 1996); for a guide of such organizations, see Carl Deal, *The Greenpeace*

Guide to Anti-Environmental Organizations (Berkeley, CA: Odonian Press, 1993). For the decline of environmentalism, see Mark Dowie, *Losing Ground: American Environmentalism at the Close of the Twentieth Century* (Cambridge, Mass.: MIT Press, 1995).

10. William Cronon, ed., *Uncommon Ground: Rethinking the Human Place in Nature* (New York: W.W. Norton, 1995).

11. Kenneth Olwig, "Reinventing Common Nature: Yosemite and Mount Rushmore—A Meandering Tale of Double Nature," in Cronon, ibid., 379-408.

12. W.M. Adams, *Future Nature: A Vision for Conservation* (London: Earthscan, 1996).

13. For an overview, see Sverker Sörlin, "Nordic Identity: Sweden and Canada in Comparative Perspective," in *Canada and the Nordic Countries*, Lund Studies in English 78 eds. Jørn Carlsen and Bengt Streijffert (Lund: Lund University Press, 1988), 333-41.

14. Karin Johannisson, *Det Mätbara Samhället: Statistik och Samhällsdröm i 1700-talets Europa* (with a summary in English: Society in Numbers: Statistics and Utopias in Nineteenth Century Europe) (Stockholm: Norstedts, 1988). See also, Tore Frängsmyr, J.L. Heilbron, and Robin E. Rider, eds. *The Quantifying Spirit in the 18th Century* (Berkeley, Los Angeles and Oxford: University of California Press, 1990).

15. A sample of central works on these issues are: Bo Sundin, "Environmental Protection and the National Parks," in *Science in Sweden: The Royal Swedish Academy of Sciences 1739-1989*, ed. Tore Frängsmyr (Canton, MA: Science History Publications, 1989); Sverker Sörlin, *Framtidslandet: Debatten om Norrland och Naturresurserna under det Industriella Genombrottet* (with a summary in English: Land of the Future: The Debate on Norrland and Its Natural Resources at the time of the Industrial Breakthrough) (Stockholm: Carlsson Bokförlag, 1988); Roger Kvist, "Swedish Saami Policy 1550-1990," in *Welfare States in Trouble*, Umeå studies in humanities 124 eds. Sune Åkerman and Jack L. Granatstein (Umeå : Umeå University, 1995), 11-26.

16. On Sweden and the UN conference, see John McCormick, *The Global Environmental Movement: Reclaiming Paradise* (London: Belhaven Press, 1989), chapter 5.

17. For the post-World War II period, see Johan Hedrén, *Miljöpolitikens Natur* (The Nature of Environmental Policy), Linköping Studies in Arts and Science 110 (Linköping: University of Linköping, 1994).

18. *Blågul Tillväxt* (Blue and Yellow Growth) (Stockholm: Swedish Social Democratic Party, 1993).

19. Recent work among cultural analysts has stressed this aspect. See *Moderna Landskap: Identifikation och Tradition i Vardagen* (Modern Landscapes: Identification and Tradition in Every Day Life), eds. Katarina Saltzman and Birgitta Svensson (Stockholm: Natur och Kultur, 1997); Sverker Sörlin and Anders Öckerman, *Jorden en Ö: En Global Miljöhistoria* (The Earth an Island: A Global Environmental History) (Stockholm: Natur och Kultur, 1998), especially chapter 5; and the contributions in *Miljön och det Förflutna: Landskap, Världen, Minnen* (The Environment and the Past: Landscape, Memory, Values), eds. Richard Pettersson and Sverker Sörlin (Umeå University: Department of History of Science and Ideas, 1998).

20. For two statements, see Glen Williams, *Not For Export: Toward a Political Economy of Canada's Arrested Industrialization* (Toronto: McClelland and Stewart, 1983) and Gordon Laxer, *Open for Business: The Roots of Foreign Ownership in Canada* (Toronto: Oxford University Press, 1989).

21. Suzanne Zeller, *Inventing Canada: Early Victorian Science and the Idea of a Transcontinental Nation* (Toronto: University of Toronto Press, 1987); Trevor Levere and Richard Jarrell, eds. *A Curious Fieldbook: Science and Society in Canadian History* (Toronto: Oxford University Press, 1974); for a case study in forestry, see L. Anders Sandberg and Peter Clancy, "Forestry in a Staples Economy: The Checkered Career of Otto Schierbeck, Chief Forester, Nova Scotia, Canada, 1926-1933," *Environmental History* 2, No. 1 (January 1997), 74-95.

22. Paul Walton, "The Group of Seven and Northern Development," *Canadian Art Review* XVII, No. 2 (1990): 171-79; Robert Stacey, "The Myth—and Truth—of the True North," in *The True North: Canadian Landscape Painting 1896-1939*, ed. Michael Toobey (London: Lund Humphries, 1991), 37-63.

23. Patricia Jasen, *Wild Things: Nature, Culture, and Tourism in Ontario, 1790-1914* (Toronto: University of Toronto Press, 1995).

24. Glen Williams, "Greening the New Canadian Political Economy," *Studies in Political Economy* 37 (Spring 1992): 5-30.

25. Quoted in Grace Skogstad and Paul Kopas, "Environmental Policy in a Federal System," in *Canadian Environmental Policy: Ecosystems, Politics, and Process,* ed. Robert Boardman (Toronto: Oxford University Press, 1982), 47.

26. George Hoberg and Kathryn Harrison, "It's Not Easy Being Green: The Politics of Canada's Green Plan," *Canadian Public Policy* XX, No. 2 (1994): 119-37.

27. Mr. Justice Thomas Berger, *Northern Frontier, Northern Homeland: The Report of the MacKenzie Valley Pipeline Inquiry,* 2 volumes (Ottawa: Minister of Supply and Services, 1977).

28. For a recent Canadian treatment of some of the same questions, see Donald Blake, Neil Guppy, and Peter Urmetzer, "Canadian Public Opinion and Environmental Action: Evidence from British Columbia," *Canadian Journal of Political Science* XXX, No. 3 (1997): 451-72.

PART I

REARTICULATING NATURE

CHAPTER TWO

TOWARDS A THIRD NATURE

CONCEPTIONS OF NATURE IN BETWEEN

EIVOR BUCHT

In 1994, the Swedish National Board of Housing, Building and Planning (Boverket) presented two new ideas on nature's role in town planning. First, it proposed that towns be surrounded by old-fashioned agricultural landscapes composed of hayfields with the herbs now endangered as haymowing is coming to an end. Boverket advised that these fields be located on the urban fringe, where they could form new attractive biotopes in the everyday landscape. Secondly, Boverket recommended that some parks be transformed into "wilderness areas." In particular the large lawn parks of housing areas from the 1960s, and the green open spaces surrounding towns, could be sites for vulnerable biotopes of endangered plant and animal species. These areas could offer a richer and more varied environment and an opportunity for people to gain a new nature experience.[1] The starting point of these visions is not, as before, the urban dweller but endangered species. Their realization would mean an erasing of the boundaries between urban and the non-urban nature in both form and content.

The landscapes that Boverket wanted to recreate are not new. In 1703, Nicolaus Wallinus, vicar on the island of Öland, marvelled over and praised the island's woods, which resembled gardens separated by promenades.[2] The promenades consisted of openings in sprout wood, a green *väng* [enclosed] field, which the farmers had created artificially to shape the vegetable kingdom to meet their demands.[3] In the nineteenth century the beauty of this "terrestrial paradise," first described by writers and painters, inspired a new landscaping orientation, the English landscape garden or park, which in its nineteenth century form became a model for the shaping of a new urban element, the public park. With few exceptions this orientation has set the style until the present.

This chapter explores Boverket's two visions during the three hundred years that separate Wallinus' description of the beauty of the farm landscape and Boverket's new vision of how to shape tomorrow's landscape for the urban resident. The focus is on urban nature, in towns and in the countryside. To facilitate the handling of the various nature forms, I borrow Jacopo Bonfadio's sixteenth century designation of garden nature as a "third nature," where nature is fused with art and where the purpose of the garden is to provide both pleasure and utility. Bonfadio separates third nature from "second nature," a notion utilized already by Cicero to describe the cultivated landscape. Thereby Cicero is implying a "first nature," although he doesn't describe any, a nature which is not worked upon by humans, i.e., wilderness.[4] Having narrative characteristics the three concepts of nature give quite new options for the discussion of what parks and gardens are as forms of nature compared to using the value oriented dichotomy of nature versus culture.

Expressions of Third Nature

Before the eighteenth century, the main form of third nature in the towns north of the Alps was the utility garden, that is, the agrarian garden which existed inside the wall-girdled towns as well as in separate cultivated areas, so-called "cabbage gardens" outside the town. Probably through the influence of the monasteries an esthetic and religious principle was added to the utilitarian concept. The step from the monastery agrarian gardens to the medieval pleasure gardens was fairly short. Both were dominated by the same formal principles. In accordance with the ideals of the Renaissance but above all the Baroque, the pleasure garden was extended and brought together with the houses to a single, grand architectonical work, where the formal language of the garden reflected the architecture in geometry, symmetry and harmony. The third garden form, the picturesque or the English landscape garden, in many respects is an opposite to the utility or agrarian garden as well as to the architectural garden.[5] It is neither based on geometrical principles of controlling nature or on utilitarian concepts. The picturesque garden reflects the human relationship to nature.

> *That garden art had become intimately allied with the picturesque vogue by the end of the eighteenth century should remind us of the essential fact that gardens, too, have always been ways of mediating the physical world...gardens are, if not ways of actually coming to terms with the first and second natures, at least retrospectively ways of registering how we have come to terms with them.[6]*

The eighteenth century English landscape garden comments on and stylizes the agrarian landscape that the industrial revolution had brought into being, but introduces also allusions on ancient civilizations. The picturesque movement was ambivalent. In its emblematic form it pointed back to the Renaissance but also forward to a modern, private and fully formal form of expression. In the expressive gardens of Romanticism from the early nineteenth century things spoke to a bourgeois public which lacked the education that the English landscape gardens of the first epoch demanded from their visitors. It was then that the picturesque style was formed in order to arouse sentiments among individuals. The shaping of the garden received an individual expression instead of being based on a commonly known iconography.[7]

Beginning in the 1820s, the English landscape garden through the expressive form of the "Victorian Garden," was introduced as the new nature form of the modern town. The eighteenth century park grounds were created to be experienced in solitude, and the experience was intimately connected to the emblematic contents of the garden. The English landscape garden which was introduced into towns in the form of railway parks or other public "promenades" worked in quite another way. Here it seldom was the lonely wanderer who was to be satisfied but collectives, from the family via school classes or sport clubs to the plethora of individuals coming together in a common outdoor room. The promenade was shaped as a public arena for social relations inside a frame that associated with the first or second natures, but without any demands on authenticity.

There are interesting parallels between the eighteenth century view of third nature and Boverket's current conception about transforming urban nature in picturesque directions. The Arcadian landscapes that the supporters of the early picturesque style admired were built in order to create an illusion of a bygone time. It was the spectator whose knowledge, imagination and associations to literature and paintings recreated the landscape image that was wished for. In a similar way, the modern person is supposed to imagine the eighteenth century farmer at work when standing in front of "oldfashionly cultivated fields" recreated on the urban fringe. The antique buildings as well as oldfashioned farmlands offer an iconography for common interpretations and experiences. But the beauty that a contemporary city dweller finds in his/her experience of the newly created farm landscape lacks the authenticity of Wallinus' description. The latter reproduces the experience of a cultivated agrarian landscape, while the modern person experiences the illusion of such a landscape, that is a picturesque stage.

Boverket recommends a transformation of the 1960s lawn parks in order to save endangered species. The primary starting point is the plants and the animals who are to live in the new biotopes, though human beings are thought to get a richer experience of nature by visiting these new biotopes. Again one is reminded of the eighteenth century landscape stage. The motives are different but there are parallels. In order to experience plants and animals in the vulnerable biotopes you ought to be almost alone. The new interesting sites are no more arenas for social but for pedagogic activities. Modern society is not confronted with an antique civilization and history but with a scientific iconography. But in both cases it is necessary to possess a specific knowledge to get the experiences that the scenery is meant to give.

In the development of the picturesque landscape image, the post-modern age represents something similar to the eighteenth century emblematic, which was backward-looking as well as future-oriented towards the individual and the modern. Even the ecologically oriented shaping of third nature looks backward as well as forward—backward by its association with precisely the farm landscape of the eighteenth and early nineteenth century, forward in its strife to demonstrate the nature contract.

Perspectives on Third Nature

In his book *The Nature Contract* Sverker Sörlin writes about three levels of analysis in environmental history, the ecological, the socio-economic and the ideological.[8] In the following, these concepts are applied to the history of urban nature from the eighteenth century and onwards.

Before the eighteenth century, i.e., before the picturesque landscape image had been developed as an idea, the cultivated landscape in Swedish towns was almost totally dominated by the agrarian landscape in the shape of plots, "cabbage gardens" and other forms of gardens. The gardens existed to produce food—the socio-economic aspects of urban nature dominated. The actual growing conditions gave the gardens their form. Intentionally shaped gardens of the flora, for example monastery gardens and profane pleasure gardens, were rare until the seventeenth century. In the course of the eighteenth century the common gardens underwent no real change. Self subsistence was troubled by population expansion in the few larger towns. The main change concerned the idea of an embellishment of the public urban room which for the first time was getting more attention in the form of trees planted on squares and along main roads. With models from the Continent the pastoral design or the picturesque landscape image was established as an ideal for the Swedish aristocracy in their garden design at the end of the century.[9]

In the course of the nineteenth century the image of urban nature changed very radically in Northern Europe and the United States. In the growth of modern towns, green areas successively developed into integrated elements of the urban structure. British developments were in many ways decisive. The motives for creating green structures were socio-economic but intimately connected to an ideological superstructure. The ruling aristocracy found the picturesque landscape image with its strong recreative symbolism very useful for establishing a literal as well as figurative counterforce to the most unpleasant sides of industrialism—cramped spaces, diseases, alcoholism—in London and other English industrial cities.[10]

When the English landscape park was developed in France and Germany, and then in Scandinavia, it was motivated by the same social arguments as in Britain. But it was given other functions too and thereby also different forms. The social problems in these countries were not of the same scale as in Britain. The industrialization came later. In continental Europe the main goal for public parks was to create a beautiful scenography for bourgeois society. The parks were often small and decorated by architecture and plants in quite another manner than the British forerunners. From 1870 to 1930 these kinds of picturesque sceneries grew up in nearly every little Swedish town as small town parks or railway parks.

In Sweden the turn of the nineteenth century marked a change in the view of nature, as manifested in the first nature conservation law of 1909.[11] The turn of the century also marked a change in the socio-economic view of parks and green areas. From now on social activities became dominant in open space planning. But it was not until after World War II that the picturesque landscape image, which had shaped urban nature since the nineteenth century, began to be seriously questioned. Now an American movement, which since the turn of the century had transformed the shaping and contents of parks in the United States, got a foothold in Sweden. Influenced by this "reform park movement," American educators had developed a program for outdoor activities. The picturesque scenery that had given scope for free-ranging recreation activities was replaced by a strictly shaped frame of functionally ordered activity areas.[12] This highly functional program dominated Swedish town and landscape planning in the 1960s and 1970s. Natural features were totally neglected in favour of geometric schemes for play and recreation.[13]

During the modernist era a great deal of urban garden cultivation disappeared. Allotment parks were extinguished for the benefit of new housing and roads. In the private garden of the bungalow, the kitchen garden plot was replaced by leisure areas.[14] In public parks, flower gardens and hedges were taken away, giving room to larger easily-handled grass areas and monotonous shrubberies. Ecological or ideological perspectives on third nature were more or less lacking in the general debate. But already in the beginning of the 1970s, there appeared a critique against the destruction of the existing cultivated landscape as well as against the activity-dominated public garden. In discussions on play-environments the role of the natural terrain for creative playing attracted attention. A more ecological attitude towards the treatment of vegetation was proposed in the latter part of the 1970s, culminating in the establishment of "nature-like parks."[15] But until around 1980 the motives were still mainly socio-economic: better outdoor environments for city-dwellers combined with lower establishment and maintenance costs.[16]

In the latter years of the 1980s there was a radical, perhaps a revolutionary but hitherto little studied shift in the attitude to parks and green areas, from socio-economic perspectives to ideologically-directing factors. Instead of the former symbiosis between socio-economic and ideological factors, we get a new symbiosis between ecological and ideological perspectives. In the 1994 yearbook of the Swedish Society for Nature Conservation on the theme of "Neighbourhood Nature," some of the headings reflect this changed attitude to urban nature: "Richer Birdlife in the Garden"; "Your Garden—a Neglected Nature Conservation Area"; and "Ecoparks as Town Surroundings." One essay, about garden cultivation, refers to Voltaire: "Then utility was the dominant theme, now we can afford cultivating for the diversity of plants and animals."[17] The socio-economic aspects should be neglected.

By the 1990s, with the implementation of *Agenda 21* in almost every Swedish local community, the ideological arguments for urban nature or green structures were strengthened and broadened. This can be seen clearest in the focus on the preservation of biodiversity, one of the conventions that Sweden signed in connection with the Rio conference of 1992. "Here, nature or parks surrounding towns may be used for preserving and stimulating the growth of those plant and animal species which demand special ecological forms that do not fit into the production landscape: that is, a deliberate use of town biotopes as refuges for endangered species."[18]

The eighteenth century forcibly rejected the until then dominant form of third nature. The new garden ought to resemble nature and thus be more "natural." With the same force, today's ecologically-oriented proponents reject this picturesque nature in favour of a new order in urban nature, which is more like "real nature" than parks and gardens. But when these new nature forms are introduced into the urban structure, they will necessarily be formed and marked by the urban physical shape, life and activity. We are confronting a paradox. By trying to erase the borders between third and second nature, and perhaps first nature, we are creating a need to develop new shapes, which are capable to build a functioning and aesthetically attractive frame for a new garden style for the twenty-first century! This is stressed in international attempts to erase these borders, such as various housing areas in the Netherlands during the 1970s and 1980s. Current studies proclaim them partial failures, revealing inconsistencies between the ecological, functional and aesthetic perspectives.[19]

The implementation of biodiversity in urban environments brings the old debate about the natural and the unnatural to the fore. In eighteenth century literary criticism, the unnatural was symbolized by the architectonical garden and nature by the free English "picturesque" landscape garden.[20] Today's critics see all garden cultures as "unnatural."[21] The "real" nature exists, according to these critics, outside the towns, in the old farm landscape or in the residues of first nature. It thereby becomes ideologically possible to let the plant and animal forms outside the town constitute the norm for nature experiences as well as for the biological diversity inside towns, neglecting the plant and animal life in gardens and parks. Thus, in the action schemes for biodiversity which the National Environmental Protection Agency and other governmental agencies have presented, as part of Sweden meeting the biodiversity demands of the Rio-convention, one tries to interpret the urban third nature with the language and grammar of the first and second natures.[22]

For millions of private home owners, owners of summer cottages and allotment gardens it must sound strange that the biodiversity in their garden-patches is in principle non-existent. From a national perspective, it is hard to explain why about 150,000 hectares of built parks, gardens and churchyards, which by evidence contain lots of plants and animals, are not included in a national plan for the preservation of plant and animal life. One reason for that is that the qualities of the urban cultivated landscape have never been chartered by the natural sciences, as by definition those qualities are not possible to interpret by the language and grammar of the first and second natures. In the rapidly expanding scientific and policy-oriented ecological literature one can only find a few isolated studies about the ecology of third nature. In one of those rare studies, about plant and animal life in an English private house garden of about 700 square metres, the investigator not only found a considerably greater species diversity than in the most diversified tropical rain forest, but also, unsurprisingly, that the plant and animal life partly looks very different and develops in other ways than in the second and first natures.[23] One may ask what importance this garden and millions of other gardens have for urban biodiversity as well as for the overall biodiversity at the local, national and global levels? We do not have any answer due to the lack of research on third nature. The neglect of gardens also includes their potential as food producers. Like the cultivated landscape outside the town border the urban nature is a product of its own cultural history. From the perspective of a growing world population increasingly living in urban environments and not in the countryside, and stressing the ecologic point of view of a sustainability, it must be of great importance to look for knowledge and experiences in the several thousand years history of the urban or third nature.

Notes

1. Boverket (National Board of Housing, Building and Planning), *Stadens Parker och Grönområden* [City Parks and Green Areas], Report 12 (Karlskrona: Boverket, 1994), 41-42.

2. Mårten Sjöbeck, *Det Sydsvenska Landskapets Historia och Vård* [The History and Maintenance of the Cultural Landscape in Southern Sweden] (Landskrona: Föreningen Landskronatraktens Natur, 1973), 46.

3. Ibid., 90

4. John Dixon Hunt, *Gardens and the Picturesque—Studies in the History of Landscape Architecture* (Cambridge: MIT Press, 1993), 3-4. The third nature is sometimes instead called "second nature," as in a book by Michael Pollan, *Second Nature, A Gardener's Education* (New York: Dell, 1991).

5. The agrarian, architectural and picturesque garden styles are discussed by Barbara Stauffacher Solomon in *Green Architecture and the Agrarian Garden* (New York: Rizzoli, 1988). The picturesque garden in England is thoroughly analyzed by John Dixon Hunt both in Hunt, ibid., and J.D. Hunt and Peter Willis, *The Genius of the Place, the English Landscape Garden 1620—1820* (London: Elek, 1975). The picturesque garden in Sweden is discussed in a dissertation by Magnus Olausson, *Den Engelska Trädgården i Sverige Under Gustaviansk Tid* [The English Landscape Garden in Sweden during the Gustavian Era] (Stockholm: Piper Press, 1993).

6. Quoted in Hunt, op. cit., 75.

7. Ibid., 9.

8. The ecological level includes studies of nature itself, of species, food chains, reproduction, diseases, as well as studies of the expression, forms, and changes of the cultivated landscape. The socio-economic level includes analyses of reproductive conditions, manners and customs, of culture, political organization, food collecting, economic structure. The third level is about

ideas: myths, religion, science, ethics, ideology and "other forms of thinking about nature," Sverker Sörlin, *Naturkontraktet* [The Nature Contract] (Stockholm: Carlssons, 1991), 24.

9. Olausson, op. cit.

10. George Chadwick, *The Park and the Town* (London: Architectural Press, 1966).

11. Ella Ödmann, Eivor Bucht, and Maria Nordström, *Vildmarken och Välfärden* [Wilderness and Welfare] (Stockholm: Liber, 1982).

12. Galen Cranz, *The Politics of Park Design: A History of Urban Parks in America* (Cambridge: MIT Press, 1982). The ideas implemented in Sweden by the architect Hans Wohlin in his lic. study, *Barn i Stad* [Children in Cities] (Stockholm, 1961).

13. Eivor Bucht, *Vegetationen i Tio Bostadsområden* [The Vegetation in Ten Housing Areas] (Lund: Byggtjänst, 1973).

14. Eivor Bucht, "Cirkeln Sluts" [The Closing Circle], *Utblick/Landskap* 4 (1989): 8-12.

15. Roland Gustavsson, *Naturlika Grönytor i Parker och Bostadsområden* [Nature-like Green Areas in Parks and Housing Areas], Landskap nr. 58 (Alnarp: Swedish Agricultural University, 1981).

16. Bengt Persson and Erik Westlin, *Grönska i Detaljplanen* [Green Areas in Town Planning] Stad & Land Report nr 25 (Alnarp: Swedish Agricultural University, 1983), 30.

17. Naturskyddsföreningen (Swedish Society for Nature Conservation), 1994 (yearbook); *Grannskapsnatur* [Neighbourhood Nature], Sveriges Natur, vol. 85, quotation, 95.

18. Boverket, op. cit., 41.

19. The Delft housing areas in the Netherlands are used as an example by Michael Hough, *City Form and Natural Process* (London and New York: Routledge, 1984). They are also studied by Håkan Blanck, "Aspects of change—influence on the character of plantation, regarding vegetation processes, management and human mentality, with examples from nature-like parks in the Netherlands." Final thesis, Department of Landscape Planning, Swedish Agricultural University, Alnarp, 1996.

20. J. Addison, *The Spectator* 414 (June 25, 1712) in Hunt and Willis, op. cit., 143.

21. This is illustrated by the following quotation: "In absence of real nature, a new relativistic concept of nature is formed out of borrowed greenhouse flora. Asian and American plants grow as well in a bungalow garden in Bunkeflo or Åkarp. Nature has been reduced to decoration, nothing that a man can walk into and shape his own world from." Per Stenberg, "Skånes Natur Har Blivit en Dekoration" [The Nature in Scania Has Become a Decoration], *Sydsvenska Dagbladet Snällposten,* April 21, 1995.

22. Naturvårdsverket [National Environmental Protection Agency], Aktionsplaner för Biologisk Mångfald [Action Schemes for Biodiversity] 1996; Boverket, *Aktionsplaner för Biologisk Mångfald* [Action Schemes for Biodiversity] 1996.

23. Jennifer Owen, *The Ecology of a Garden, the First Fifteen Years* (Cambridge: Cambridge University Press, 1991).

CHAPTER THREE

THE OLD AND NEW HOMETOWN

Cultural Heritage as Environment

Bo Sundin

environment, n.—Syn. Conditions, living conditions, circumstances, surroundings, ambiance, encompassment, entourage, scene, external conditions, milieu, background, setting, habitat, situation. —*Websters New World Thesaurus, 1985*

The concept of the environment is ambiguous. It typically conjures up images of pollution, that is anything that threatens to destroy or contaminate our surroundings in their natural state. The environment, however, is not just nature but also culture. The environment consists of a landscape (or townscape) of historical remains which are the product of interaction between the labour of people and geography, geology and biology. The preservation of this heritage is indeed an environmental concern and a challenge of sustainability.

Certain historical remains and monuments have, ever since the birth of the nation State, been considered as an important part of the environment. In the case of Sweden the concern for the preservation of antiquities and of relics of the past has a long history. The origins of the Swedish Central Board of National Antiquities can be traced back to the beginning of the seventeenth century, and in 1666 Sweden became the first country in the world to promulgate an Ordinance on Ancient Monuments. However, it was the antiquarian associations established in Sweden during the second half of the 1800s which provided the foundation for a more formally authorized structure for preservation to be established at the turn of this century. The general background to the breakthrough of systematic preservation was the dissolution of agrarian society and the growth of industrial society and the modern nation State, which aroused reflections about cultural and national identity amongst different groups; the emphasis was upon the common heritage and Sweden's distinctive cultural character. This in turn led to a re-evaluation of old customs, symbols and artifacts, a consolidation of preservationist legislation, the establishment of museums like *Nordiska museet* and the open air museum *Skansen* in Stockholm and the growth of a popular movement organized in numerous *hembygdsföreningar* (local homestead societies). All these expressions of a new sense of the past were nourished by a strong wave of nationalism and rural nostalgia.

Before coming to the purpose of my paper, I have to stop for a conceptual exercise. The Swedish word *hembygd* is central to my discussion. The word indicates a strong sense of place and time and has, like the corresponding German word *Heimat*, very deep emotional connotations. It is impossible to find a proper English translation, but in the following I will use the word "hometown" which has about the same emotional implications. Still, a short explanation is needed to clarify the meaning of the Swedish concept *hembygd*:

> *...the word is basically constructed from two single words, hem and bygd. Hem is home. Bygd denotes a geographic district, but it also has a lot of specific connotations. It is mostly a small district that is first and foremost a cultural unit, but secondly it is a unit bound together both socially and economically. It is not necessarily however an area that coincides with a government administration district or a Church parish. Bygd is a topographical or rather chorological term which divides or unites districts across administrative borders. When you put the words hem and bygd together you get hembygd. Today the chorological meaning is dominant—both the physical setting and the mental landscape are included, but the second element is the most important. The two elements come together in the cultural heritage. The name of the site, the village or the neighbourhood that has given the hembygd its name is sacred on a symbolic level. The symbolic level of the concept is important, because without it, it is impossible to understand that the term can be interesting and analytically elaborated.*[1]

Hembygd was first introduced in the literature about 1870-1880, and a couple of decades later it became the centre of an alternative idea about the shaping of modern society. The Swedish popular movement organized in homestead societies, the *hembygd*-movement, was strongly motivated by fears of a growing rootless proletariat and it can be argued that the movement expressed the environmental concerns of its time. Many believed that industrialism had made the industrial worker an alien without any concern for the values of nature, rural life and the nation. As the country was threatened by a "non-national" proletariat which could rip apart society in a devastating class war, it was necessary to restore a "feeling of homeliness" and belonging in the lives of the proletariat. Thus, the symbols of the rural community and the peasant way of life obtained a moral and fostering significance. They were to integrate the proletariat and protect society from subversive ideas. It became a symbol of roots, of the preservation of a cultural heritage of mainly agrarian origins, which could master the evils of industrial society.

However, the *hembygd*-movement should not only be regarded as a conservative, nostalgic movement. Humans have an existential need for continuity and roots in their existence, and in the movement this need was often matched with a modernistic attitude towards life, where one seeks to acknowledge the developments and changes which have gained a foothold in one's history and traditions. The establishment of homestead societies and the local folklore movement of the early 1900s can also be seen as a form of regional politics, promoting the unique character of the region in question. This preliminary conceptual discourse has been necessary to give the non-Swedish reader an idea of the connotations of *hembygd*. To sum it up: *hembygd* has very much to do with roots, identity and a sense of time and place.

Now to the question which gives the original purpose of this chapter: is there a *hembygd* (*Heimat*, hometown) in the postmodern global village? I will discuss and answer the question by personal examples—I am going to discuss my old and my new hometown. But the conclusions have general validity and I will end up with a question on the heritage of the modern welfare State—a heritage which in my view rightfully could be considered as an environmental issue and a challenge of sustainability.

My old hometown, where I spent the first half of my life, is Frösön in the county of Jämtland in Sweden. I will try to describe my relationship to it by relating an episode in my academic life. Some years ago I participated in a symposium on "Components of a National Culture—the Cultural Face of the Swedish Model." In my paper I discussed *Hembygdsrörelsen*—the Swedish home town movement of the last turn of the century—and its longing for existential homeliness and obsession with "the good home." My argument was—and still is—that this movement was a distinctive element in the modernization of Sweden. I based my paper on developments in my hometown and opened with a quotation from the music drama Arnljot by the Swedish composer Wilhelm Peterson-Berger. The drama—influenced by Wagner and Nietzsche—debuted in 1910 and is sometimes considered as the Swedish "national opera." It is based on an Old Norse saga and tells the story of the Viking Arnljot, who has returned home from Constantinople to Jämtland, and who finally, after some complications, converts to Christianity and dies the death of a hero at the side of king Olav Haraldsson, better known as Saint Olav.

By quoting Arnljot's exalted words when he saluted the beautiful scenery of Jämtland, I intended to open in an ironic tone, declaring my distance to the cult of *hembygden*, and to the pompous national romanticism of the turn of the century. Arnljot is a pretentious drama, best surviving in the melodramatic world of opera. There is, however, one more place for the drama. Since 1935 it is performed with spoken dialogue outdoors by amateurs in my hometown. The young boy or girl, who hasn't been sitting through the drama a wet and chilly day in the summer, is not worth considering him/herself a true native of the county of Jämtland. And memories, and pictures: scents of rain, the flowers of midsummer and wet seats of wood; pictures of a landscape with snow-covered mountains, medieval churches and ice-blue lakes; and memories of horns, shields and Viking spears made of golden masonite. But there were also memories of a tall man, a mental hospital nurse and fellow-worker of my father, the man who year after year acted Arnljot in the amateurs' performance, the man whose blue and white striped uniform jacket I bought for a few cents when the hospital abolished uniforms, the jacket which I decorated with a "no to nuclear arms" button...And so on, and so on.

Suddenly the person who intended to demonstrate his irony and distance is sinking into bitter-sweet nostalgia. It was, of course, memories from a lost childhood which aroused my emotions. But the reason the memories are emotional is that they are part of my identity which, to a certain degree, was formed by the heritage interpretation of the national romanticism and the home town movement, the *hembygdsrörelse*, of the turn of the century, and by a childhood in an *environment* where, in fact, the main marks of sustainability were the romantic historical landmarks—medieval churches, ancient tumuluses and tombs, Old Norse place-names, a Rune Stone, and remnants of an ancient fortification.

But my web of nostalgic memories has also, as I have implied, other threads. There is the community of work, family and living, gathered around the hospital where my parents worked as nurses. And also the knowledge of the past—let's call it the spontaneous heritage interpretation—which is intimately linked to a locality where families have lived for many generations, where recollections of the past is mainly created in conversations, where learning the past becomes a process of maturing, amassing experiences, gaining knowledge of people and events and becoming familiar with the locality in a physical sense, where—in short—the past becomes rooted in each individual's biography and, consequently, is inseparable from the environment.[2]

My new home town, Umeå, is the town where I have spent most of my life as grown up and—more important—where my children are growing up and should find their roots. Owing to the establishment of a university in 1965, Umeå has completely changed in twenty-five years. It is a town which seems to exist not in the past but in the present and the future. I live in a typical modern suburb where everything is new. No historical landmarks, no tourism and no heritage interpretation, just shopping malls and pizzerias, daycare centres and schools, a medical centre, a library branch, a social welfare office, and so on. In short, my new home town has all the attributes of the modern Swedish welfare state. And, I would like to add, thanks to satellites, cable television and the like, it has also all the attributes of the global village.

Obviously, there is a great difference between my old and my new home town when it comes to the interpretation of the past. On a general level it's possible to discern two ways to experience space and time. The Swedish historian Lennart Lundmark has illustrated them with two pillars.[3] The first—still characterizing my old home town when I grew up—might be called the pillar of cospatiality (Figure 1). It rests on a limited locality and extends itself over a long span of time. Here, where the perspective of

The first—still characterizing my old home town when I grew up—might be called the pillar of cospatiality (Figure 1). It rests on a limited locality and extends itself over a long span of time. Here, where the perspective of space is reduced to a limited area, there is place for more concern and interest in the time dimension of this small section of space. All generations from the same locality are central in the formulation of basic cultural attitudes and the past becomes more important than the contemporary in foreign and distant space.

Figure 3.1: The Pillars of Cospatiality and Contemporaneity

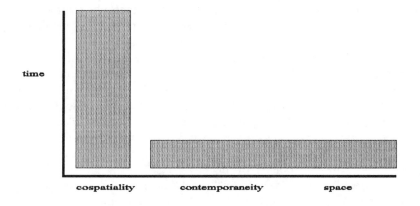

Modern society, my new home town, on the other hand, is directed at contemporaries. The pillar of contemporaneity rests on a much wider space but covers a shorter time span. Contemporaries in foreign and distant space have more influence on cultural attitudes than past generations in the locality. We can readily move ourselves to foreign countries and cultures, and with the help of modern media we are informed of events all over the world practically the moment they happen. The space is wide, the time span experienced compressed. Electronic media shortens distance and broadens the experience of "here" while the experience of "now" becomes more narrow. Information is aging faster and faster and cause and effect are more and more understood to be confined to space and contemporaneity instead of being interpreted as a process in time.

Still, we do use the past. We have all heard about the heritage industry and are familiar with the big business of nostalgia.[4] In fact, it seems to be a characteristic of contemporaneity and a consequence of the broadening of "here" and the narrowing of "now." Nostalgia means "homesickness." But today, writes Fred Davis, the existential salience of "home" in its concrete locational sense is diminished due to the tremendous mobility of persons in their occupations, residences and localities.[5] Home is no longer where the hearth is. Instead, media products serve memory where once houses, streets, and persons did. This has, no doubt, contributed to a sense of constant change, disappearance, and discontinuity.

We are also growing more ignorant of the central biblical and classical traditions which gave a frame of reference for interpreting the past. Our precursors, as David Lowenthal puts it, "identified with a unitary antiquity whose fragmented vestiges became models for their own creations. Our own more numerous and exotic pasts, prized as vestiges, are divested of the iconographic meanings they once embodied. It is no longer the presence of the past that speaks to us, but its pastness."[6] In my context I could add to the biblical and classical traditions also the Old Norse tradition. Without knowledge of these traditions, which gave a frame of reference for interpreting the heritage, Arnljot, e.g., is at best a picturesque costume play.

In my new hometown—my new *hembygd*—to my children, the frame of reference is rather given by popular culture, by satellite and television, by the world of Disneyland, by the virtual landscape, the virtual environment of Internet. I could go on like this and end up in a conservative reflection on how we seem to be living in a rootless society. Or I could end up in a resigned and cynical postmodern discourse on the ephemeral character of our society where the picture, the surface, has supremacy, where cultural life is reflecting more what's in vogue than eternal values, and where the past has been reduced to a box of toys, theatrical collages and pastiches. Does this mean that the young generation—to me personified by my three children—is growing up in a rootless society, in an environment without the heritage one could find in my old hometown? I'd like to answer yes—and no. Yes, simply because there is much in the postmodernists' diagnosis of our time. But no because I refuse to accept that history has come to an end and that there is no heritage to be interpreted.

In fact, everything has its history. Alfred Rowse gives a nice example when he reflects on the history of the pen-nib with which he is writing, and finds that "in fact a pen-nib implies the universe, and the story of it implies the story of the universe."[7] All things have a time-aspect. Accordingly, even in a modern suburb, one doesn't have to walk around for a long time to find more or less hidden traces of a past. In most cases the modern physical environment is nothing but the last layer in an old cultural landscape. In my hometown, for example, I have at a closer look found scattered remnants from the old agrarian society. One way of heritage interpretation could be to mark these remnants in one way or the other, preserve them as local monuments and found an old homestead museum.

That is not, however, what I would suggest. It is important not to forget the very recent history. In *What Time is This Place?* Kevin Lynch has argued "that the quality of the personal image of time is crucial for individual well-being and also for our success in managing environmental change, and that the external physical environment plays a role in building and supporting that image of time." A desirable image, says Lynch, "is one that celebrates and enlarges the present while making connections with past and future."[8] So, where in the environment do you find a heritage from the recent past, local monuments from the hometown of my children, monuments that celebrates and enlarges the present while making connections with past and future? Why not look for day care centres and other public institutions which symbolize the modern welfare state! It is the heritage of the modern welfare state that should be interpreted and considered as part of a sustainable environment.

Heritage interpretation can never be ideologically or politically neutral. Today we are facing a situation where the gradual dissolution of the nation state seems inevitable. And with it goes much of the welfare state and the collective norms and values that have been hegemonic for a long time. We now witness a general shift towards a much more competitive individualism as the central value of an entrepreneurial culture has penetrated many walks of life. All this is part of the postmodern condition. It is time to form counteracting forces, to regard the collective norms and values as a heritage, a heritage able to link the past to the future.

The sense of place and time indicated by concepts as *hembygd* (hometown) is important. In the postmodern global village it is even more important. The national romanticism of the old hometown movement might be outdated. But a local heritage interpretation certainly is not. And in that interpretation it is important not to forget the more recent, the heritage of modernism.

Notes

1. Maria Björkroth, "Hembygd—A Concept and its Ambiguities," *Nordisk Museologi* No. 2 (1995).

2. Bengt-Erik Borgström, "The Mazeways of the Past: History as Experience and Construction in a North-Swedish Parish," unpublished manuscript, Department of Social Anthropology, University of Stockholm.

3. Lennart Lundmark, *Tidens Gång & Tidens Värde* (The Passing and Value of Time) (Stockholm: Författarförlaget Fischer and Rye, 1989). For a more general discussion of space, see David Harvey, *The Condition of Postmodernity* (Oxford: Blackwell, 1990).

4. Robert Hewison, *The Heritage Industry: Britain in a Climate of Decline* (London: Methuen, 1987); Peter J. Fowler, *The Past in Contemporary Society* (London: Routledge, 1992).

5. Fred Davis, *Yearning for Yesterday: A Sociology of Nostalgia* (New York: Free Press, 1979).

6. David Lowenthal, *The Past is a Foreign Country* (Cambridge: Cambridge University Press, 1985).

7. Alfred Leslie Rowse, *The Use of History* (Harmondsworth, England: Penguin, 1971).

8. Kevin Lynch, *What Time is This Place?* (Cambridge, Mass.: MIT Press, 1972).

CHAPTER FOUR

VALUES OF NATURE IN EVERY-DAY LIFE

Words Versus Action in Ecological Behaviour

ANNA-LISA LINDÉN

Environmental attitudes and behaviours are characterized by personal contradictions and individual differences. For some individuals, environmental concerns can lead to some degree of change in behaviour of everyday life while for others such concerns are no more than empty phrases. In order to understand the different expressions of ecological behaviour, we need to understand aspects of socialization, the individual's socio-economic context as well as the structural aspects of social life. The aim of this paper is to present various ways of exploring ecological behaviour in Sweden. I begin by looking at how personal costs, generation and gender influence ecological behaviour.

I then proceed to explore how a value orientation, based on individualism or collectivism, may affect ecological behaviour. Such values stress perspectives of ethics and morals on environmental problems, and how the effects of a problem can be judged as favourable or unfavourable either to individuals or society. The discussion suggests a typology of actors, namely the egoistic exploiter, the egoistic conservationist, the collectivistic conservationist, and the collectivistic exploiter.

Personal Costs and Ecological Behaviours

Since 1990, three out of four Swedes have reported a high concern for the environment. The latest opinion polls show that the problems with the ozone layer, nuclear waste disposal and the deforestation of the rain forests are on top of the list of concerns.[1] Very close to the bottom of the list we find problems caused by automobile gas emissions. The figures reflect at least two kinds of problems. First, it is well known that individuals have a tendency to worry about huge problems at a far distance whose consequences are likely to affect them several years from now. Secondly, it is more difficult to accept nearby problems which must be handled individually here and now, and that affect a highly valued standard of living.

Environmental concern and the ranking of environmental problems reflect the relationship between individuals and their social environment as well as the relationship between the individual and nature. A constructionist perspective suggests that environmental problems are culturally and socially defined.[2] Environmental concerns, attitudes and behaviour differ between countries as well as among groups of individuals within the same social and cultural sphere.[3]

Words, however, are easier to express than to act upon. In surveys which have scored ecologically oriented behaviour, the recycling of paper, glass bottles and plastics have scored the highest.[4] Composting has scored much lower. The use of public transport instead of private cars has scored the lowest for almost ten years. This seems to suggest that it is possible to classify behaviour in relation to how much it affects a person's lifestyle.[5]

Those ecological behaviours which normally score very high cost very little in extra effort or in money. Most often these are activities people avoid doing, for example, not throwing garbage on the street. A second type of actions takes more physical effort and involves some financial cost, for example, the buying of ecological food or other environmentally-certified products. A third type of action indicates a planned change of behaviour which may involve an extra time commitment. The buying of more fresh rather than canned or frozen food, for example, could mean prolonged cooking times. A fourth set of actions involve some proactive measures on the part of a whole neighbourhood. If there are no composting facilities in a residential area, for example, a group of individuals may have to execute a plan collectively to rectify the situation. A fifth type of action involves a change in several aspects of a person's life. A change of use from the private car to public transport, for example, may force an individual to change his/her time schedules, and shopping and dress habits. This position leads clearly to a change in lifestyle.

Most often surveys on environmental attitudes and behaviour analyze the first three types of action. The findings show quite a good relationship between words and action, that is, between attitude and behaviour. The more effort, costs or consequences a change introduces, the weaker grows the relationship between words and action. Swedes in general have a high degree of environmental concern. When measuring behaviour, however, Swedes scored 4.1 out of ten measured indicators of ecologically oriented behaviour in the year 1993 compared to 3.7 in 1990.[6]

One of the weaknesses with studies on the relationship between attitudes and behaviour is that they do not take account of individual or group differences within a population. A further set of studies have shown that ecological behaviour in social groups indicate large differences in relation to sex, socio-economic belonging, generation and regional factors.

Generations and Ecological Behaviour

Belonging to different generations means shared experiences and social conditions with the same generation and at the same time differences compared to other generations. Belonging to a generation can partly be compared with class belonging.[7] With the same generation you share a time bound solidarity which is deeply rooted and means more than just group belonging. According to Karl Mannheim, the first twenty years are an extremely important socialization period in life. The values and norms acquired during that period function as standards of comparison later in life. They may have been forgotten, but can easily be activated when so needed. Many aspects of ecological behaviour coincide with behaviour common in less affluent times. Low consumption levels, the reuse of material and organic gardening are examples.

During the life time of now living Swedes, the urban population has almost doubled (Table 1). Many persons of the older generation have their own direct experiences of living in the countryside close to nature. Still others have relatives, for example grandparents, in rural areas. The older generations have a close connection to the rural history of Sweden. These generations get low scores in studies testing environmental knowledge, although they are very good in ecological behaviour. In some way or other they have an earlier experience which quite easily can be activated. The younger generations get high scores in environmental knowledge. They are, however, not so good in ecological behaviour. The step from theoretical knowledge to behaviour in everyday life seems to be a large one. The younger generations have more often spent their life time in urban areas and have fewer experiences of living in rural parts of the country. Theory and practice in ecological behaviour belong to separate spheres.

Table 4.1: Ecological Behaviour of Four Different Generations of Grownups as Related to Income, Urbanization, and Car Ownership

Generation born before	Income	Urbanization	Cars/1000 inhabitants	Ecological behaviour
the pre-war generation (1930)	2	47	2	4.9
the II-world war generation (1945)	3	59	8	4.3
the welfare generation (1965)	13	77	231	3.9
children of the welfare generation (1980)	45	83	347	3.7

* Index calculated on mean income in the year 1990. 100= SEK 125,600.
** Towns with at least 200 inhabitants.
All indicators refer to the years 1930, 1945, 1965, and 1980 respectively.
Sources: Lindén, 1994, see note 8, and Bennulf, 1995, see note 4.

It has been shown that older persons score higher in ecological behaviour than younger persons.[8] That trend has been going on for at least ten years. On the other hand, younger persons score higher in knowledge on environmental processes than older persons. The findings indicate the importance of the social and cultural situation for individual behaviour also in other aspects than urban or rural experiences. An analysis of generations is something more than a comparative analysis between age groups. An analysis of generations is related to indicators of the social and cultural situation of an individual's early years and its impact on behaviour later in life.

The older generations are far better in ecological behaviour (number of scores out of ten) compared with younger generations (Table 1). There is also a quite clear dividing line, both in behaviour and social indicators, between the two older generations and the two younger generations. The two youngest generations are more or less bound to social welfare developments, which are characterized by a high standard of living and a high consumption level. Their environmental concern is more closely related to an adequate and theoretical knowledge of environmental problems than practical living. Exactly the opposite situation is typical for the two older generations. Their corresponding standard of living comes from the pre-war social and cultural situation when the consumption level was low, and the reuse of material was an almost daily occurrence. For older generations it is easier to activate practices experienced as children or youngsters in a less affluent society. Behaviour from those days happens to be today's ecological behaviour. In interviews with older persons they do not refer to ecological aspects legitimating their ecological behaviour. They more often refer to behaviour they have had for a very long time as habits. Experiences from their socialization are well integrated in their daily behaviour. The social and cultural situation for generations is evidently of importance in affecting ecological behaviour.

Gender and Ecological Behaviour

Men and women report themselves to be equally concerned about the environment.[9] Three out of four are very concerned about the environment. Women worry more over environmental problems and consider them to be more serious than men, 64 percent compared to 52 percent for men. Women are more concerned about the effects on human health and on the welfare of the household.[10] In analyzing the correlations in scoring environmental problems women seem to be more oriented to "green" aspects of the environment and men more oriented to dimensions of cleaner technology. Women are better at environmental behaviour compared to men. In 1993 women scored 4.4 and men 3.8 out of ten behavioural dimensions asked for.[11] Women in all age-groups scored higher than men. The lowest score was found among young, unmarried men. Findings from studies in other countries show similar results.[12]

There are at least two major explanations for the differences in men's and women's attitudes and behaviour. First, most studies ask for environmental concern and behaviour related to concrete phenomena, as for example the reuse of glass bottles, the recycling of paper products, the buying of ecologically-produced food, and the composting of kitchen refuse. Most activities polled belong to women's rather than men's spheres of life. Most women are more or less unaware of the environmental aspects of men's spheres of life, such as the choice of oil products for the car, the use of ecologically-produced paints, or the buying of energy saving household machines. Secondly, women live closer to the reproductive sectors of life.[13] They are mothers, often working within the care sector, responsible for social and caring relations in the family. Men, on the other hand, are more connected to the instrumental spheres of life, such as getting a job, obtaining a high salary and raising the family's standard of living.

Both explanations are of course valid as far as we are looking at attitudes and related behaviours. One problem with attitudes is that they tend to be quite unstable and easily affected by time bound information from political debate or accidents. Attitudes and related behaviours are closely bound to concrete phenomena and situations. To be able to make comparative analysis it would be better to study environmental values, which tend to be more deeply rooted and resistant to time bound fluctuations in the flow of information. Measuring behaviour, on the other hand, has to change from focusing on concrete situations to analysing the localization of behavioural orientation within private spheres or collective spheres of life.

Value Orientation and Ecological Behaviour

Values are more deeply rooted in the conception of social phenomena and thus more resistant to the daily flow of information. The relation between humans and nature in the discussion has been transformed to a continuum of value orientation with the poles *conservation of the environment* and *exploitation of the environment*.[14] The conception of nature develops in a cultural process of understanding the relations between humans and nature. The outcome in attitudes is closely bound to a process of claims-making where the individual is weighing consequences of proposed measures in relation to social and economic development.[15]

The relationship between humans and society is a classical theme in sociological research. In this analysis it is used in a behavioural dimension defined by the opposite poles *individualism* and *collectivism*. In the first case the actor is prepared to do things to restore or repair environmental problems as long as they do not affect him/herself and his/her neighbourhood. A collectivist, on the other hand, is prepared to do things him/herself, even if the measures have negative effects for him/herself and his/her convenience.[16] Generally it seems easier to deviate from values held than to accept a certain amount of consequences negatively impact one's standard of living. On the other hand the social costs of deviating from specified attitudes to problems is more difficult and inconvenient to legitimate than a deviance from values.

The third step is to establish a two dimensional analysis of the dimensions of value orientation and behavioural dimension. In Figure 1 it is graphically shown. The model gives us possibilities to discuss a four-fold typology in relation to environmental problems. The four types are: 1) an egoistic exploiter, 2) an egoistic conservationist, 3) a collectivist conservationist and 4) a collectivist exploiter.

The empirical example used in the discussion is taken from an ongoing debate in Sweden about the location of nuclear waste storage.[17] A few geographical places have been identified as suitable for storing from a technical and scientific point of view. In every case the local opinion has mobilized a large resistance. On the other hand there has also been investigations analyzing more generally held values on environmental issues including energy production and use. The empirical background gives us possibilities to analyze the resistance in its variations of values, attitudes and willingness to accept or not accept the consequences in the local area.

1) *The egoistic exploiter* has the value orientation that development is closely bound to energy needs. Nuclear energy is extremely important from this perspective. The negative aspects of nuclear energy is the long-lasting waste problem. According to the egoistic exploiter, the best way to take care of this problem is to find far-away storage facilities. This person is most likely a man. He is likely to work in blue-collar or white-collar positions in the industrial sector. He is most likely to be found in regions of high unemployment.

2) *The egoistic conservationist* has a cautious value orientation in relation to nuclear energy. S/he is more bound to explore other forms of energy, which are less harmful to both people and nature. This person is prepared to take care of the nuclear waste produced though in safe places far away from populated areas. Individuals in this category are both men and women, quite well-educated and often working in the public sector.

3) *The collectivist conservationist* has a value orientation which is against the use of both nuclear and fossil forms of energy. S/he believes that renewable energy resources are the best for the environment and coming generations, tough s/he is also prepared to take care of the waste produced by living generations. This individual also believes that everyone has to take measures to lower their energy use, and to accepting waste storage and disposal in their immediate surroundings. This group is represented by both men and women. Ideologically they vote for green or left wing parties.

4) *The collectivist exploiter* has a value orientation in which development is closely bound to energy use. S/he thinks that nuclear energy is extremely efficient. The waste problem is considered a minor problem when compared to the urgent need for energy. It is believed

that the waste problem will be solved some time in the future. Until that time, waste has to be stored as far from human settlements as possible. Persons in this category are dominated by young men, working in the industrial sector.

Figure 4.1: Typology of Value and Behavioural Orientation

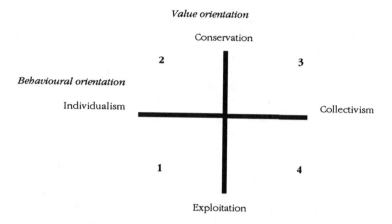

Source: Anna-Lisa Lindén, "Från Ord till Handling: Individuella Möjligheter och SamhälleligaRestriktioner, in *Fråga, Forska, Förändra* ed. Lars J. Lundgren (Stockholm: Naturvårdsverkets Förlag, 1996)

The example presented shows us the extreme positions in relation to one problem. It is of course possible that one actor has different positions in the typology on other problems.

Conclusion
One advantage with this kind of analysis is that it is possible to compare positions in at least three ways: to make comparisons between different environmental problems; to compare value and behavioural orientation in time perspectives; and to make comparisons between actors which differ from each other in demographic, socio-economic and structural terms. It is well known from studies that a person's position in the labour market affects both value and behavioural orientations in relation to environmental problems.[18] Maybe the fact that women work in the care sector to a larger extent than men is much more important for their ecological values and behaviour than gender. Professional status and personal experiences may be more important in influencing value orientation and behaviour than gender, age or income level.

Notes

1. Anna-Lisa Lindén, "Från Ord till Handling: Individuella Möjligheter och Samhälleliga Restriktioner" [From Words to Action: Individual Possibilities and Societal Restrictions], in *Fråga, Forska, Förändra*, ed. Lars J. Lundgren (Stockholm: Naturvårdsverkets Förlag, 1996).

2. Steven Yearley, *The Green Case: A Sociology of Environmental Issues, Arguments and Politics* (London: Routledge, 1991).

3. Pierre Bourdieu, *Distinction: A Social Critique of the Judgement of Taste* (Cambridge: Harvard University Press, 1984).

4. Martin Bennulf, "Vad är det Gröna? Om Livsstilar och Miljö i Olika Sociala Grupper" [What is Green? On Lifestyles and Environments for Different Social Groups], in *Miljöstrategier—Ett Företagsekonomiskt Perspektiv*, eds. Peter Dobers and Rolf Wolff (Stockholm: Nerenius & Santérus Förlag, 1995).

5. Lindén, 1996, op. cit.

6. Martin Bennulf and Mikael Gilljam, "Snacka Går Ju—Men Vem Handlar Miljövänligt?" [Words Come Easy—But Who Acts Environmentally?], in *Åsikter om Massmedier och Samhälle*, eds. Lennart Weibull and Sören Holmberg (Gothenburg: Report 7, Department of Political Science, Gothenburg University, 1991); Bennulf, op. cit.

7. Karl Mannheim, *Essays in the Sociology of Knowledge* (London: Routledge, 1952).

8. Anna-Lisa Lindén, *Människa och Miljö: Om Attityder, Värderingar, Livsstil och Livsform* [People and the Environment: Attitudes, Values, Lifestyle, and Lifeform] (Stockholm: Carlssons, 1994); Lindén, 1996, op. cit.

9. Lindén, 1994, op. cit.

10. Åsa Thelander and Åsa Waldo and Anna-Lisa Lindén, *Malmöbon och Närmiljön* [The Malmö Resident and His/Her Immediate Environment] (Lund: Department of Sociology, Lund University, 1996).

11. Bennulf, op. cit.

12. Paul Hackett, *Conservation and the Consumer: Understanding Environmental Concern* (London: Routledge, 1995).

13. Jens Goul Andersen, *Kvinder og Politik* [Women and Politics] (Århus: Politica, 1984).

14. Anna-Lisa Lindén, "Perspectives on Man, Value Orientation, Behaviour and Sustainable Development," in *Thinking, Saying, Doing: Sociological Perspectives on Environmental Behaviour*, ed. Anna-Lisa Lindén (Lund: Department of Sociology, Lund University, 1997).

15. John A. Hannigan, *Environmental Sociology: A Social Constructionist Perspective* (London: Routledge, 1996).

16. Lindén, 1997, op. cit.

17. Ibid.

18. Hackett, op. cit.

Chapter Five

BARGAINING THE SACRED

The Approach from "Immanent Holism"

Peter Harries-Jones

"Resource wars" characterize post-cold war international development. Of the 82 armed conflicts that have occurred between 1989 and 1992, and increasingly since 1992, most have been internal to nation States, and a significant proportion have had some concern with resources. In the same period many important ecosystems such as arctic tundra, tropical rain forests, coastal zones, wetland and semi-arid regions have come under continued pressure for agricultural or industrial development. These areas are the homeland of indigenous populations many of whom do not accept territorial boundaries imposed by national political authorities. Their awareness of the increasing importance to industrial societies of the value of environmental resources in their homeland, former "marginal" areas, has increased the urgency with which claims for ethnic self-determination are put forward. These have accounted for some of the conflicts.

A recent edition of *Cultural Survival Quarterly*, an activist publication of the discipline of anthropology recently devoted its entire contents to conflict about ecological resources and possible approaches to conflict management in the new era of resource wars. Among the questions raised are who intervenes? what is the appropriate timing of intervention? what sort of strategy should be employed? In particular, the issue asks whether there is a range of decision making processes that enable bargains to be struck over economic development without polarizing issues of cultural identity and ethnic self-determination.

If there is any consensus arising among authors in this issue, it is that the impact of resource wars on regional and international peace are so great that the old rules of non-interference by international organizations in the internal affairs of a nation state no longer seem to apply. Instead, all resource conflicts are multi-tiered, involving not only states but strong sub-state and trans-state accords organized in a myriad of ways, some of them formally instituted arenas for "stakeholders," some of them informal negotiations entered into by non-governmental organizations. This makes the whole process of bargaining far more complex than conflict in the colonial era or during the various phases of the cold war. The new bargaining strategies seek to take into account structural problems and inequalities in a manner quite different from the older rationalistic approach of the Westphalian state.

There is a further concern. Not all resource development issues examined in *Cultural Survival* seemed to be negotiable. A feature of many of the cases presented were distinctions drawn in the bargaining process between the indigenous concept of custodial responsibility toward land and western notions of ownership. Several authors argued that unless indigenous concepts of custodial responsibility, including special reservation for sacred places were given validity, there could be no proper partnership in the negotiation process. In the case of Australian Aboriginal negotiations, any proposed development abutting upon sacred sites, development became non-negotiable. The only viable option for non-Aboriginal negotiators was to back away, and not to pressure the Aboriginal delegates "to deny or abrogate their values and custodial responsibilities." However, Aboriginal negotiators "often have alternate and more sustainable development visions for their regions, or may be willing to allow development elsewhere on their land." [1]

But where are the specific international organizations that are able to bargain in a manner that is different from the well understood principles of rationalism? And with what authority could these international organizations enter into the bargaining process, specifically with bargains about the sacred? More significantly, from the usual scientific-rationalist perspective the whole notion of "bargaining the sacred" is a contradiction in terms. In this article I intend to pursue this conundrum. Though epistemological contradictions may, in the process of bargaining, give way to pragmatic resolutions, no case by case resolution can easily resolve this post-Westphalian conundrum. Between the practical world of negotiation and the "rational" response to structural problems of "resource wars" lies an evident cognitive gap. This gap, in turn, prevents the development of institutions responsive to this global predicament.

The existence of this conundrum is, perhaps, one element in the collapse of the high hopes of the Earth Summit in Rio in 1992. Today, it would appear that the United Nations is less and less at the centre of a global process for managing environmental crises, and that there is a groping for an alternative to the 1992 idea of a single global centre dealing with environmental crises. One option suggested is the establishment of a code of conduct by multinational corporations, but skepticism surrounding the efficacy of a code of conduct, in which the foxes promise not to harm the chickens, is high—certainly among environmentalists. Another option is that centralism gives way to devolution and that international grass roots environmental organizations, supported by a global consensus, take up the process of negotiation in place of UNCED. Such a proposal has been put forward by Robert Cox, as part of a general proposal for a "new multilateralism" and a return to "civil society."[2] I support Cox's proposal, but the emergence of "a new multilateralism" will still require a well worked epistemological approach to environmental resource wars.

Elements of this approach would appear to lie a) in changing western conceptions of rationalism, which many environmentalists are evidently agreed is necessary, and b) changing western conceptions of the sacred, which is certainly not agreed upon, but which environmentalists do at least agree requires examination.[3] I am going to put the case for "immanent holism" which, I argue permits both science and spirituality within its framework of enquiry, though immanent holism transforms both narrow definitions of rationalism in science and contests transcendental definitions of spirituality that usually surround western notions of the sacred.

Left Biocentrism

One author in *Cultural Survival* argued that designating culture or spirituality as the key variable hides as much as it informs. As a practical matter, when one gets down to real life situations, he said, particular individuals and organizations with different class, generation group or educational background are of equal importance to any blanket concepts of spirituality or culture.

At first glance it is easy to dismiss the dissenter's opinion, particularly in a Canadian context, where there have been several severe crises over sacred sites involving stand-offs and bloodshed between federal soldiers, provincial police on one side and armed groups supporting the First Nations (Aboriginal Peoples) on the other. Nevertheless to regard any claim for spirituality and sacred places as absolute and inviolate is to ignore the very different implications of the claim for each party to the bargaining process. Acknowledging absolute validity of the sacred requires both parties to agree to the primacy of transcendent powers over political process and this position is unlikely to be held by the negotiators for the state.

Transcendent spirituality, when juxtaposed with cultural relativism, becomes even more problematic. The most recent occasion I came across this was in a conference at the Canadian Learned Societies held in 1995 at the University of Québec, Montreal, while on a panel co-sponsored by the Society for Socialist Studies and the Environmental Studies Association of Canada. My interest as a panel member was both in the elaboration of the concept of "left biocentrism," a concept that has emerged in environmental discussions of "red" versus "deep green" and also in the way in which the panel's discussion paper took a critical stance toward certain political claims by representatives of First Nations in Canada.[4]

The central tenet of left biocentrism is a required dismantling of our present industrial society by abrogating free trade capitalism, and its corollaries: endless economic growth, consumerism, progressive privatization of property rights. Left biocentrism can only have one agenda for industrial economy and that is to put it into reverse. A similar but non-socialist position has been put forward by Herman Daly, formerly a member of the World Bank.[5] Left biocentrists engaging in the sort of bargaining strategies depicted above would enter any negotiation on natural resources prepared to cut back globally on industrial processes.

We have noted that First Nations in Canada, like other indigenous peoples, insist on their spiritual relationship to land and resources. Yet the Left biocentrist discussion paper argued that there was a troubling alliance between environmentalists and First Nations leaders which had resulted in uncritical acceptance of a number of issues in the name of the Aboriginal notion of "deep stewardship." Among these were the belief that aboriginal cultures and their traditional livelihoods were models of rectitude defining appropriate relations between nature and culture and that this model should carry over into the contemporary situation—especially in Canada. Another belief of deep stewardship, the paper stated, was that only Aboriginals can define the appropriate use of land and resources in aboriginal areas; and that aboriginal claims, statements and demands must define the terms of reference of any alliance with non-native environmentalists.

Further, a mainstream political position had emerged with respect to First Nations land claims, namely that claims for social justice must take precedence, even if the outcome of bargaining between First Nations and the various governments, provincial and federal, resulted in political compromises that were almost indistinguishable from the platforms of sustainable development. No Left biocentrist could accept this state of affairs. Thus, while First Nations may benefit politically from the settlement of a land claim, such settlements and the compromises they contain, should be regarded critically by those that have any attachment to the principles of left biocentrism.

The panel discussion itself came to little resolution either on the topic of cultural relativism or in defining a critical approach to the claims of deep stewardship. Chief Ron Ignace (Secwepemc Nation, Interior Salish, B.C.), in particular, argued that rights for self-determination include integrated resource management and principles of biodiversity. He gave voice to deep stewardship as a way of living among First Nations people, when he stressed that the relation between his own band and salmon fishing was so tightly bound to one another that "When the salmon go, we go." It was inconceivable that Secwepemc would overfish, he said, and already they had imposed upon themselves a total ban on salmon fishing wherever the stock of salmon were threatened. Industrial corporations not indigenous peoples had created the environmental crisis, indigenous peoples themselves could never harm the environment.

Orton made the case that the generally depleted nature of biodiversity and all wildlife resources have created a new set of ecological circumstances, a totally changed ecological context for traditional practices which overrides claims made in the name of the sacred. For Left biocentrists, the well-being of Earth remains the ultimate yardstick for all environmentalists, natives and non-natives alike. Thus, given the choice between being green or being red, the former must prevail. The primary claim, where any fundamental choices have to be made, "must come down on the side of wild nature. Humans have options. Animals, plants and the physical environment do not have options."[6]

On Spiritualist Visions

Orton was willing to accommodate to North American Indian animism. Animism, he says, is one way to reintegrate the human species into the community of all species. Deep ecology from which Left biocentrism has derived, "is compatible with traditional animistic beliefs."[7] But his position is at best ambiguous. In the publication above he argues that North American Indian animism is ultimately, anthropocentric, self-centred, whereas the principles he espouses are biocentric; and because they are not human-centred, biocentrism goes beyond animism.

These ambiguities embrace a wider field of interpretation. The panel discussion in Montreal has a link to prior events described and published by the Swedish anthropologist Alf Hornborg. In Hornborg's discussion of environmentalism, ethnicity and sacred places among the Mi'kmaq in Nova Scotia, he describes how Orton and his organization, Green Web, "converges with Mi'kmaq traditionalists in demanding a radical and spiritually informed conceptualization of the role of humankind in the biosphere." Hornborg argues that for the Mi'kmaq, as for others, the concept of sanctity or sacredness posits irreplaceable and incommensurable local values. Such concepts radically oppose modernity for they are an example of an attempt to redesign the definition space of environmentalist discourse against "the decontextualizing cosmology of the economists, which aspires to engulf all local systems of meaning, [and] is a means to open local communities and ecosystems to outside exploitation."[8] Epistemologically Hornborg brings the support of postmodernism to the contentions of Mi'kmaq traditionalists; but, as the evidence suggests above, his postmodern epistemology does not completely accord with Orton's position.

Hornborg's sympathy for a spiritualist vision is modest compared to other examples of epistemological support for the transcendentalism in the environmental literature. The literature is replete with a range of spiritual solutions for western environmentalists. There is, for example. the eco-theology of Henryk Skolimowski who tries to construct a notion of world as sanctuary. Ecological spirituality in such a world goes far beyond simple recognition of the interconnectedness of all life and requires, in addition, our deepest intuition of the sacred, a sense of deep communion with all beings.[9] The New Age environmental literature also advocates a return to "divine reality, cosmic meaning and an enchanted nature," in effect, a return to organicism accompanied by an almost medieval frame of thinking. The adoption of spiritual values is also promoted by some eco-feminists. Charlene Spretnak argues for a quasi-religious transformation of contemporary cultures in order to bring about a new state of environmental grace, which, it would seem, would emerge from wholesale borrowing of the mysticism of native North American thought.[10] Many other environmentalists have called for a borrowing of Buddhist or Taoist ideas of spirituality since the Christian church has explicitly refused all doctrines expressing adoration of nature.

Of the choices available for building trust and developing pro-active initiatives, designed to prevent conflict cycles over resources, borrowing other people's cosmologies seems to me to be the least satisfactory because it would be the least stable solution. I would contest this tactic on other grounds as well. Western premises of the authoritative role of religion are precisely those not assumed by other religions or beliefs. Nor, as anthropology's comparative investigation of religions has shown, does the existence of coherent cosmological thinking necessarily lead to a set of well defined practices. For other cultures, the translation of belief into efficacy in every day life always requires—as in our own case—construction of context and relevance. Every cosmological system requires interpreters and here is a source for a wide range of variation as to what is or is not spiritual. Certainly societies who exhibit social practices that remain isomorphic with their cosmological system, and spiritual exhortations associated with that system, are rare.[11] In effect, our own western notions of authority inherent in transcendental spirituality and other cultures' very different views of spiritual practices give rise to false comparisons which, in turn, yield grave difficulty in assessing the relevance of either. To bridge this gap brought about by false comparison requires a lot of hard work.

Immanent Holism

I am going to argue that the first step in resolving the dilemma is to recognize that *transcendental spirituality*, whether ours or those of other cultures, is simply unnecessary for conceptualizing holism or biocentricity. One may have a deep awareness of holism, to which one attaches a vision of the spiritual, without denoting any more than the *immanence of holism* in nature. Gregory Bateson, for one, proposes this form of resolution to the vexed question of *the sacred*. The problem, he argues, is the tendency in our own society to take what is not immediately knowable and throw it unexamined into the realm of the supernatural. This is a habit which arises from the dualism of mind and body that western sciences created and entrapped themselves in during the seventeenth century.

Our own propensity, therefore, is to think in dualistic terms, but not to be aware of implicit dualism in our epistemological position, scientific, religious or political. That makes the sacred so difficult to talk about as an ecological concept. Another difficulty, Bateson says, is the fact that the sacred is so intimately related to healthy integration in ecosystems. Yet it is very perplexing to talk scientifically about integration in any living system that is healthy and doing well. Most of our current scientific understanding of environment, as in our current understanding of genetics or evolution, arises from a study of pathology, not of healthy integration. So any evocation of the sacred as some sort of bridge between our own understanding and the unknown must be treated with the greatest of care.

An ecological system in many respects shares similar forms with an ecology of ideas. By this Bateson means that the sacred, far from being a concept of the transmundane, is an immanent idea, with an immanent reference to the tangled web of consciousness that constitutes ecological order. And just as the connectedness in human ideas may be approached immanently, so too can connectedness in ecology. Indeed, the two are linked. The connectedness of human ideas exhibits a combination of both indicative-type consciousness open to sensibility and ordinary perception and of metaphor. Nature may lack indicative consciousness but it certainly responds to the injunctions of oscillation over time, and from these we derive our metaphors of evolution. So too the richest use of the word sacred in ecological understanding is that use which denotes and connotes the combination of the two—the descriptive and the metaphorical, getting the two together. "And that any fracturing of the two is, shall we say, anti-sacred."[12]

In other words, to evoke a notion of the sacred in an immanent context, is to evoke a relation between the more abstract, unconscious parts of mind, and the more prose parts of linguistic understanding. In apprising ourselves of ecological order and of its temporal integration among its multitude of parts and interconnection of parts, we must first learn how to keep different levels of description "*not* separate, because they can never be separate, and *not* confused, because if they get confused, then you begin to take the metaphoric as absolute, as the schizophrenic does."[13] From Bateson emerges an recursion between natural form and ideas that requires no transcendental spiritualism—but may draw on spiritual notions and notions of the sacred as analogues to help learning about holism.

Can one hope for modern science to support Bateson's line of argument and so bring western science beyond dualism, in alignment with a version of immanent spirituality? There are some hopeful signs. Today there is a wing in the study of theoretical biology which resists both dualism in science and transcendent notions of the sacred. According to this wing, if "there is an underlying physical law which we, through interaction with the outside world, are attempting to describe...we do it only within the context of rules [of recursive interpretation] which we impose." These theoretical biologists mark self-description as the fundamental feature of living organisms. Description of self-description (together with what rules may be derived from this phenomenon of recursiveness) is the object of its scientific enquiry and process. "Anything with an internal description or self-description, cannot be characterized solely in terms of space, time, matter and energy, in terms of physics...the study of life from that (latter) point of view is necessarily a half-truth."[14]

This sort of theoretical biology obviously takes issue with the study of living systems being screened through assumptions of objectivity, value free logic and of independent control over nature. Instead, they argue, conditions of context-dependency no longer permit study of living systems to be reduced to single level numerical calculations. In fact, sense data of human beings, far from being discrete from natural order, are a necessary component in any loop of description of biological order: "there are many ways of describing the same thing (i.e., art, poetry, music) and each description presupposes a set of rules or constraints. Reality has innumerable descriptions."[15]

Conclusion

In this paper I have suggested an approach to issues raised both in a global aspect, namely an increasing number of resource wars in which culture, spirituality and notions of the sacred arise, and in the more local manifestations of a meeting in Montreal and Hornborg's paper. Extrapolating from Bateson we can argue that a reformed science of immanent holism would be free of many ambiguities of dualistic thinking that are still common both in environmental and political circles. It would recognize an immanent ecological order that neither merges into, nor grants a separate status to, cosmology of other peoples. In so doing, it would extract itself from the messy opposition between one particular state of mind "biocentricity" and another state of mind "anthropocentricity" in which it is still mired. To a large degree, arguments surrounding these latter two concepts merely substitute different names for the older dualism of reality as being either matter or spirit.

Left biocentrism must generate its own dialectical order and its terms with regard to social justice and the sacred are evidently not worked out as yet. Because Left biocentrism insists on the dismantling of our present industrial society as a precondition for resolving ecological issues, I would argue that it is a superior framework with which to undertake genuine "partnership bargaining" in the coming resource wars than the mainstream notions of sustainable development to which it is politically opposed.

Notes

1. *Cultural Survival Quarterly* 19, No. 3 (1995): 36.

2. Robert Cox, ed., *The New Realism: Perspectives on Multilateralism and World Order* (Tokyo: United Nations University Press, 1997).

3. J. Baird Callicott, *Earth's Insights: A Survey of Ecological Ethics From the Mediterranean Basin to the Australian Outback* (Berkeley: University of California Press, 1994).

4. David Orton, "The Wild Path Forward: Left Biocentrism, First Nations, Park Issues and Forestry—A Canadian View," *Wild Earth* 5, No. 3 (1995): 83. In Orton's view "left biocentrism"

is part of an emerging trend in the green and environmental movements which gives critical support to deep ecology, generally embracing its principles—subordination of human interest to a wider eco-reform on a global scale so that land, water, and air, become the common inheritance of all living beings—while challenging its many impractical stances with respect to political activism.

5. Herman Daly, *Beyond Growth: the Economics of Sustainable Development* (Boston: Becon Press, 1996), 145. Daly writes, "my problem with my fellow economists is not their frequent state of disagreement, but rather their near unanimous support of basic policies [i.e., Free Trade and Globalization] that are killing us." See also Peter Harries-Jones, Abraham Rotstein and Peter Timmerman, "A Signal Failure: Economy and Ecology After the Earth Summit," in *Future Multilateralism: Tasks and Political Foundations,* ed. Michael G. Schechter, in press.

6. David Orton, "The Environment and Relations with First Nations," *New City Magazine,* 16, No. 2 (1995): 32. Parts of this panel discussion were published in *New City Magazine.* A pre-circulated discussion paper, together with its supporting case studies on which the panel were to comment, received heated replies by e-mail from members of Environmental Studies Association of Canada (ESAC). His discussion paper was regarded as so "controversial" that there were calls to cancel the panel.

7. David Orton, "Aboriginal Tradition or Commercial Trapping," *Earth First! Lugnasadh* (1995): 24. "If it is part of a cultural revival among indigenous peoples, and to that extent that it is food for the soul and not public relations or commercial veneer, animism offers hope both for respectful relations with the Earth and for building real alliances with ecocentric environmentalism."

8. Alf Hornborg, "Environmentalism, Ethnicity and Sacred Places: Reflections on Modernity, Discourse and Power," *Canadian Review of Sociology and Anthropology* 31, No. 3 (1994): 262, 263.

9. Henryk Skolimowski, *A Sacred Place to Dwell: Living with Reverence upon the Earth* (Rockport, MA: Element Press, 1993), ix—xii.

10. Charlene Spretnak, *states of Grace: The Recovery of Meaning in the Postmodern Age* (San Francisco: Harper and Collins, 1993), 27.

11. Bali is a good case. While there is a remarkable concordance between cosmology and practice in some areas of Bali, the introduction of a type of rice, IR 36, as part of Southeast Asia's green revolution led to a set of practices with regard to its sowing and harvesting that were only partial replications of prior practices and, hence of cosmological order. See Andrew Duff-Cooper, "The Balinese Rice-Planting Rite of *Nuasén* and the Magic Square of Three," in *Cosmos,* ed. Emily Lyle (Edinburgh: Traditional Cosmology Society, 1989), 41-57.

12. Gregory Bateson, *A Sacred Unity: Further Steps to an Ecology of Mind,* ed. Rodney Donaldson (New York: Harper-Collins, 1991), 269.

13. Bateson, op.cit., 267, and Peter Harries-Jones, *A Recursive Vision: Ecological Understanding and Gregory Bateson* (Toronto: University of Toronto Press, 1995), 212-234.

14. Howard Pattee, "A Symposium in Theoretical Biology" in *Glimpsing Reality: Ideas in Physics and the Link to Biology,* eds. Paul Buckley and David Peat (Toronto: University of Toronto Press, 1995), 127.

15. Ibid., 149. They are therefore in broad agreement with the ecofeminist critique. Carolyn Merchant identifies five scientific assumptions prevalent since the seventeenth century to which she raises objections. These assumptions are: (a) matter is composed of particles (the ontological assumption); (b) the universe is a natural order (the principle of identity); (c) knowledge and information can be abstracted from the natural world (the assumption of context independence); (d) problems can be analyzed into parts that can be manipulated by mathematics (the methodological assumption); (e) sense data are discrete (the epistemological assumption). See Carolyn Merchant quoted in Charlene Spretnak, op. cit., 301n.

PART II

COMMON OR UNCOMMON GROUND?

CHAPTER SIX

A FOREST OF FIRE

FROM ABORIGINAL HOME TO ECOSYSTEM MANAGEMENT IN THE BOREAL FOREST

PETER J. MURPHY

The boreal forest in Canada runs in a wide belt across northern Canada. The focus of this paper is the northwestern part, which ranges from the western Yukon to northwestern Ontario. In this area the forest has evolved under the influence of recurrent fire, and the resulting mosaic of forest cover types can be clearly identified from the air. In the western boreal forests, forest fires and people are linked. Forest fires have affected the forests and people, and people, in turn, have affected fires. These relationships are described for three generally-defined eras: Aboriginal, European, and Ecosystem Management. The story reflects changing values and philosophies, and some elements of *deja-vu*.

Aboriginal Home
The forest was home to the Aboriginal people. It was also their cultural and spiritual home. Fire made life possible in these northern forests, providing heat for year-round living, and for cooking. Recurrent forest fires also created the earlier plant succession stages and the mosaic of habitats that were necessary to sustain the plants and animals on which they depended. The Aboriginals were hunters and gatherers, moving to take advantage of seasonal opportunities. The moose was a staple, providing meat, clothing, footwear, coverings for lodges and boats, and sinew for sewing. Surplus meat was dried to preserve it. The same traditions of hunting and gathering remain today. It is important in contemporary forest management planning to maintain those opportunities for Aboriginals as part of their cultural heritage.

Many of the plants and animals on which they depended were post-fire related, such as berry-bearing plants, birch used for bark and syrup, willows and aspen, and the beaver that used them in turn for food and dam building. The canoe represented a high state of technology, using native materials—framed with saplings or split wood, covered with bark, sewn with split spruce roots, and sealed with conifer pitch. As a result, the keepers of fire and the fire-bag were important parts of their lives.

Life in the northern forests was not always idyllic, and starvation was a constant threat. Although post-fire vegetation supports a variety of life, the immediate aftermath of fire may be relatively barren. This excerpt from a Hudson's Bay Company post record for Fort Edmonton on October 12, 1812 illustrates the immediate problem of obtaining meat after large burns. In these regions, with such continuity of fuels, fires could become very large, with effects extending over vast areas.

> *The Plains are, and have been these several Days past, burning in a most dreadful manner. Fires are raging in all Directions, and the sun obscured with Smoke that covers the whole Country, and should the remarkable dry weather which has now continued so long, not change very soon, the plains must be burnt to such an Extent as to preclude all Hopes of our getting a large supply of dry provisions, for which appearances on our Arrival here were very flattering.*[1]

In prairie or parkland areas the Aboriginals learned to set back fires to help to protect themselves. More significantly, they also learned to use fire—fires deliberately set to enhance their hunting and gathering activities and ease of travel.[2] David Thompson, the noted explorer and map maker for the Hudsons Bay Company, commented on the relationship between Aboriginals and fire as follows in June 1796:

> *...the Natives are frequently very careless in putting out the fires they make, and a high wind kindles it among the Pines always ready to catch fire; and [they] burn until stopped by some large swamp or lake; which makes many miles of the country appear very unsightly, and destroys many animals and birds especially the grouse, who do not appear to know how to save themselves, but all this devastation is nothing to the Indian, his country is large.*[3]

Thompson, with his European upbringing, perhaps misjudged what he observed. Colonel Sam Steele, who led the Northwest Mounted Police into western Canada, saw things differently in his 1874 comment:

> *Indians...wilfully set the prairies on fire (in the autumn) so that the bison would come to their part of the country to get the rich green grass which would follow in the spring.*[4]

Louis Martel, a Beaver Indian in northwestern Alberta, conveyed a clear understanding about fire during an interview by Dr. Henry T. Lewis in 1975.

> *Fires had to be controlled. You couldn't just start a fire anywhere, anytime. Fire can do a lot of harm or a lot of good. You have to know how to control it...It has been a long time since my father and my uncles used to burn each spring. But we were told to stop. The Mounties arrested some people...The country has changed from what it used to be—brush*

and trees where there used to be lots of meadows, and not so many animals as before.[5]

There is growing evidence that Aboriginals significantly affected landscapes through their use of fire, but their use appeared to be tempered by an understanding of the ecosystem, their place in it, and the need to constrain fires to the areas that they wanted to burn. For example, they would burn stream and river margins for ease of travel, to provide grass for horses, encourage willows for moose and aspen for beaver, open areas on which to camp and to stimulate berry production. They would also burn meadows to encourage willows and sedges, and would burn some stands of living trees to create sources of dry wood for fires.[6]

European Settlement

The arrival of Jacques Cartier at Hochelaga in Quebec in 1530 marked the beginning of major changes. The early European fur traders quickly adopted Aboriginal skills and knowledge, and typically travelled and lived in harmony with Aboriginals. The Aboriginals were encouraged to trap furs, a natural extension of their hunting and gathering activities. The extension of trading posts brought European trade goods such as axes and guns which were quickly adapted to enhancing their ways of life.

The European use of the forest for timber at those times was light. Pitsaws were used for lumber for the few buildings and for the wooden York boats used to move trade goods, supplies and furs on the northern waterways. Probably the greatest demand was for fuel wood to provide heat during the long winters. Early travellers marvelled at the features of this new country, but forest fires were alien to them, and their perception of burns was invariably described in terms of destruction, devastation, darkness and danger. Evidence suggests that fires had been frequent in the boreal forests. However, in the European mind, fires were bad, a phenomenon to be prevented if possible.

Three major influences resulted in a greater value to be attached to the timber component of the forests. The first was sea power—the need to provide timber for the sailing ships so vital to exploration, trade and national defence. Both the English and French established royal reserves of timber in eastern Canada as early as 1763, particularly to maintain a supply of timber for masts. Napoleons blockade of the Baltic around 1800 caused the British to turn more specifically to North America to provide substitute sources of timber. This led to the start of the white pine trade that firmly established the traditions of logging, camp life and river drives in New Brunswick and Nova Scotia, then up the St. Lawrence through Quebec and into Ontario up the Ottawa Valley and into the Great Lakes region.[7] The great log drives down the Ottawa River also caused our first Prime Minister, Sir John A. MacDonald to write in 1871:

The sight of the immense masses of timber passing my windows every morning constantly suggests to my mind the absolute necessity there is for looking into the future of this great trade. We are recklessly destroying the timber of Canada, and there is scarcely a possibility of replacing it. The quantity of timber reaching Quebec is annually decreasing, and the fires in the woods are periodically destroying millions of money. What is to become of the Ottawa region generally, after the timber is cut away, one cannot foresee. It occurs to me that the subject should be looked in the face and some efforts made for the preservation of our timber. The Dominion Government, having no lands, has no direct interest in the subject, but it seems to me that it would be a very good thing for the two Governments of Ontario and Quebec to issue a Joint Commission to examine the whole subject and report: 1st. As to the best means of cutting the timber after some regulated plan, as in Norway and on the Baltic; 2nd. As to replanting so as to keep up the supply as in Germany and Norway, and 3rd. As to the best means of protecting the woods from fires.[8]

The second influence was Confederation in 1867 that linked the four eastern colonies of Nova Scotia, New Brunswick, Quebec and Ontario into the Dominion of Canada. Sir John A. MacDonald immediately launched two actions. One was to encourage British Columbia to join Confederation by building a trans-continental railway to link it to eastern Canada. He also arranged to acquire Ruperts Land from the Hudsons Bay Company in order to ensure Canadas territorial integrity. Both results were achieved in 1870 when British Columbia joined the union and Ruperts Land became Dominion Lands within the North West Territories of Canada. Construction of the Canadian Pacific Railway created a great demand for wood for ties and bridges, and to construct new communities that sprang up around the railway stations. When the railway arrived in Calgary, Alberta in 1883 it led to a demand for building materials which gave a monetary value to the timber on the eastern slopes of the Rocky Mountains—timber which lay on the newly-acquired Dominion lands. Large steam-powered sawmills supplied by timber driven on the east-flowing rivers launched the forest industry in the central interior west.

The third influence was that of homesteading. Once the prairies were settled and homesteading moved into forested areas, land clearing became a major preoccupation. Homestead regulations required a minimum area to be cleared in order to gain title to the land. Tree falling was difficult, and fire was often seen as an easier way to clear the land. Many fires escaped into adjacent forests, raising concerns about the need to develop an agency for fire prevention. On the prairies, wood was in short supply and settlers travelled a long way to forested areas to obtain the building materials they needed. On the short-grass prairies irrigation showed great promise for increasing agricultural production, and led to increased value of the dryland prairies. Promoters recognized that the water source was in foothills and mountains, and they urged the government to protect those sources from fire. In 1899 a Superintendent of Timber and Forestry was hired in Ottawa to develop plans for managing the forests on Dominion lands. Surveys and investigations led to passing of the 1911 Forest Reserves Act which established protected areas throughout the west, coupled with fire ranging districts in the intervening forested areas.

The mandate of the Dominion Forest Service was to encourage tree planting on the prairies, but especially to stop forest fires on the Dominion lands. Prevention was the first step. There were few resources and not many people so fire laws were passed, notices posted, and seasonal rangers hired. In northern areas canoe patrols on the waterways carried a prevention message. As well, Dominion Forest Rangers accompanied Treaty Parties in the north, encouraging Aboriginal peoples to take a pledge of fire prevention. However, it became quickly evident that there were limits to the effectiveness of prevention.

Wildfire was a constant threat. For example, the community of Lac La Biche, Alberta was burned out in May of 1919. Subsequent investigations show that this was part of a larger series of forest fires that occurred over a 400 km area from west of Lac La Biche to somewhere northeast of Prince Albert, Saskatchewan—a burn that may have affected 8 million ha. Other communities in forested areas were also affected during these times. For example, Matheson, Ontario burned in 1916, and an estimated 350 people were killed as a result of the fire, especially among those in outlying settlements who could not escape the rapidly-moving fire. Events such as these led to major efforts to develop a fire fighting capability. In western Canada this included constructing trail access to enable patrols, building of lookouts, and improving roads for fire access. Initial fire fighting was done with wet sacks in prairie areas and hand tools in the forests.[9] Tools have become increasingly sophisticated, including the CL-415 Air Tanker, highly-trained helicopter-borne initial attack crews, and flying drip torch. Research and technology have also enabled development of computer-based systems for predicting forest fire behaviour under a variety of weather and fuel conditions, and the construction of fire attack models.

Ecosystem Management
The growth of the forest industry sector has contributed substantially to the economy. However, it has also led to concerns about sustainability of the forest ecosystem. The emergence of the concept of ecosystem management requires that we manage to respect ecosystem processes, and to constrain disturbances to those within the ranges of natural variation. This, in turn, entails studying more closely the influence of fire on the forest to develop guidelines for forest protection and harvesting to meet human needs—to balance ecosystems and economics.

A study of forest stand age-class data provides evidence about the former extent of forest fires. Charles Van Wagner described how the age-class distribution in forests subjected to recurrent forest fires took the shape of a negative exponential curve in which younger age-classes were in the majority, with fewer and fewer older stands.[10] The shape of the curve makes it possible to calculate the average annual rate of burn. In northern Alberta, the historic rate of burn before the advent of fire control was conservatively estimated at 2.6 percent of the area per year.[11] This has been subsequently reduced to approximately one tenth of one percent, largely as a result of improved fire management capabilities. The shape of the present age-class curve shows that we may have transformed our forest over the last ninety years, reducing the areas of younger forests and increasing the area of older age-classes.

Historic photographs also showed the pervasive influence of fire at the turn of the century. Comparison of these shows how the old burns have since grown back as green forests, contributing to the perception of the current generation that "green" is natural, and disturbances such as burns are unnatural. Another influence, besides regrowth of previously burned areas, is the spread of homes, cabins and resorts into forested areas, sharply increasing the values at risk, as well as concerns about safety to human life in those forest-urban interface areas. As well, the forest industry is inherently dependent on the forests for wood supply.

In our context, it is therefore important to maintain a fire control capability in order to protect those values at risk from forest fire. However, we must also consider the role of fire. For example, fire by prescription is being increasingly applied, reintroducing some of the Aboriginal concepts. Examples include use of fire in an extensive blowdown area to reduce the risk of intense wild fire and to control an emerging outbreak of bark beetles, creation of timberline wildlife habitat such as bighorn sheep range, and rejuvenation of winter range for moose and elk along river bottom lands. Fire has been reintroduced into parts of our park systems, for example on the Panther River in Banff National Park for the dual purpose of restoring fire to the ecosystem and creating fuel breaks along the park boundaries to enhance future opportunities for natural fire management.

Fire was the original harvester of forests. As there was forest renewal after fire, so is there renewal after logging. However, we need to learn more about specific fire influences, since fire has been so pervasive in wild forests. There is a research need both to assess the influence of fire and the results of its patterns on the landscape. For example, some fires are of low intensity while others burn under conditions of very high intensity—each creating different post-fire effects. Most fires are small, while fewer are large, but over 90 percent of the area burned is as a result of large fires. Fires of one million ha and greater are not uncommon. Seasonal fires, such as spring fires, may be more diverse as a result of greater diversity in moisture. Fall burns may be of higher intensity with more complete burns. We need to learn more precisely what the influence of fire size, pattern, shape and the unburned residuals is on post-fire recovery and the influence on wildlife so that these conditions may be more closely replicated in forest harvesting in support of biological diversity. The challenge is to balance fire and harvesting with the requirements for forest sustainability.

Notes

1. Hudson's Bay Company, Post Record for Fort Edmonton, NWT (Winnipeg: Hudson's Bay Archives, 1812).

2. Stephen J. Pyne, *Fire in America—A Cultural History of Wildland and Rural Fire* (Princeton, NJ: Princeton University Press, 1982).

3. Richard Glover, ed., *David Thompson's Narrative 1784-1812* (Toronto: The Champlain Society, 1962).

4. Colonel Samuel B. Steele cited in George W. Arthur, *An Introduction to the Ecology of Early Historic Communal Bison Hunting Among the Northern Plains Indians* (Ottawa: National Museums of Canada, 1975).

5. Louis Martel interviewed by Henry T. Lewis, "Maskuta—The Ecology of Indian Fires in Northern Alberta," *Western Canadian Journal of Anthropology* 7, No. 1 (1977), 15-56.

6. Ibid.

7. Donald MacKay, *Heritage Lost—the Crisis in Canada's Forests* (Toronto: Macmillan of Canada, 1985).

8. Macdonald to John Sandfield MacDonald, June 23, 1871, Sir John A. MacDonald Papers, MG 26 A, volume 518, part 4, L.B. 15, p. 963, National Archives of Canada.

9. Peter J. Murphy, *History of Forest and Prairie Fire Control Policy in Alberta*, ENR Report T/77 (Edmonton: Alberta Energy and Natural Resources, 1985).

10. Charles E. Van Wagner, "Age-Class Distribution and the Forest Fire Cycle," *Canadian Journal of Forest Research* 8 (1978), 220-227.

11. Peter J. Murphy, *Methods for Evaluating the Effects of Forest Fire Management in Alberta*, Ph.D. Dissertation, Department of Forestry, University of British Columbia, 1985.

Chapter Seven

LANDSCAPE CHANGE AND BIODIVERSITY CRISIS

A Forest History of Boreal Sweden

Lars Östlund

The human impact on the boreal forest of northern Sweden can be divided into three distinctive phases: an early period dominated by agricultural use of the forest ecosystem, an intermediate period with a diverse forest use including agricultural and pre-industrial activities, and a final industrial era. The shift from the first to the third phase occurred within the last two centuries. During this period the forest of northern Sweden was transformed from a forest shaped mainly by natural processes towards a forest strongly influenced by human activities. Agricultural, pre-industrial and early industrial forest utilization was generally aimed at specific forest resources, such as leaf-fodder, pine-stumps or very large pines. In the twentieth century, forest utilization and forest exploitation were replaced by forest management. This increased the overall growth-rate and standing volume of the northern Swedish forest but at a high ecological cost. During the period of intensive silviculture in the twentieth century, biologically important structures were consistently removed from the forest and biological diversity was reduced. Historical studies allow the detection of long term changes in ecologically crucial structures and components of the forest landscape.

Humans have altered forest ecosystems and transformed the forest landscape of northern Sweden fundamentally. The present forest is radically different from any preceding forest vegetation. The human impact has taken different forms throughout history. In the sixteenth century, sawmills were erected to furnish the Swedish king with sawn wood and masts for sailing ships.[1] In the seventeenth and eighteenth centuries, iron works were relocated from the mining district of central Sweden to the northern Swedish coast. This was done because wood for charcoal production and water power, limiting factors for the iron production in other parts of the country, were abundant in northern Sweden.[2] In the nineteenth century, tar was produced from old-growth pine stumps and snags and then exported. Potash extracted from broadleaved trees also became an important export item at this time.[3] In the nineteenth century, northern Sweden also constituted a timber frontier. The large old-growth pines became a prime target for a rapidly developing sawmill industry. In a short time, Sweden became the world's leading exporter of sawn wood. At the beginning of the twentieth century, there was a period of transition between large scale forest exploitation and the introduction of sustained-yield forestry and intensive silviculture. In the early years of the century the Swedish Parliament passed a modern forest legislation based on sustained yield principles and a mandatory provision to provide for regeneration after logging.[4]

Parallel to the pre-industrial and industrial forest exploitation, a more diffuse agricultural utilization of the forest occurred. During the last millennia, more and more of northern Sweden has been populated. Agriculture has increased at the expense of hunting and fishing and other forms of traditional and extensive land-uses. The most prominent waves of settlement came in the sixteenth and nineteenth centuries. Although the agricultural impact on the forest ecosystems have increased successively, the sparse populations of humans and domestic animals in northern Sweden have never exerted an impact comparable to the situation in the southern parts of the country.

In our time, many different opinions have been advanced regarding the history of human impact on the forest and the historical state of the northern forest. Very little research has, however, been done. The nature of the change is complex due to the cumulative effect of many different human activities. The magnitude of change is also difficult to estimate. At the present time, there is also a lack of forest reserves which could serve as points of comparison to the managed forest landscape.[5] Even if there were such forest reserves, it is not certain that they could be used as references to the managed forest landscape. Fire exclusion and atmospheric pollution have also changed forest areas which have been exempt from exploitation. One way of analyzing the human impact and the resulting changes on the forest ecosystems is to study forest history. Quantitative information from historical sources and biological archives on changes in the forest ecosystems can be analysed. I believe, however, that very important changes in the northern Swedish forest have occurred within the last few centuries, and that it is possible both to document and quantitatively analyze these changes.

One motive for forest historical research is that it may yield important knowledge for the present and future management of forest resources. Today, as was the case in the beginning of the twentieth century, we are in a period of transition. Forest legislation and forest management are changing and the debate is again focused on the concept of sustainability in forestry. At this time, though, the emphasis is not on forest yield, but on biological sustainability.[6] Of particular importance right now is knowledge that will enable us to restore some of the biological legacy and natural processes to the forest landscape, upon which many endangered species depend.[7] Forest historical studies will allow us to understand long term changes in ecologically crucial structures and components of the forest landscape. It will also help us to understand changes in forest ecosystem dynamics and functions.

Boreal Sweden in Geographic and Ecological Context

In the present paper I will discuss the forest history of boreal Sweden. It can, in ecological terms, be placed in the northern coniferous forest region, dominated by the tree-species Scots pine (*Pinus sylvestris L.*) and Norway spruce (*Picea abies L. (Karst)*).[8] Other important tree species are the broadleaved birches (*Betula sp.*), aspen (*Populus tremula*), grey alder (*Alnus incata*) and rowan (*Sorbus aucuparia*). Boreal Sweden is characterized by the Scandes mountain range which separates Sweden from Norway. From this range the country slopes gradually eastward towards the Gulf of Bothnia. Approximately fifty-five percent of the land-area is covered by forests; wetlands comprise fifteen percent; arable land including pasture comprise only two percent; and the rest consists of mountains above the tree line.[9] The large rivers generally run in a southeastern direction, draining the Scandes mountain range and the forest land. The large rivers together with their medium-sized and small tributaries constitute a comprehensive network of waterways that cover the forest land.

Boreal Sweden is distinguished from the southern part of the country in several respects. Land-use has traditionally been much less intensive and the cultivation of crops has only affected smaller areas. It was primarily the coastal areas and the lower reaches of the larger rivers that were occupied by farmers for an extended period of time. The inland forested areas have in contrast been used by hunters, fishermen and to some extent by the Saami population. The Saami changed their way of life considerably in the seventeenth century when the scale of their traditional reindeer-herding changed and they started to move longer distances with larger groups of animals.[10]

Domestic Forest Utilization, Cattle Ranging and Firewood

The start of commercial logging in northern Sweden changed forest utilization from being a local and small-scale activity to a large-scale exploitation covering almost all of the forest land. The diverse agrarian forest utilization, which was largely dominant until the nineteenth century, was limited to the immediate surroundings of the existing settlements and towns. The intensity and areal extent of the effects on the forest ecosystem depended on the population density and the age of settlements. This assumption is not based on specific investigations but on general descriptions of the agrarian forest utilization.[11] Firewood, often consisting of dead standing trees, was usually gathered in the immediate surroundings of the villages. Construction timber which had to meet certain standards often had to be hauled from further away.

Cattle ranging has been an important part of the rural economy of northern Sweden. Cattle grazed in the forest during the summer, and winter fodder was collected from sedge fens and alluvial meadows along rivers. Cattle grazing generally took place over large areas in the outfileds at some distance from the villages. The grazing had direct effects on forest regeneration, but the effect obviously was highly dependent on the kind of animals as well as the grazing intensity.[12] Farmers also used fire for grazing improvement and in some regions slash and burn cultivation, a practice which altered the natural fire regime of the forests. In general, the pre-industrial agrarian impact on the forest in northern Sweden can be inferred from the demography of northern Sweden. Consequently, an important conclusion is therefore that the agrarian impact on the forest prior to the nineteenth century was rather limited and geographically concentrated to the more densely settled areas, leaving the larger parts of the inland forest relatively unaffected. This conclusion must be viewed in the light of the difficulty of assessing this type of human impact on the forest.[13] It is easy to over- or under-estimate the impact because of the difficulties in measuring it adequately. It is even harder to assess the long-term effects on the forest vegetation caused by this type of utilization.

Pre-industrial Forest Exploitation: Charcoal, Tar, Masts, and Potash

Prior to the industrial revolution, other forms of forest exploitation influenced the northern Swedish forest. In the seventeenth and eighteenth centuries, iron works were relocated from the mining districts of central Sweden to the Gulf of Bothnia.[14] These new locations, near rivers and vast forests, were selected to allow the industry to benefit from water-power and large supplies of wood for charcoal production. In general, the reason for the relocation was not due to a depletion of forest resources in the mining districts of central Sweden, but to the larger resource base in the North, and its promise for increased production.[15] The impact on the forest arising from the new iron works in northern Sweden was probably local and did not extend far into the forest.

Tar produced from pine stumps and fire-scarred snags also became an important export product in the eighteenth and nineteenth century.[16] Before the nineteenth century tar was mostly produced in Finland, which until 1812 was a part of Sweden. After that time tar production expanded considerably in the far north of Sweden to compensate for the lost production in Finland. In contrast to the domestic forest utilization and the charcoal production for the ironworks, tar production could take place in the sparsely populated inland parts of the country. The tar trade introduced close and lasting business relations between farmers and merchants operating in the coastal towns of northern Sweden. The rise and decline of tar production was closely linked to the world market. Tar was used to maintain and preserve sailing ships. The magnitude of this enterprise therefore declined when such ships started to disappear in the early twentieth century. The tar trade introduced close and lasting business relations between farmers and merchants operating in the coastal towns of northern Sweden.

In the late eighteenth and early nineteenth century shipbuilding enterprises were established in several locations on the Bothnian coast. While tar was extracted from the interior and mainly exported, sailing ships were mostly built for domestic use. The shipbuilding required special timber assortments and tree-qualities. Such trees were rare, but their value could cover the cost of transport even over a long distance. The most valuable items were masts longer than twenty meters with a minimum diameter of twenty centimeters. Other important items were buttress parts of large trees and curved timber.[17] Many shipyard enterprises developed into large integrated forest companies which built sailing ships, owned forest land, sawed their own timber and exported the deals abroad. One such company was Wifstavarv AB, located near the town of Sundsvall.[18] This company was in operation from 1798 to 1966 when it was bought by the Swedish Cellulose company (SCA).

Potash was another typical pre-industrial forest product exported from northern Sweden. The potash (K_2CO_3) was obtained from wood-ashes of broadleaved trees, primarily birch and aspen. The potash was highly refined with a dryweight-ratio of approximately 1000/1 between the raw-material and the produced potash. This fact allowed for long transports and exploitation of forests far from villages and settlements. In some areas, particularly in the counties of Västerbotten and Norrbotten, the production expanded considerably in the early nineteenth century but declined in the 1860s. Previous research concerning the potash production in northern Sweden has concluded that the production declined because of a shortage of raw-material,[19] but more recent work suggest external factors, especially the use of other chemicals, as the primary reason for the decline.[20] The rise and decline of this specific form of forest exploitation shows a similar pattern in Scandinavia and North America at this time.[21] Nevertheless this forest exploitation probably had a large impact on tree species distribution in certain areas.

The Nineteenth Century Timber Frontier

The rapidly increasing international demand for sawn timber in the nineteenth century introduced a new era of forest exploitation in northern Sweden.[22] This exploitation differed from the domestic and pre-industrial forest utilization in several important aspects. First, the scale of operation was much greater. Large amounts of timber were hauled from forests which had previously been little influenced by humans. The exploitation came to affect almost all the forest land of northern Sweden. Secondly, the exploitation was aimed at one specific forest resource: high quality large diameter pine timber, which was abundant all over northern Sweden. Thirdly, the impact on the forest ecosystem was much greater than the previous forest utilization. Almost all old-growth pine was removed from the forest. In some places large numbers of dead standing trees were also cut as construction material to be placed in creeks and rivers to facilitate the floating of timber. The initial exploitation of the old-growth timber was followed by secondary waves of exploitation aimed at spruce timber and smaller trees used for pulpwood after the turn of the century.[23]

The introduction of large scale commercial logging of virgin forests in the nineteenth century was not confined to northern Sweden. Norway was the traditional supplier of sawn-wood on the European market. Timber from the Norwegian forests was readily abundant and the harbours on the Norwegian coast were open all year round, and situated close to the markets. But when the demand started to rise in the early nineteenth century, timber from the Norwegian forests was not sufficient, and the focus of the Scandinavian sawmill industry shifted towards the Swedish west-coast and then further north.[24] Although the relative importance of the Norwegian sawmill industry decreased in the nineteenth century, Norway still was an important exporter of sawn wood products, and the export rose considerably during that century.[25] In Finland the development was quite similar to northern Sweden. The sawmill industry expanded into old-growth forests in the northern parts of the country. It became the most important export industry during the latter part of the nineteenth century.[26] In North America a timber frontier also moved across the continent during the nineteenth century. The first forests to be exploited on a larger scale were pine forests in the north-eastern part of the United States and the eastern parts of Canada.[27] Later during the nineteenth century the frontier moved towards the pine forests around the Great Lakes and then to the pine forests of the south.[28] At the end of the century the final phase of exploitation of virgin forest had started in the Pacific Northwest.[29] In this part of North America many valuable coniferous species were used, such as Douglas fir, Western red cedar and Sitka spruce.[30]

There are many similarities between the nineteenth century timber exploitation in North America and Scandinavia. The logging was in both cases primarily aimed at large trees in virgin forests. The forest was virgin to a varying extent, used and maybe even transformed to some extent by humans, but it had never been subjected to large-scale exploitation before.[31] Most of the exploitation in North America encompassed pine forests, resembling the exploitation of pine-dominated forests in northern Scandinavia. The timber frontier was also intertwined with agrarian colonization in both Sweden and North America. Especially during the early phase of the exploitation in the sparsely populated northern Swedish forests, the work of the farmers was important for the logging and the log-driving in the rivers. Later, as the logging expanded, professional loggers became more important, but they never entirely replaced the farmers in the forest.[32] In the

United States the rapid agrarian colonization also served as an internal force driving the timber exploitation. Large amounts of sawn boards and other wood products were needed by the settlers, especially in areas where wood was scarce, such as the Great Plains. An important distinction from Sweden is, therefore, that there was a large internal demand for wood products in the United States. In Sweden, most of the sawn products were exported, which made Sweden the largest exporter of wood in the world at the end of the nineteenth century. Canada, Finland and Russia were also large exporters of sawn timber in the late nineteenth century.[33]

The large scale forest exploitation in the nineteenth century brought up the issue of property rights in Scandinavia as well as in North America. In Sweden two events received special attention. One was the acquisition of timber from public land by the Baggböle sawmill in the county of Västerbotten. On several occasions the sawmill company was engaged in legally dubious activities and it was claimed that the company had persuaded farmers to cut timber illegally on public forest land. The trials and the public debate that followed became a symbol of the large-scale exploitation of the northern Swedish forest, which in many respects was ruthless.[34] Another process of principal importance was the acquisition of forest land from independent farmers by sawmill companies between 1880-1900. This large-scale shift in land ownership raised questions about the future of the farming population in northern Sweden, and led to a 1906 law prohibiting the sale of private forest land to companies in northern Sweden. In the United States similar property rights questions arose in connection with the accelerating timber exploitation in the nineteenth century. Especially in the Great Lakes and southern states, large scale land speculation, through legal or illegal land claims, was practised by the lumber companies.[35]

The Transformation of the Forests of Northern Sweden

The present forest landscape in northern Sweden is very different from the pre-industrial forest landscape. Two major phases can be distinguished in the transformation of the forests of northern Sweden. The first phase is the nineteenth century exploitation, which can be characterized as a non-sustainable "mining" process carried out by the sawmill industry. The main effect of this phase was simply that the larger timber trees were logged from the forest. The exploitation was generally done without regard to the long-term yield of the forest, although legislation was introduced in the late nineteenth century restricting the exploitation to some extent. The second phase comprises the twentieth century sustained-yield forestry, characterized by intensive silviculture and forest management. This phase is to some extent a product of the first phase, in the sense that the debate over the intensive exploitation in the nineteenth century initiated forest legislation in the early twentieth century.[36] The growth of pulp mills, which could utilize smaller trees, also sped up and facilitated the introduction of sustained-yield forestry.[37] The introduction of intensive silviculture included a wide spectrum of measures carried out in accordance with detailed management plans. The effects of this phase are numerous and include increases in standing volume and forest yield as well as the division of the forest landscape into relatively well defined and uniform forest stands.

Forest transformation on a landscape level has also been documented in detail.[38] A case study of Orsa forest common in the province of Kopparberg in Sweden indicates major changes during the last one hundred years. This forest of approximately 55,000 hectares was exploited for the first time in the 1890s. At that time the forest was dominated by old-growth pine with a large stock of large old and dead trees. The logging severely reduced the number of large living trees and the standing volume was halved within a twenty-year period. After the logging much effort was put into silviculture with the aim of restoring the standing volume and increasing the yield from the forest.[39] Today the standing volume of the forest approaches the pre-exploitation level. The twentieth century silviculture and forest management have also produced a forest of relatively young forest stands, typically even-aged, and dominated by only one tree species. The species composition of Orsa forest common has fluctuated considerably during the last one hundred years. The pre-exploitation forest was dominated by pine, which constituted approximately seventy-five percent of the standing volume. The nineteenth century exploitation reduced the dominance of pine, but silvicultural measures during the twentieth century have strongly favoured pine over other species, and the standing volume of pine once again reaches approximately seventy-five percent of the total volume.[40]

The Ecological Significance of the Human Impact on the Boreal Forest

The changes in the northern Swedish forest ecosystem during the last two centuries are complex and encompass many different aspects. Old-growth forests have diminished in extent and their qualities reduced. Typical old-growth characteristics include the presence of large trees, old trees, dying trees and dead trees within a forest.[41] Changes in the presence of such structures may result in negative consequences for biological diversity in the forest,[42] since many endangered and threatened species of plants and animals in the boreal forest of Scandinavia, and elsewhere, are dependent on old-growth structures.[43] In Sweden, more than 200 species of plants and animals are seriously threatened by extinction because of current forest management.[44] Although the importance of the old-growth structures are widely recognized, we know surprisingly little about the changes of such structures in the boreal forest during the last few centuries. I have shown that typical old-growth characteristics of the Orsa forest common have diminished drastically during the last one hundred years.[45] The nineteenth century exploitation of the forest reduced the number of large trees in the forest significantly. These trees were not only large in size but also old (250 years), and many were described as senescent and dying at the time of exploitation.

A second old-growth forest structure of great importance is dead trees. The reduction of standing dead trees has been dramatic in the Swedish forest during the last century. It is important to stress that the figures presented only include standing dead trees that were of sawtimber quality. The reduction in the number of standing dead trees of lower timber quality as well as of down-logs has most likely been even greater.[46] Although dead trees were used for various purposes prior to the twentieth century, the major reduction occurred during the present century. Removal of dead and old trees were mandated to reduce the risk of insect outbreaks. There was also a policy to "clean-up" and "rejuvenate" the forest during the twentieth century, expressed in forest legislation as well as in management policies of forest owners.[47] It is thus a combination of several factors that lie behind the rapid reduction of dead trees in the northern Swedish forest. An important conclusion is that the twentieth century forest management, which has increased overall growth rates and standing volumes of the northern Swedish forest, has had an ecological price. During the period of intensive silviculture in the twentieth century, biologically important structures have been consistently removed from the forest and biological diversity has been reduced.[48] The process of forest transformation is comprised of many different aspects, including the spread of clearcut areas, the decrease in old-growth forests, the promotion of single species and even-aged forest stands and the introduction of exotic tree species. I believe it is appropriate to point to the importance of historical knowledge as a prerequisite for nature conservation and forest management aimed at maintaining biological diversity in forest ecosystems. The first step in understanding the effects of modern forestry on biological diversity must be to identify crucial forest structures and analyse their changes over time. At present, such knowledge is not used widely even though current trends in Swedish forestry and forest legislation are strongly emphasizing multiple use and biological diversity.

Exploitation and utilization of different resources in the forest almost by definition changes the forest. But other more indirect measures also have had effects on the forest ecosystems. Perhaps the most important of these is fire exclusion from forest ecosystems. One of the major concerns of foresters in the early twentieth century was to suppress wildfire. The different methods (fire-towers, roads, fire crews) were so successful that fire almost ceased to be an ecological factor in the Boreal forest landscape. The implications of successful fire-exclusion are far-reaching and complex. One important consequence is the diminished presence of dead trees. The combination of large-scale exploitation and declining frequency of fires has severely reduced the abundance of dead trees in the forest.[49]

Some of the more recent general shifts in vegetation cover can also be related to anthropogenic changes in quality and quantity of disturbances over the last two centuries. The shift from "fire disturbed" to "logging disturbed" forest ecosystems has generally favoured ericaceous plant communities. As an effect, competitive dwarf shrubs like *Empetrum hermaphroditum* have increased on clearcuts especially within the northern boreal zone. *Empetrum* is a fire-sensitive species which previously played a minor role in fire disturbed plant communities. Under prevailing non-pyrogenic conditions however, *Empetrum* has become a clear winner. Selective cuttings in the late nineteenth and early twentieth century, and clearcutting after the 1950s, has furthered its growth. As this species has an unusual ability to monopolize plant communities, a general reduction of plant diversity has occurred at these sites. Natural regeneration by conifer species and broadleaved species are also strongly inhibited by *Empetrum* vegetation through allelopathic interference and resource competition.[50] The example of *Empetrum* illustrates the far-reaching consequences of multiple anthropogenic influences on complex ecosystems. It is typical, however, that the replacement of one natural disturbance factor, i.e., fire, with a human influence, i.e., logging, results in large scale changes of ecosystem function and structure.[51] We also suspect similar but even more complex interactions between human interference and ecosystem functions related to the case of potash production in northern Sweden in the nineteenth century. We believe that the pre-industrial forest landscape contained a larger stock of old-growth deciduous trees in different forest ecosystems compared to the present.[52] We also believe that they were especially important keystone species in the boreal conifer-dominated forest. Such trees therefore strongly influenced biodiversity and ecosystem production in a complicated pattern. The reduction of deciduous trees by pre-industrial potash burning probably changed fundamental relations between tree-layer, ground vegetation and soil properties, even before the industrial exploitation took place. Our current knowledge leads us to such a hypothesis but only further interdisciplinary research in forest history can verify it.

Notes

1. Wilhelm Carlgren, *De Norrländska Skogsindustrierna intill 1800-talets mitt* [The Northern Swedish Forest Industry Before 1850] (Uppsala: Almqvist & Wiksell, 1926).

2. Gunnar Arpi, *Den Svenska Järnhanteringens Träkolsförsörjning 1830-1950* [The Consumption of Charcoal by the Swedish Iron Industry, 1830-1950] (Uppsala: Almqvist & Wiksell, 1951).

3. Lars Östlund, Olle Zackrisson, and Håkan Strotz, "Potash Production in Northern Sweden—History and Ecological Effects of a Pre-industrial Forest Exploitation," *Environment and History*, in press.

4. Per Stjernquist, *Laws in the Forest* (Lund: CWK Gleerup, 1973).

5. Per Anders Esseen, Bengt Enström, Lars Ericsson, and Kjell Sjöberg, "Boreal Forest—The Focal Habitats of Fennoscandia," in *Ecological Principles of Nature Conservation: Applications in Temperate and Boreal Environments*, ed. L. Hansson (London: Elsevier Applied Science, 1992): 252-325.

6. Lars Hultkrantz and Sören Wibe, *Skogspolitik för ett Nytt Sekel* [Forest Policy for the 21st Century], Report No. 31 (Stockholm: ESO, 1991).

7. Lars Erik Liljelund, Börje Pettersson, and Olle Zackrisson, "Skogsbruk och Biologisk Mångfald" [Forestry and Biodiversity], *Svensk Botanisk Tidskrift* 86 (1992): 227-232.

8. Hugo Sjörs, "Forest Regions," *Acta Phytogeogr. Suec.* 50 (1965).

9. Göran Kempe, et al., *Rikskogstaxeringen 1983-87—Skogstillstånd, Tillväxt och Avverkning* [National Forest Inventory 1983-87—Fibre Supply, Growth and Harvesting], No. 51, Institutionen för skogstaxering (Umeå, SLU, 1992).

10. Lennart Lundmark, *Uppbörd, Utarmning, Utveckling. Det Samiska Fångstsamhällets Övergång till Rennomadism i Lule Lappmark* [Taxation, Impoverishment, and Development: The Change from Reindeer Hunting to Nomadism in Saami Society, Lule Lappmark], (Lund: Lunds Universitet, 1982).

11. Lars Östlund, *Exploitation and Structural Changes in the North Swedish Boreal Forest 1800-1992*, Department of Forest Vegetation Ecology (Umeå, SLU 1993).

12. Olle Zackrisson and Lars Östlund, "Branden Formade Skogslandskapets Mosaik" [The Influence of Fire on the Forest Landscape], *Skog och Forskning* 4 (1991): 13-21.

13. Mikko Mönkkönen and Daniel A. Welsh, "A Biogeographical Hypothesis on the Effects of Human Caused Landscape Changes on the Forest Bird Communities of Europe and North America," *Ann. Zool. Fennici* 31 (1994): 61-70.

14. Arpi, op. cit.

15. Ibid.

16. Lars-Erik Borgegård, *Tjärhanteringen i Västerbottens Län under 1800-talets Senare Hälft* [The Tar Trade in Västerbottens Län, 1850-1900], (Umeå: Kungl. Skytteanska samfundet, 1973).

17. Östlund, op. cit.

18. Ibid.

19. Lars Tirén, "Skogshistoriska Studier i Trakten av Degerfors i Västerbotten" [Studies in Forest History in the Degerfors Region of Västerbotten], *Meddelanden från statens skogsförsöksanstalt* 30 Nos. 1-2 (1937): 67-322.

20. Östlund, Zackrisson, and Strotz, op. cit.

21. Lars Östlund and Hans Lindersson, "A Dendroecological Study of the Exploitation and Transformation of a Boreal Forest Stand," *Scandinavian Journal of Forestry Research* 10 (1995), 56-64.

22. Jörgen Björklund, "From the Gulf of Bothnia to the White Sea—Swedish Direct Investments in the Sawmill Industry of Tsarist Russia," *Scandinavian Economic History Review* 32 No. 1 (1984): 17-40.

23. Anders Holmgren, "Skogarna och deras Vård i Övre Norrland intill År 1930" [The Forests and their Care in Northern Norrland before 1930], in *Sveriges Skogar under 100 År,* ed. Gunnar Arpi (Stockholm: Kungliga Domänverket, 1959): 375-443.

24. Björklund, op. cit.

25. Francis Sejersted, "Veien mot Öst" [The Road to the East], in *Vandringer. Festskrift till Ingrid Semmingsen,* eds. S. Langholm and F. Sejersted (Oslo: Aschehoug, 1980): 163-201.

26. Jussi Raumolin, "Formation of Sustained-yield Forestry System in Finland," in *History of Sustained-yield Forestry: A Symposium,* ed. Harold K. Steen (Santa Cruz, CA: Forest History Society of America, 1984).

27. David Smith, *A History of Lumbering in Maine 1861-1960,* (Orono: University of Maine Press, 1972). Michael Williams, *Americans and Their Forest: A Historical Geography,* (Cambridge: Cambridge University Press, 1989).

28. Charles E. Twining, "The Lumbering Frontier," in *The Great Lakes Forest* ed. Susan Flader (Minneapolis: University of Minnesota Press 1983): 121-155.

29. Thomas Cox, "Trade, Development, and Environmental Change: The Utilization of North America's Pacific Coast Forest to 1914 and its Consequences," in *Global Deforestation and the Nineteenth-Century World Economy,* eds. Richard P. Tucker and J. F. Richards (Durham: Forest History Society, 1983): 14-29.

30. Williams, op. cit.

31. Ibid.

32. Göran Rosander, "Skogsarbetaren och hans Verktyg" [The Forest Worker and his Tools], *Kungliga Skogs—och Lantbruksakademiens Tidskrift* 127 (1988): 145-162.

33. Björklund, op. cit.

34. Gunnar Balgård, "Ödemarken, som Bevittnat Dåden är, Stum" [The Wastelands Who have Witnessed the Deeds are Silent], *Västerbotten* 1 (1980): 15-40.

35. Williams, op. cit.

36. Stjernquist, op. cit.

37. Leif Mattsson, and Einar Stridsberg, *Skogens Roll i Svensk Markanvändning—En Utvecklingsstudie* [The Role of the Forest in Swedish Land Use—A Study in Development], (Umeå: SLU, 1981).

38. Östlund, 1993, op. cit.

39. Gustav Kolmodin, "Skogen och Storskiftet i Orsa" [The Forest and Land Organization in Orsa], in *Orsa, En Sockenbeskrivning*, eds. Johannes V. Boethius and Olle Veirulf (Stockholm: Nordisk Rotogravyr, 1953): 222-586.

40. Östlund, op. cit.

41. Jerry F. Franklin, Herman H. Shugart, and M.E. Harmon, "Tree Death as an Ecological Process—The Causes, Consequences, and Variability of Tree Mortality," *BioScience* 37 No. 8 (1987): 550-556.

42. Lennart Hansson, "Landscape Ecology of Boreal Forests," *Trends in Ecology & Evolution* 7, No. 9 (1992): 299-302.

43. Kari Heliövaara and Rauno Väisänen, "Effects of Modern Forestry on Northwestern European Forest Invertebrates: A Synthesis," *Acta Forestalia Fennica* 189 (1984): 4-29.

44. Anon, *Hotade Arter* [Endangered Species], (Stockholm: Naturvårdsverket, 1990).

45. Östlund, 1993, op. cit.

46. Per Linder and Lars Östlund, "Förändringar i Norra Sveriges Skogar 1870-1991" [Changes in the Forests of Northern Sweden, 1870-1991], *Svensk Botanisk Tidsskrift* 86 No. 3 (1992): 199-215.

47. Anders Öckerman, "Städning i Skogen. Om Skogshygien, Hyggesrensning och Jägmästare" [Cleaning Up the Forest: On Forest Hygiene, Slash Removal and Foresters], C-uppsats i idéhistoria, Institutionen för idéhistoria (Umeå: Umeå Universitet, 1993).

48. Hansson, op. cit.

49. Östlund, 1993, op. cit.

50. Olle Zackrisson and Marie-Charlotte Nilsson, "Allelopathic Effects by *Empetrum hermaphroditum* on Seed Germination of Two Boreal Tree Species," *Canadian Journal of Forest Research* 22 (1992): 1310-1319.

51. Zackrisson and Östlund, op. cit.

52. Lars Östlund, Olle Zackrisson, and Anna-Lena Axelsson, "Forest Structure Consequences of Forest Transformation Since the Nineteenth Century, and Ecological Consequences: The History of a Scandinavian Boreal Forest Landscape," *Canadian Journal of Forest Research* 27 (1997): 1198-1206.

Chapter Eight

CULTURE VERSUS NATURE IN THE HISTORY OF SWEDISH FORESTRY

A Case for Pluralism

Anders Öckerman

In the 1940s, the American forester and naturalist Aldo Leopold identified two types of foresters.[1] Type A foresters viewed nature as productive ground, forests as a crop, and used industrial methods in the production of cellulose. Type B foresters regarded nature as an ecosystem, and forestry as a way to use, not to transform, ecosystems; these foresters were also interested in species protection and biodiversity. Leopold, himself a former type A forester, placed his hope for the future among type B foresters, who, he thought, worked towards an "ecological consciousness." At the time of Leopold's writing, type A foresters were clearly in command. In more recent years, however, type B foresters appear to have gained a stronger foothold in the profession.

In this chapter, I propose to explore four historical epochs of Swedish forestry. Previous studies suggest that the first and the third are narrowly focussed on type A forestry, large scale clearcutting and subsequent silvicultural treatments, while the second and fourth are centred on type B forestry, selection cutting and natural regeneration. In contrast to this interpretation, I argue that the forestry debate and forest practices have been more characterized by variety and uncertainty, especially during the second era, when intermediate forms of management were commonly practised. The dual scheme of A and B foresters, though still useful as an ideal type, is thus too simple. The historical record show that intermediate forms of forestry have co-existed in the past, suggesting that they could also coexist and inform each other in the future.

The account is mainly an intellectual forest history: a history of forestry ideas. I seek to understand it as *environmental* history: how the structure of the forests interacts with human minds and technology. I employ a relatively narrow definition of "forestry." I define it as the theory and practice of producing a sustained yield of primarily wood.[2] I therefore do not centre my discussion on the Leopold-inspired debate on anthropocentrism versus ecocentrism, but more on the ways in which type A and B forestry may modify sustained yield. As I see it, Swedish forestry has been inspired by two tendencies: one based on intensive management, maximum yield and ecosystem transformation (tending towards type A forestry), and the other based on multiple use, sustained yield, and ecosystem preservation (tending towards type B forestry).

The Patriarchs of Swedish Forestry

The Swedish Royal Academy of Science expressed a concern for diminishing resources as early as the mid-eighteenth century, when it turned to German forestry schools for an answer.[3] When Swedish forestry emerged in the nineteenth century it was thus uncritically supportive of German clearfelling systems. In 1828, higher forestry education was established in Stockholm, and in the middle of the century (1859) a governmental agency (*Domänverket*, Swedish Forest Service) was created. In 1822, the father of Swedish forestry, Israel Ström, wrote in *A Proposal for an Improved Forestry Economics*, for decades the main textbook for prospective foresters (*jägmästare*), that the "selective method, as practised widely in Sweden, has for good reason been rejected in both France and Germany…[I shall here]…exclusively treat the clearcutting system and its subdivisions."[4] The word "subdivision" was well chosen here, as the first step of transforming a forest into a clearcut system is to subdivide it into annual cutting areas.

Ström and his contemporary forest economists taught and defended clearcutting in an era when unregulated forest use was common. Peasants practised swidden cultivation, burned forests to create pastures and cut whatever tree they needed here and there. Ström wanted to produce state controlled *order*, mainly on Crown lands, which he also wanted to expand. Ström and his successor Gunnar Segerdahl taught nothing but ordered clearcutting for almost half a century. With a few exceptions, forest economics were synonymous with mapping, clearcutting and promoting sustained yield growth in even age stands. But something changed in the last few years of nineteenth century.

The nineteenth century clearcutting forestry mission of the "forest economists" was not very successful, and northern Sweden was very far from being an ordered clearcutting system based on sustained yield. The industrial boom of the late nineteenth century led to extensive cuts, and a concerned agitation by conservationists and preservationists. Clearcut areas were seen as scenes of devastation. In the early twentieth century, a new league of conservation-minded foresters and many non-foresters, seen as dilettantes, aspired to work in tune with nature, and not to force and control it. Selection cuttings were seen as more gentle, harmonious and less risky. At the end of the century forestry turned more and more to conservation matters, and clearcutting systems were blended and complemented with selection cutting systems (*blädning*). One of the world's first general regeneration laws was put into effect in 1903, and the first national parks were established some years later. In 1897, a most influential forester, Uno Wallmo, argued that "We shall seek to diminish clearcutting to a minimum and introduce selection systems...that incorporate every means possible to promote the individual tree's comfort as well as the security of the stand's regeneration."[5] This became the code of a new generation of foresters, some of whom proposed selection methods to be used extensively, but even the strongest proponents not wanting them to be used everywhere.

In the middle of the twentieth century, the modernistic generation of forest officers were the first to succeed in introducing a standardized method of forestry. The method was, as in the rest of the world, modernistic clearcutting. One of the strongest advocates of modernistic forestry, Fredrik Ebeling, blamed past forest exploitation, including pasturing and timber exploitation (all of which he called selective forestry) for reducing the northern forests of Sweden to what he called "green lies." The answer to these lies was what he called "modern conservation" (*modern skogsvård*), which included "restoration," modern and modernistic clearcutting and the replanting of genetically superior seedlings. A journalist, hired to write the centenary jubilee text for the Swedish Forest Service [Domänverket] in 1959 captured the inherent conflict of "restoring" something by removing it completely and putting something else in its place:

> ...*seen with the eye of a tourist, it may look dreadful. Black burned and littered clearfelled hills, clearcuts as sad open wounds in nature. Is this the so famous deep forest? No, this is modern conservation. A sign that the forests of these surroundings are at last being restored after exploitation.*[6]

The former non-intensive use was called exploitation, and the new intensive management was called restoration. The public, however, viewed it mostly the other way around. Soon preservationists and environmentalists thought of restoration as a rationalization (if not a fraud) for clearcutting (both technically and psychologically). But throughout the 1950s, the critical voices were either silenced or rebuffed in the name of progress.

The modern clearfelled areas were large, cleaned of all woody plants, sprayed with herbicides to kill the deciduous broad leafed trees, planted with conifer seedlings dipped in DDT, and thinned into more or less perfect artificial forest plantations. A Canadian, supposedly high productive pine species (*Pinus contorta*; lodge pole pine), was introduced on hundreds of thousands of hectares. The growing wood stock has almost doubled in Sweden since 1923, the date of the first reliable Swedish forest assessment. Production increased considerably as the landscape was transformed. To describe this forestry, the actors used concepts like conservation (*skogsvård*) and multiple use (*mångbruk*). But this play with words, and the attitude that "everything worked fine," masked what was really going on, what Paul Hirt has called a "conspiracy of optimism."[7]

Many modernistic foresters still view this project as truly heroic. A couple of years ago, one district forest officer expressed disappointment with the new ecological forestry of the 1990s and with the critique from biologists and environmentalists: "It seems to me like the forest sector meets contemporary values with a crashed time perspective and that foresters fail to explain the greatness of the forest restoration of the 1950s."[8] Still, not even at the time, did all people appreciate the forest restoration. Recently an influential retired forester described the initial difficulties of clearcutting the formerly thinned stands (the so-called "green lies") in the 1950s as follows: "The liquidation of the 'green lies' often met with resistance. We had to go easy, to take the worst first and to compromise in the beginning."[9]

At the present, all forest companies and forest boards produce a steady flow of written material on ecological landscaping, biodiversity, alternative forestry methods, new forestry and green industry. In May, 1996, the Royal Academy of Forestry and Agricultural Science held a conference on how to put wood ashes from industrial furnaces back into the forest ecosystem. The main objective was on how to imitate the ecological cycle. Such conferences used to be dedicated solely to questions on how to raise wood productivity.[10]

Out of this story, four rather distinct eras of theoretical forestry, more or less implemented (less in the beginning) is taking form:

1) Forestry economics (skogshushållning)1820-1890
   Ordered clearcutting systems
2) Conservation (skogsvård)1890-1940
   Pluralism
3) Modernistic forestry (modernt skogsbruk)1940-1990
   Strict clearcutting
4) Postmodern or ecological forestry 1990-?
   Pluralism and biodiversity

Culture Versus Nature or Something in Between?

It is very tempting to interpret this historiography in structuralist terms. We have a dichotomy of A and B foresters, and as Leopold defines them, the first era is A, the second is B, the third is A and the present is B again. The analysis implies that type A forestry will be back as dominating paradigm sooner or later. One main concept used for the type A forestry argument is "culture," as in silviculture; this concept contains terms such as ground preparation, planting, and thinning which are all part of the crop/agricultural metaphor of forestry.[11] One of the key concepts of type B is "nature," such as in natural regeneration and the expression "to follow instead of controlling nature." A non-forester, C.A. Agardh, was the first influential person in Sweden to oppose clearcut forestry. He stood alone as a selection cut defender in the mid-nineteenth century. In a typical reference to nature, he wrote: "Nature produces the greatest and most pleasant forests without any cost. It demands...nothing else than being left alone and time..."[12]

He went on to argue that the Crown had a surplus of time because the state is eternal. Therefore land should be owned by the Crown. He called clearcutting an "artificial" (and therefore bad) system and selection cutting "natural," in accordance with a divine national and a pre-Darwinistic benevolent nature. Ström, Segerdahl and later the modernistic foresters basically only talked about silviculture (skogsodling). The cultural, the human-made, was the norm and the highest good. Even though "culture" was normally used, "nature" was used rhetorically. Segerdahl, the head of the Higher Forestry education in Stockholm, argued that the forester must harvest not from the capital, but only from the "natural" growth (interest). The one who harvested from the capital was "acting against nature" (naturvidriga angrepp).[13] The concept of "nature" was clearly used by both clearcutters and selection cutters, but much more frequently by the selection cutters. Looking at the Swedish situation then, it seems like periods of type A forestry are dominated by clearcutting theory and practice, while periods of type B forestry are characterized by selection methods. Clearcutting is cultural and type A. Selective cutting is natural and type B. The structuralist analysis is complete.

The dual systems of selection and clearcutting practices are, however, much more complex. In the interface of theory and practice, there are lots of complications, especially during the first conservation-oriented era. The relevant but scarce historiography describes this era as one of selection cutting. Due to the economic crisis, the forests were thinned, especially in the 1930s.[14] Since there had been a regeneration law since 1903, it was accepted generally that the cuttings were in line with the principles of selection cutting, and that natural regeneration would appear. But the extent to which selection systems were implemented is debatable. Table 1 illustrates that the topics debated did not relate to the theoretical question of whether to use clearcut or selection harvesting systems, but how to use intermediate cutting practices. The modernists nevertheless later used a simplified narrative about their predecessors as professing and implementing selection systems as an unsustainable exploitative form of forestry, and that modernistic clearcutting overcame this misuse.

Table 1 illustrates that much of the debate over forestry methods revolve around intermediate concepts that blurred the distinction between selection and clearcut systems. In practice, the forestry methods used can be placed on a continuum, with large cleaned square clearcuts at one extreme, and repetitive cutting of all dimensions in fully stratified forests at the other extreme. For the non-professional (and professional), the actual result of clearcut and selection methods may be identical, but still viewed as coming from diametrically opposed systems or methods. Perhaps the classified methods stem from a mere abstract dichotomy.

Table 8.1: Synonymous Operations in the Selection and the
Clearcut System Concepts[15]

SELECTION SYSTEM CONCEPT (BLÄDNINGSTERM)	CLEARCUT SYSTEM CONCEPT (HYGGESTERM)
strip selection system (kantblädning)	strip clearcut (kulissbyggen)
group selection system (luckblädning)	small clearcuts (små byggen)
areal selection system (traktblädning)	thinning (gallring)
dimension felling (dimensionsblädning)	high thinning (höggallring)
preparatory felling (förbuggning)	shelterwood (högskärm)
regeneration cutting (föryngringshuggning)	seed tree method (fröträd/timmerställning/ högskärm)
opening up felling (ljushuggning)	seed tree method (fröträd/timmerställning/ högskärm)

In the forest, then, different kinds of cutting operations have been carried
out without a broader theoretical base. The question of which system of
forestry a particular cut belongs to seems to be of a later approximation and
a historical construction. Usually it takes more than a hundred years to
grow a tree and during that time conceptions of forestry have changed
several times.

The ground for classification has usually been the cutting operation used.
In English the concepts are simply "selection cutting" and "clearcutting." The
more relevant questions to put might be on how to view natural regeneration
(non-planting forestry) and thinning. Thinning is a true hybrid, a concept that
sits between the selection and clearcutting system. It is an accepted and
important part of both systems.

In Sweden the two ways of cutting has been abstracted and assumed
to be two diametrically opposed ways of forestry. Modernistic forestry has
viewed selection cutting as being opposed to rational sustained yield
forestry. An earlier historiography, produced mainly by retired foresters, has
judged selection cutting harshly, and as an impossible system to promote
forest conservation. There is good ground, however, for revising these
assumptions of selection cut forestry.[16]

There is an interesting dialectic in the story between clearcut and selection cut ideology and practice. In fact, there has been great quasi-scientific and forester (jägmästare) debates, said to be polarized between the two ideal type forestry systems. The first forestry economic era was based on clearcutting theory. The second was more pluralistic (said by modernists to be selection-biased). The third modernistic era was effectively clearcut-oriented. And now the clearcutting practice of the modernistic decades is being nuanced and sometimes even challenged. We're entering a legally liberal and pluralistic forestry era. "Ecology" might be the strongest candidate for an emerging new paradigm.[17]

Doing intellectual history, focussing on theory, one comes across several set of problems. One is how theory, conceptions and "policy" are related to actions, implementation and ecosystems. I assume here that there is such a connection, though it is sometimes not so easy to detect it historically. For instance most of the forest practices recommended by foresters in the nineteenth century were not implemented, and the actors continuously complained about their unheeded proposals. When it comes to modernistic forestry after the Second Word War, it was fully implemented on a large scale, and the landscape was transformed according to the vision of a few men who were intent on controlling the forest resource. The detrimental side effects of that agenda are now subject to scrutiny through the postmodern lens.

To sum up, it is clear that "sustained yield" has been and continues to be a central concept in Swedish forestry. It cannot, however, be equated with the recent concept of "sustainability," where components such as "biodiversity" stand in direct opposite to traditional forestry. Traditional forestry is part of the enlightenment project and early science, where nature is considered a mechanical clockwork, and a willing labourer and producer of human goods and services. The result is species loss and simplified ecosystems.18 On the other hand, other aspects of sustainability stress long-term production for human use, which is the same as the idea of sustained yield. It seems like the old concept of sustained yield is part of—but not everything—in the new envisioned era of "ecology" and "sustainability."

But there is also a dialectic between conformism and pluralism. While Swedish forestry theory started out as a standardizing project, an imagined matrix to be forced upon the ecosystem, forestry theory switched in the early twentieth century to a conservationist pluralism, and forestry methods were thoroughly debated. Then, after modernistic forestry was dominant in the post-World War Two era, pluralism and arguments in favour of "nature" re-emerged in the 1990s.

In this emerging ecological and "new" forestry I think different kinds of foresters are needed, types A and B and the rest of the alphabet. The uniform thought structures and grand narratives that characterize modernistic forestry result in uniform and impoverished forests. Ecosystems, on the other hand, are, as Aldo Leopold discovered, complex and beautiful. If pluralism is desirable in forestry theory and practice, we must continue to promote alternatives to the still dominant practice of clearcutting.

Notes

1. Aldo Leopold, *A Sand County Almanac: With Other Essays on Conservation from Round River* (New York: Oxford University Press, 1966 [1949]).

2. Thus defined, forestry begins in the German "Kleinstaaten" of the eighteenth century. It has recently been argued, though, that Japan also practised sustained yield forestry in the eighteenth century. Conrad Totman, *The Green Archipelago: Forestry in Preindustrial Japan* (Honolulu: University of Hawaii, 1989).

3. Kungliga vetenskapsakademien, prisfråga "Blädning contra trakthuggning," 1771.

4. Israel Ström, "Förslag till en Förbättrad Skogshushållning i Sverige" [Proposition for an Improved Forest Economy in Sweden], (Stockholm: n.p., 1822). Quoted in Carl A. Agardh and C.E. Ljungberg, *Försök till en Statsekonomisk Statistik öfver Sverige 3*, No. 1 (Karlstad: n.p., 1857), 318.

5. Uno Wallmo, "Rationell Skogsafverkning: Praktiska Råd till Såväl Större som Mindre Enskilda Skogsägare" [Rational Forest Harvesting: Practical Advice for Large and Small Private Woodlands Owners], (Örebro: n.p., 1897). Quoted in Gunnar Schotte and Anders Wahlgren, *Sveriges Skogar* [Sweden's Forests] (Stockholm: n.p., 1928), 589.

6. Erik Goland, *I Skogslandet: En Berättelsesvit mest över Tider som Svunnit* [In the Land of the Forest: Stories of Past Days] (Stockholm: Kungliga Domänstyrelsen, 1959), 76.

7. Paul W. Hirt, *A Conspiracy of Optimism: Management of the National Forests Since World War Two* (Lincoln: University of Nebraska Press, 1994).

8. Ingemar Eriksson, "Skogsvårdsepoker i Norr" [Epochs of Forestry in the North], *Skogshistorisk Tidskrift* 1 (1992).

9. Svante Fahlgren, "Skogsbruket i Kramfors Bolag" [The Forestry of Kramfors Company], *Skogshistorisk Tidskrift* 5 (1996), 9.

10. Kungliga Skogs- och Lantbruksakademin, "Askåterföring," May 21-23, 1996.

11. Hirt, op. cit., argues that the agricultural metaphor is typical for post-World War II U.S. forestry.

12. Carl A. Agardh, "Om Sveriges Skogsväsen", in Agardh and Ljungberg, op. cit., 78.

13. G. Segerdahl, Svenska Landtbruksmötet 6, Part 5 (1853), 43.

14. Fahlgren, op. cit.; Thorsten Andrén, *Från Naturskog till Kulturskog* [From a Natural to a Cultural Forest], (Bjästa: CEWE Förlag, 1991).

15. Concepts from "Chief Foresters' Discussion Protocols," Domänverket 1910-1921, Domänverket's Archives, Falun, Sweden.

16. The view established in Gunnar Arpi, ed., *Sveriges Skogar under 100 år* [Sweden Forests during a Hundred Years], (Stockholm: Ivar Hæggströms, 1959); see also Erland von Hofsten, *Domänverket 125 år* (Falun: Domänverket, 1984).

17. See, for instance, Kathryn A. Kohm and Jerry F. Franklin, eds., *Creating a Forestry for the 21st Century: The Science of Ecosystem Management* (Washington: Island Press, 1997).

18. Carolyn Merchant, *The Death of Nature: Women, Ecology and the Scientific Revolution* (San Francisco: Harper and Row, 1980).

Chapter Nine

THE SWEDISH FOREST COMMONS

Challenges for Sustainable Forestry?

Lars Carlsson

The Swedish forest commons consist of 25,000 individual shareholders with property rights in the forests. Based on a medieval pattern of ownership, the commons appear quite prosperous within the realm of modern society with its highly competitive forest industries. This chapter explains why the Swedish forest commons have survived as vital and competitive actors in the timber market. Two main explanations are discussed: the commoners' conscious attempts to reduce transaction costs, and their general ability to adjust to changing political and economic circumstances.

Historical Development

Even before Sweden adopted its first written constitution in 1350, different types of commons were codified in the old county-laws. Two hundred years later, in 1523, the country became independent and united under King Gustav Wasa. Huge areas of land were confiscated from the nobility and from the church. The monarchy became hereditary; Lutheran Protestantism replaced Catholicism as the official religion, and a new Protestant state Church and a strong, national bureaucracy were created. Under the monarchy, all "unclaimed land" was declared to be the property of the Crown/state. This precipitated a process of land delimitation in the seventeenth century, followed by a process of land redistribution in the middle of the eighteenth century. Both these procedures shared two common purposes: to create bigger and more productive farms (thus strengthening local economies), and to widen the basis of taxation.

As a result of land delimitation, farmers were allotted their own, private forests—which to many at the time had only minor value. Arable land was scarce, the forest areas were enormous, and the farmers were not yet aware of the market value of their forest resources. In the early period of industrialization, it was therefore possible for timber companies to buy rights to harvest vast areas, and to sometimes possess whole villages. This situation called for state control, and it was suggested that one third of the lands allotted to the farmers be detached and made into forest commons. Although this idea was not popular amongst farmers, the first common was created in 1861. One of the ancient medieval types of common was used as an organizational blueprint for the new forest commons. Eventually, in a process that lasted well into the beginning of this century, thirty-three forest commons were created, today encompassing a total area of about 730,000 hectares. These commons are regulated by a single law—codified in the 1950s—whose principles have virtually stayed the same over the last one hundred years.

The Concept and Organization of the Forest Commons[1]

For purposes of taxation each farm was designated as containing a certain number of "assessment units of land," based on the amount of arable land. These units were used as the basis for each farmer's share of the common. Only via ownership of "share holding farms" (i.e., farms assigned rights to a forest common) do single farmers, and other types of owners, hold property rights in the commons. The only way an outsider can get access to a forest common is to buy, inherit, or in some other way acquire a share holding farm. Consequently, not only single farmers but also groups of people, companies, the church, and even the state can be legal owners, and thereby also shareholders, in the Swedish forest commons. Currently, about sixty-eight percent of the shares are in the hands of private persons, eighteen percent belong to companies and the remaining fourteen percent are held by the church, the state and other corporate owners.

A great number of the commons are located in sparsely populated areas, and about twenty percent of the 25,099 owners can be regarded as non-resident owners. The general management and financial administration of the common is the responsibility of a board, elected by the shareholders. According to the law, a professional forest manager must be attached to the common. This person, who usually is employed by the common, is responsible for forest management. As is the case for all forest owners, the commons are subject to control from the County Forestry Board. In addition, the state County Administrative Board controls the commons (although this is largely a formality). Today, many commons are run like big forest companies and some of them have a sizeable workforce and inventory of machinery. Among the three largest commons each possesses about 60,000 hectares of productive forest lands. About half of all the commons also run subsidiary companies or pursue commercial enterprises.

The benefits for a single shareholder are threefold. First, s/he is eligible to appropriate revenue from the forest—as annual cash payments—in accordance with her/his number of shares. Second, s/he may lay claim to monetary subsidies paid to the shareholders for drainage projects, the construction of buildings, and the purchasing of fodder. Finally, the shareholders benefit from the commons' general support to the local area, such as the presence of roads and fishing areas.

Combined Provision of Private and Public Goods and Services

The fact that Swedish forest commons have succeeded fairly well in comparison with other big forest owners is remarkable. Companies owning comparable areas of forests basically "produce" timber. The costs of this production are reflected in timber prices. The commons, however, also provide public goods and services. They regularly subsidize farmers, build and maintain roads, support local villages, and provide hunting and fishing areas. Accordingly, the commons have to pay more attention to the costs related to the provision of *both* public and private goods.[2]

Consequently, a forest common faces *a broader set of costs*, so-called transaction costs, compared to a forest company, which mainly engages in the production of timber for sale. In addition, the control of access, and the exploitation of forest resources, are generally more costly for a forest common than a private forest company. These high transaction costs—the costs associated with the exercise of property rights—are related to the collective quality of the common. Thus, for example, one would expect the regulation of access among thousands of shareholders in a common to be more costly than the management of owners in a private company. Similarly, one would expect it to be more expensive to regulate the exploitation of the forest resources of a common compared to a company. A forest company can probably keep up with technology more easily than a common, and is likely to have established channels for the gathering of market information, all of which is part of what we call transaction costs. In addition, it can be assumed that a company can more easily conform to rules and regulations connected to modern forestry; a good deal of competence and knowledge is needed to follow and adjust to the numerous laws and regulations governing Swedish forestry. How, then, do the Swedish forest commons deal with this problem?

Means of Reducing Transaction Costs

It was assumed in the above discussion that all commercial actors, commons as well as forestry companies, are faced with the same types of problems—such as gathering information about rules, regulations, markets, competitors and forestry technology. In this section five concrete problems, related to these more general problems will be discussed.

1. Coping with the Share Holding System

One problem with the Swedish forest commons is the increased number of non-resident owners. People move from the countryside, but they tend to keep their farms and therefore also a right of access to the benefits of the commons. Moreover, an increased number of shares are owned by forest companies (in 1995 eighteen percent of all shares). This jeopardizes the intentions of the founders of the commons. In the last ten years, about 3,000 new shareholders have been added. Clearly there has been a widening of the access to the commons. What methods have been used to solve these problems?

The adding of new private owners is mainly the result of inheritance. Under the current legislation, this is hard to do anything about. In general, the commons have adopted the principle that every farm owned by more than two persons must appoint a deputy. This person votes on behalf of the others at the assembly meetings. S/he is also the recipient of the annual cash amounts or other types of support supplied by the common to the farm. This principle is based on a law guiding the relationship between state authorities and farmers, but the commons have simply decided it is also convenient for their purposes.

The companies that have bought into the commons find themselves in a different position. With the power of their shares—in six of the commons they possess more than forty percent of the shares—they have the legal right to a significant part of the harvest. In none of the commons, however, do they execute their rights in proportion to their share holdings. Generally, in those commons where cash is distributed, the assembly of shareholders have decided to leave the companies without such endowments. It is also usual to avoid electing representatives from companies to the boards, although companies could succeed in doing so if they utilized all their shares. Even when companies have representatives on the board of a common, they generally hold a very low profile. Company representatives explain this behaviour by referring to costs, but they are also interested in maintaining good relations with local people. If they do not, they risk problems with the purchasing of timber from private forest owners and the use of private logging roads. Their "voluntary" abandoning of revenue from the commons is thus a rational decision.

2. Keeping Up with Rules and Regulations

The commons have different ways of meeting the regulations connected to their forestry activities. Some rules are treated as obsolete. For example, the commons are still required to inform the County Forestry Board regarding harvesting levels and silvicultural practices, but they neither do nor are asked to do so. Other rules they simply evade. For example, some of the commons are not allowed to endow their individual shareholders with cash amounts but by renaming a cash amount a "general subsidy for forestry purposes," the rule is circumvented. Significant information costs are connected to the fulfilment of the demands codified in forest and conservation legislation. The forest commons have tackled this problem by building alliances with the authorities which are supposed to enforce the laws. They regularly purchase the services of the authorities for forest assessments (in the form of a cruise) before cutting. They also buy services from the forest authorities to perform inventories and to check on their own shareholders. The latter requires an explanation.

About seventy-four percent of the commons distribute their residual income for common purposes, or as direct "subsidies" to individual shareholders for operations on their own private land. A single farmer may be subsidized, for example, for the number of cows s/he owns, trees planted, or hectares of land drained. Since all shareholders have an incentive to cheat or at least exaggerate their entitlement, the system must be controlled. When it comes to forestry subsidies, the most common solution is to utilize the bureaucracy already built up for the control of state subsidies. state employed and locally stationed extension foresters are responsible for all forestry-related controls. For example, they can easily also check whether a single shareholder has actually planted the number of pine trees for which s/he has claimed a subsidy from the common. In practice, no money is paid until the shareholder can provide a signed form from the local extension forester.

3. Keeping Up with Technology
When forestry was a manual enterprise, all commons had their own staff of loggers. Today there are virtually no loggers left in Swedish forestry. The commons have faced significant pressure to adjust to these changes. Only some of the largest commons have their own machinery operated by their own personnel. The largest common has forty-five employees.

One method of dealing with technological change is to externalize the costs for its renewal. Thus, most commons dispose of wood through stumpage sales and timber auctions. In this way, the buyer is responsible for the cost of harvesting machinery and forest renewal. Where no market for stumpage sales exists, delivery agreement and renewable felling contracts are common. These agreements can be based on harvesting with the commons' own machinery, but generally most commons have kept their machinery ownership to a minimum, and externalized the costs to the companies.

4. Conflicting Claims on the Rights of Using the Forests: the Saami Population
The majority of all forest commons are located in areas in which reindeer herding by the indigenous Saami people is practised. Paragraph 20 of the Silviculture Act stipulates that consultations must be held with the Saami population before any logging can be performed on lands they use on an all-year-round basis. The commons have solved the problem by negotiating with the Saami people before constructing roads and harvesting wood.

This "co-management" seems to function quite well. Since 1971 there has been only one appeal against a logging decision made by a common. Another indicator of the relative harmony between the reindeer herders and the forest commons is the manner in which the Saami treat the commons. The Saami can legally use wood for building fences and shelters from the forest commons.[3] Yet this right is hardly used on forest common land, but instead exercised on state-owned land. Finally, those Saami families who are shareholders in commons have not adopted a different position on forest management. Essentially, since the commons adjust their activities to reindeer herding, the relationship with the Saami has been remarkably free of conflicts.

5. Hunting and Fishing as a Problem of Access

One of the effects of industrialization is urbanization. This has also affected the Swedish forest commons. When people move into cities, the commons gradually lose their base of local people. Paradoxically, however, although there is a decreasing number of farmers, the Swedish forest commons are faced with increased pressure, because although the younger generations frequently live and work in the cities, they tend to retain some form of ownership in the share holding farms. This is done in different ways such as splitting the farms and joint ownership.

The purpose of joint ownership is twofold. The main reason is to maintain the rights to hunting and fishing that are connected to the share holding. A second but probably almost as important reason is the desire to maintain some social ties to the native districts.[4] Consequently, the commons have to regulate the number of hunters; fishing is a minor problem. The problem is not a question of over-consumption, as exploitation is regulated by the state (moose hunting is licensed by the County Administrative Board). It is rather a question of who should be allowed access to the system.

The commons have tried to solve this problem by creating hunting regulations. They always reflect local circumstances. For example, there are commons where only local citizens and their children are allowed to hunt, while other commons have developed more generous rules. Some observers have found it odd that shareholders can spend significant time and mental energy discussing access to hunting, while the same people do not engage themselves in financial issues, which represent millions of dollars. If one appreciates that the access to the commons—and by this also access to one's native district and to hunting—represents significant, non-monetary value, this behaviour is quite logical.

Performance

Clearly the commons have endeavoured to address each of the five problems above, but is their way of solving the problems satisfactory? In this section, the assessment of institutional performance developed by Ostrom, Schroeder and Wynne is used to evaluate the Swedish forest commons.[5] Five different criteria are applied: *economic efficiency, fiscal equivalence, redistribution, accountability,* and *adaptability.*

A rough estimate of the *economic efficiency* of the forest commons can be made by answering two questions: are the forest resources managed in a sustainable manner, and does the economic output exceed the resources that are spent on operating the commons? The answer to both questions is yes. The commons do generate a "residual" which does not cut into the forest capital as only 70% of the annual increment is harvested. This is likely to continue. The commons have existed for more than one hundred years without devastating their forest resources.[6] Research has also shown that the commons adopted a conscious silviculture policy earlier than other forest holders.[7] Recent research has also given more support to the observation that commons have a tendency to harvest less when prices rise. Thus, contrary to private forest owners in the same district they seem to have a "target income," a behaviour which is likely to retain the commons' forest resources in times of high timber demand.[8]

Fiscal equivalence is the idea that those who benefit from an institutional arrangement also ought to bear a proportional burden of its maintenance. This is not the case with the Swedish forest commons. There is no direct flow of resources from the single shareholders to the commons. The shareholders have all the benefits of being members of the system, but they make no direct contributions to the commons. The only way they contribute is indirectly—in that the cost of maintenance of the commons is already deducted when the shareholders receive their endowments. Since the share holding companies do not receive economic resources in accordance to their amount of shares, it can be argued that they have to contribute proportionally more than they gain. Taken these observations together, the fiscal equivalence can be regarded as fairly low.

The same is true for *redistribution*. There is no policy allowing the redistribution of resources among the shareholders; everyone is supposed to be endowed with cash amounts in proportion to her/his share holdings. The fact that the companies do not receive economic resources proportionate to their shares might indicate a policy of conscious redistribution from rich to poor, but as indicated from the discussion above, this would be an overly hasty conclusion. Since shareholders are subsidized for activities such as planting and draining (carried out on their own private lands), resources are allocated to active farmers. This, however, is a reflection of a local policy to strengthen the district economically, which prevailed when the commons were created. In general, it cannot be argued that the Swedish forest commons have adopted a conscious strategy of redistribution.

The degree of *accountability* depends on the quality of the connections between those who are making decisions and the members of the commons, i.e. the shareholders. Accountability varies according to local circumstances, but at the organizational level, it is generally high—with two assembly meetings per year, open elections, free access to records of the meetings, fiscal transparency, and legal rights to appeal. Logically, high accountability should be related to high community activity. For example, do shareholders attend meetings, or do they try in other ways to influence the decisions made? However, the matter cannot be assessed quite so simply. Some commons have a significant number of elderly people, who rarely attend the assembly meetings. In these commons, the formation of groups competent to make decisions can be problematic, although this is not necessarily indicative of a lack of shareholder interest.

There are many local variations of the organization of the commons. Two of the commons practise an administrative system retained from the first part of the seventeenth century. In these commons the geographical area is divided into "rotar" with a responsible farmer in each one of them. The farmers elect this person. On behalf of the commons s/he keeps track of all the changes in ownership and share holdings in her/his "rote," and also distributes the cash amounts in the area. As a consequence, these commons have very good records of their owners, which is not necessarily the case in other commons in the same district.

One of the commons (in a high mountain area) does not have assembly meetings at all. The villages elect representatives who form a mini-assembly whose members elect a board. The representatives are held responsible at local village meetings. The northern-most forest common is collectively owned by "all the people in the community." Today this is interpreted as the "municipality." Thus, this common is regarded as a branch of the municipal government, comparable to the public bus company. Although the above discussion indicates the complexity involved in assessing accountability, it must be concluded that the commons score well on this criterion of performance.

Both present activities and historical research demonstrate the *adaptability* of the commons. When the forest commons were created, Sweden was an agricultural nation. Therefore, the income from the commons was designated to support agriculture. Soon the commons began to support a general mechanization of the farms, the establishment of dairies and insemination stations, and renewal of farm buildings. The fact that the commons still exist as vital producers of timber is an indicator of their capacity to adapt to change. Over time, there has been a clear and gradual shift from policies supporting agriculture to policies, which support forestry. Today the main part of all subsidies is designated for forestry.

Another example of the commons' adaptability is the modernization of their forestry. This is primarily reflected in mechanization, and a reduction in personnel. Harvesting techniques used by the commons are as good as those used by other forest owners who possess comparable amounts of land. The larger commons also utilize digitised maps and computerized accounting systems. The commons have adjusted to different demands arising from different policies regarding nature conservation and other environmental concerns. The same is true concerning the adaptation to certain types of formal rules related to taxation, accounting, labour conditions and social services. As noted earlier, the commons have utilized the formal rules that regulate them with significant discretion. Furthermore, the commons have voluntarily adopted state regulations, which were not primarily designed for the commons.

Conclusion

Despite facing the problem of combining the provision of private and public goods and services, and the high transaction costs associated with this, the Swedish forest commons survive as vital and competitive actors in the timber market. Indeed, they score high in three out of five criteria used for assessing institutional performance.

In these concluding paragraphs, it is instructive to consider briefly the "life" of the commons within industrialized society, and in particular their relationship with the state and society. An important point to note is that the state cannot be conceptualized as a unity.[9] "The state" provides the formal legal framework for the commons, it controls and supervises their day-to-day operations, and it uses them as policy tools to promote local economic development. However, in its relationship to the commons, *different* units of "the state" have established different commercial, political and legal terms. County Forestry Boards have been and continue to be particularly influential. They sell their services to the commons, and they even control the commons' individual members. The Swedish forest commons are neither completely managed by local people, nor are they composed solely of individual shareholders.

As providers of private goods, the commons have also (and simultaneously) developed close relationships with various societal actors. Private companies are provided with felling contracts and stumpage sales. In addition, as providers of public goods, the commons have developed systems of co-management with local public institutions, such as schools and non-profit making organizations.

One conclusion drawn from the Swedish example might be that the commons have survived as prosperous timber producers and providers of public goods, not only because of their ability to lower transaction costs, but also because of their interaction with a fragmented state and various societal actors. This interaction has provided a local "opportunity structure" which the commons have utilized. This has been possible because the commons, their forest managers, boards and assemblies of shareholders still possess sufficient local, current knowledge to be able to adjust the commons to industrialized society. The main lesson to be learned from the Swedish forest commons might be their successful integration in, rather than their separation from, the logic of the negotiated economy and industrialized society.

Whether this integration is also conducive for promoting the environmental aspects of sustainability is very much an open-ended question. In spite of biodiversity goals being considered equally important to production objectives in the most recent Swedish forest legislation, the Swedish forest sector remains production-biased. Thus, by working closely with the County Forestry Boards, the forest commons may shield themselves from future disputes over, and public demands for, biodiversity. The current dispute over the harvesting of timber in the high mountain area between one of the larger forest commons in the County of Västerbotten and environmental groups may be a reflection of the forest commons' unwillingness to meet ecological demands. On the other hand, if the Swedish state and its forestry boards decide to commit more resources to enforcing the current forest legislation on biodiversity, the forest commons might be uniquely positioned to become pioneers promoting both economic and ecological goals.

Notes

1. Lars Carlsson, *Skogsallmänningarna i Sverige* [The Forest Commons in Sweden], Research Report, TULEA 1995:22 (Luleå: Luleå University of Technology, 1995). See also Lars Carlsson, "The Swedish Common Forests: A Common Property Resource in an Urban, Industrialized Society," *Rural Development Forestry Network* No. 20 (Winter 1996/97): 1–13.

2. Elinor Ostrom, Larry Schroeder, and Susanne Wynne, *Institutional Incentives and Sustainable Development: Infrastructure Policies in Perspective* (Boulder: Westview Press, 1993), 73 ff.

3. See also Bertil Bengtsson, "The Legal Status to Resources in Swedish Lapland," in *Law and the Management of Divisible and Non-Excludable Renewable Resources*, eds. Erling Berge et al. (Aas, Norway: Department of Land Use and Landscape Planning, 1994).

4. This is discussed in Håkan Blix, *Utbors Motiv för och Attityder till Skogsägande* [The Motives and Attitudes of Non-Resident Forest Owners], Examensarbete No. 22 (Stockholm: Institutionen för fastighetsekonomi, Tekniska Högskolan i Stockholm, 1986).

5. Ostrom et al., op. cit.

6. See Carlsson, 1995, op. cit., 38 ff.

7. Linder and Östlund compare the changes in standing volume at Orsa forest common with an adjacent state-owned area. See Per Linder and Lars Östlund, "Förändringar i Sveriges Skogar 1870-1991," *Svensk Botanisk Tidskrift* No. 86 (1992), 199-215. See also Lars Östlund, *Exploitation and Structural Change in the North Swedish Boreal Forests 1800-1992* Dissertations in Forest Vegetation Ecology 4 (Umeå: Sveriges lantbruksuniversitet, 1993).

8. See Carlsson, 1995, op. cit., 38 ff; Jerry Blomberg and Mats Nilsson, "Institutional Arrangements and Firm Behavior: The Case of Common Forests in Sweden," *Journal of Economic Issues* XXXI, No. 2 (1997): 401-408; and Niklas Johansson, "Hur Agerar Skogsallmänningarna på den Svenska Rundvirkesmarknaden?" [How Do the Forest Commons Act in the Swedish Roundwood Market], D-level thesis (Luleå: Divison of Economics, Lulea University of Technology, Sweden, 1997).

9. Vincent Ostrom, "Multiorganisational Arrangements in the Governance of Unitary and Federal Political Systems," in *Policy Implementation in Federal and Unitary Systems: Questions of Analysis and Design,* eds. K. Hanf and T. A. J. Toonen (The Hague: Martinus Nijhoff, 1987).

CHAPTER TEN

MANAGING UNCOMMON GROUNDS

Swedish Forestry Policy and Environmental Sustainability

Katarina Eckerberg

The aim of this chapter is to discuss the recent developments in Swedish forestry policy in relation to environmental goals.[1] Conflicts over environmental sustainability in forest management have been defined differently during the last few decades both by environmentalists and the forest industry sector.[2] Beginning in the 1970s, the use of herbicides was the hot topic of public debate, with environmentalists questioning the methods and goals of modern Swedish forestry. Large clearcuts, conifer monocultures, highly mechanized equipment along with chemicals were introduced during this period. The conflict was intense between environmentalists and the forest industry. In the 1980s, the most debated issues were how the montane forests could be preserved and how government subsidies to the felling of low productive, but environmentally valuable, forests could be stopped. During this period, the environmentalists gradually won recognition in the debate, which eventually halted the government subsidies to forestry. In the 1990s, biological diversity became fashionable in Swedish forestry. From having fought on different sides in the debate, the environmentalists and the forest industry began to speak the same language. The question is, however, to what extent Swedish forestry lives up to its reputation of being a world leader in environmental sustainability, particularly in relation to biological diversity goals?[3]

I will take a critical position in answering this question. I will briefly review the goals and achievements in forestry policy towards biodiversity goals, including government programs and private forestry initiatives. Self-regulating strategies for environmental sustainability have been developed during the last decade, including environmental auditing, Environmental Impact Assessments (EIAs), and environmental labelling. Are such initiatives part of a new way of thinking within the forest sector, or are they largely of a symbolic nature? What is it that forces Swedish forestry to introduce new management policies—is it mainly the national or the international policy community? Does Swedish forestry take a leadership role in environmental sustainability or is it simply responding to new "green" demands from the market? To what extent does government policy pay mere lip service to the international agreements that have been made within this policy area?

Biodiversity Goals and Strategies in Swedish Forestry

Environmental goals in Swedish forestry are to:

> ...preserve natural conditions for production, biological diversity and genetic variety. Forest management must allow all animal and plant species that belong naturally to the forest environment to survive in vigorous populations. Threatened species and biotopes must be protected. Cultural values in forests as well as aesthetic and social values must be upheld.[4]

This implies the protection of forest areas of high value for biological diversity in order to preserve living populations of animal and plant species.[5] The status of different species in Sweden is monitored by the Threatened Species Unit of the Swedish University of Agricultural Sciences in Uppsala. They estimate that five to ten percent of wild species of plants and animals are threatened today, in the sense that their long-term survival is uncertain. This means that the Swedish situation is similar to the global figures of threatened biodiversity.[6] Many of those species belong to forest ecosystems—among threatened plant species more than half of them (fifty-one percent). Some forest areas are especially rich. Seventy percent of threatened species depend on dead and dying wood and fifty-six percent live in southern broad-leaved forests.[7] Such substrates and biotopes are therefore especially important to protect. The Forestry Agency has developed lists of environmentally rich forest biotopes.[8]

Three interdependent strategies are used:[9] 1) large reserves in a network[10]; 2) many small reserves (biotopes); and 3) environmental considerations in all commercial forestry. These strategies are endorsed by government policy as well as by private forest companies. However, more precise formulations indicating how large areas should be protected and how environmental concerns should be weighed against commercial interests are still debated. The extent to which these strategies are implemented will be further discussed in the following.

Protection of Large Forest Reserves

Among international comparisons, Sweden has small areas of protected forests. In 1991, 690,000 hectares of forest land, or 3.4% of the entire forest area, was protected.[11] Most of the reserves are located in the montane forests. If montane forests are excluded, only 0.6% of the forest area is reserved. At the same time, Sweden has ratified international agreements where increased protection of environmentally valuable forests is high on the agenda, for example the UNCED Forest Principles, *Agenda 21*, and the Helsinki agreement on sustainable forestry. Compared to tropical rain forests, (9.32% protected of the total area of such forests), or other tropical forests, (circa 4.7% protected), the Swedish figures are low.[12]

Moreover, the areas that have been protected so far are unevenly distributed among representative forest ecosystems. The large part is, as earlier pointed out, located in the northern counties of Norrbotten and Västerbotten, where almost ten percent of the land area is protected. In many southern counties the protected land area (including other ecosystems than forests) is below one percent. Since biodiversity is much higher in the south, those figures indicate that protection has not come about for only environmental but also financial reasons. It is much cheaper for the state to purchase land in the north. Of the protected forest land, eighty-seven percent is montane forests. Many southern counties have almost no forest reserves, for example in Östergötland where 0.09% of the forested area is protected.[13] The tendency is clear; in those counties where the state (the Swedish Forest Service, AssiDomän) owns a small portion of the forests, the protected forest area is also low. For several reasons, it is more difficult to preserve forests owned by private individuals or private companies, but unfortunately such ownership often coincides with high biodiversity values. When the National Environmental Protection Agency has used its small budget available for preservation purposes,[14] virgin forest areas and montane forests have been prioritized.[15] A group of experts appointed by the Nordic Council has recommended that actions be taken immediately to preserve at least five percent of the productive forest area below the montane region; that montane and northern conifer forests be protected well above this five percent goal; that a network of natural forest areas larger than 500 hectares be established, in particular among those ecosystems that are currently under-represented; and that in addition to such reserves, forest management in general be developed according to natural ecological processes.[16]

Protection of Small Forest Areas

A new instrument to protect small areas of great value for threatened species (so called biotopes) was introduced in 1992. Since then, the National Board of Forestry has initiated an inventory of such biotopes. Some 70,000-80,000 objects covering around one percent of the entire forest land area will be included in this classification. It has been estimated that a total of 2-4 billion SEK will be required in order to preserve these areas up to five hectares each. The present annual budget is 20 million SEK. This means that it would take 100-200 years to protect those biotopes that have been identified. To date, only 200 areas have been protected through this instrument. The process is slow for several reasons: first, the inventory is not finished and therefore it has been considered difficult to prioritize sites;

secondly, the county level environmental agencies have limited resources and staff for providing expertise in the consultation process; and thirdly, the amounts that are paid out to forest owners by the County Forestry Boards have been criticized for being overly generous. Regardless of those constraints, it is evident that the new instrument cannot suffice as long as the budget remains at such a low level. The hope is thus directed to voluntary agreements with private forest owners for protecting small, environmentally valuable, forest areas.

One such voluntary instrument is "nature protection agreements" (*naturvårdsavtal*), through which the forest owner may receive financial compensation for protecting an area. These agreements can only be upheld for a certain period (that is, they must be renewed after forty-nine years). The forest owner may negotiate the agreements with the state or with other juridical persons, such as an environmental organization. In Sweden, this instrument has not yet been frequently used. However, a few agreements covering rather large areas of forests have been made.[17]

The large forest companies (who own half of Swedish forests) have set aside some areas on a voluntary basis. According to their own figures, between five and ten percent of their forest land is protected, including environmentally valuable biotopes. AssiDomän, the semi-state forest company, retains one percent of its productive forests as reserves, three percent due to technical impediments, and around ten percent is saved at clear-cuttings. It should be emphasized, however, that such protected areas may be felled in the next round of clearcuts. There are no legal barriers to commercial extraction of timber from previously protected biotopes.

Environmental Considerations in Commercial Forestry

The Swedish Forestry Act requires environmental considerations with all forest management since 1974. In 1979 special regulations were introduced that made it possible to punish forest owners who did not live up to these stipulations. In practice, however, very few sanctions have been used.[18] In the new Forestry Act of 1994, the environmental goal is for the first time made equal to the production goal. Like previously, environmental considerations cannot be required to the extent that it "considerably damages present land use." Hence, economic profit from timber extraction is still the guiding principle, since biodiversity gains are not included in the economic calculations. The official interpretation of how much can be protected without demands for economic compensation to the forest owner is around 0.5-1 hectare, or less than ten percent of the area to be clearcut.

Several studies have been made to evaluate how environmental considerations are implemented on forest clearcuts. The first of those, which I conducted myself in 1981-84, showed that approximately fifty percent of those environmental measures which were required according to the Forestry Act were indeed implemented. Aesthetic values were protected to a much larger extent than pure biodiversity values, and more environmental protection measures were achieved in areas where the recreational pressure was high.[19] Later follow-up studies by the National Board of Forestry showed that although the environmental consciousness of forest owners has been raised, there remains a lot to be done. In 1992-93 satisfactory environmental measures were achieved on three-quarters of the clearcut area, while only half of the area was satisfactory in 1989-90. Most of the improvement occurred on low-productive boglands and rocky areas. Species-rich biotopes were still the least retained.

The large forest companies have recently conducted their own evaluations of environmental considerations in clear cuts. For example, MoDo finds that its "acceptable" share of clear cuts has increased from thirty-five percent in 1988 to eighty-one percent in 1993. As in my early studies, it is shown that most of these environmental measures are prioritized in recreational areas and those close to urban settlements, whereas small wetlands, steep ravines and small streams are the least protected. AssiDomän is the foremost "environmental" forest company according to its ecological account from 1994. AssiDomän protected on average 0.8 out of 6.9 hectares per clearcutting in southern Sweden, and 4.2 out of 26.1 hectares in the northern parts of the country. As earlier noted, these "protected" areas are not legally protected since they can be cut at a later stage.

Efforts are also made to change forest management towards more "ecologically" based principles. Retention of old trees, increased proportion of broad-leaved trees in conifer-dominated forests, selection cuttings, burning of clearcut areas, and seed-trees instead of plantations are examples of management practices that are now becoming fashionable. However, recent reports from the Forestry Agency indicate that natural regeneration is often used for financial rather than ecological reasons. Many recent clearcuts have not achieved satisfactory regeneration because the conditions for natural regeneration have not been favourable. Even if more ecological thinking is integrated into commercial forest management, representatives from both the environmentalists and the forest sector agree that it can never become a substitute for the three strategies of large reserves, small reserves and general environmental considerations. It may, nevertheless, become an important complementary measure to those three strategies. So far, research is lacking on the practical application of new methods in forestry, and it is difficult to say to what extent various species can be preserved through "alternative" forest management.

New Forest-Environmental Policy Instruments

Different types of new instruments are currently being introduced in the Swedish forestry industry which may affect the future attainment of biodiversity goals. These include landscape planning, ecological forest planning, environmental labelling of timber and pulpwood, EIA and various other European Union (EU) regulations. At present, it is too early to evaluate the influence of such new instruments on Swedish forestry. Some reflections can, however, be made at this stage.

All the large forestry companies are currently revising their forest inventories to include landscape features, and to divide previously large management units into smaller and more ecologically-based units. The revisions are to be finalized by 1998. Within those forests owned by private individuals, environmental considerations were earlier attained to a higher degree than in company-owned forests.[20] In those private forests, it is often difficult to include landscape analysis into forest planning. The National Board of Forestry as well as Forest Owners' Associations are now working on strategies to involve groups of forest owners in larger management units. Simultaneously, some private forest owners are also developing new "green" forest planning which includes ecological concerns to a greater extent than before.[21] Environmental auditing is practised by some forest companies and will probably be enhanced by future environmental labelling. Within Mälarskog, (the Forest Owners' Association of central Sweden), a "Nature Protection Document" was introduced in 1995, to which any forest owner can commit him/herself. This "document," which is based on an evaluation of the extent to which the individual forest owner lives up to environmental standards, will guarantee an extra financial bonus in timber and pulpwood prices.

The Swedish forestry industry has agreed with environmental organizations to introduce environmental labelling. From two parallel systems, the Forest Stewardship Council was accepted in 1997.[22] The system includes environmental indicators which will ensure that forest products derived from a certified forest owner have been extracted in an environmentally sustainable manner. In order for this system to become accepted, it must be sufficiently flexible to regional variation in natural conditions. It must also be sanctioned by the international environmental community. Several of the large forest companies are now testing different systems within their territory, some of which follow international standards of ISO-14000 and EMAS.

EIAs are not used in Swedish forestry other than within research projects in limited geographical areas. The County Environmental Administration can require an EIA prior to drainage operations and other activities that may "considerably change the natural environment." Since 1991, when this possibility was introduced in Swedish legislation, only one county has required an EIA to be made. The National Board of Forestry can require EIAs prior to introducing new management practices, exotic species or liming of forest areas. In practice, however, it is not possible to prohibit measures through an EIA. By international standards, Swedish EIA legislation is thus very weak.[23]

Through Swedish membership in the European Union in 1994, new instruments might be introduced which can affect forestry. So far, the attempts from EU to regulate forestry have been lacking, largely due to the political resistance from the Nordic countries to streamline European forestry policy. They fear that regulations that are valid in a southern European context may be totally inappropriate in the Nordic context. The Natura 2000 network is a EU initiative to create a system of nature reserves all over Europe. It is based on the EC Directive on the Conservation of Natural Habitats and Wild Flora and

Fauna 92/43/EEC, which all member states must adher to. The Swedish way of implementing this directive was simply to include already protected nature reserves in the network, rather than trying to create new ones. So far, the EU membership has not implied any change of national forest-environmental policy.

Conclusion
It is beyond doubt that environmental conflicts have changed in Swedish forestry during the last thirty years. Through intensive educational campaigns, the private forestry sector has now become aware of ecological relationships in forest ecosystems, and has adopted several new instruments to follow up on the achievement of environmental goals. However, even if the Swedish forestry industry now speaks the same language as the environmentalists in terms of goals for environmental sustainability, the above analysis suggests a clear distinction between policy statements and forest management practice.

In my view, there are three ways that Swedish forestry could possibly change this shortcoming. First, the legal interpretation of what environmental considerations are required without economic compensation is comparably generous to land owners. In industrial policy, by contrast, the owner must pay for any investment that is required in order to live up to environmental standards. Land ownership rights are thus regarded with different eyes than other types of private ownership that affects the environment. As long as the interpretation of forest-environmental legislation requires compensation by the state (or other funds) of any protected areas that exceed 0.5 to one hectare, substantial funds will be needed to maintain biological diversity. Secondly, much of the discrepancy between goals and practices can be attributed to the shortage of public funds to compensate for the preservation of forest areas. As long as Swedish voters (and taxpayers) do not demand higher budgets for nature preservation, this picture will not change. Different sources have been suggested to raise the state funding for forest protection, including the allocation of so called "infrastructure development funds" for this purpose as well as introducing special taxation measures for forest owners that would go towards a nature conservation fund. Thirdly, the attitudes within the forest sector might change as to what forest management policy is considered profitable in the long run. In this respect, the demand from the international (mainly EU) market is a key factor. If European consumers request "green" management in order to purchase Swedish forest products, there is no other way out than trying to implement environmentally sustainable forestry.

Present government policy would succeed in protecting the required forest area for preserving biological diversity within 100-200 years. It is most unlikely, however, that Swedish forest owners will await such a procedure by voluntarily retaining virgin forest areas and species-rich biotopes for such a long time. It seems likely that only the pressure from the international community of environmentalists and consumers of wood products can affect national policy-making in this field. The Swedish forestry industry wants to appear in a favourable light in terms of environmental sustainability, and considers itself to be at the forefront internationally. It remains to be seen, however, whether voluntary instruments such as environmental labelling can take over where national agencies have failed in their action programs for maintaining, (and improving), biological diversity in the forestry sector.[24] To conclude, the international community and the environmental movement will continue to play a leading role in pressuring Swedish forestry towards environmentally sustainable practices.

Notes

1. The paper builds on a more extensive analysis in Swedish on Swedish forestry policy in relation to biodiversity goals. See Katarina Eckerberg, *Att Skydda Biologisk Mångfald med Alternativa Metoder i Skogsbruket—Räcker det?* [To Protect Biodiversity through Alternative Methods in Forestry—Is it Sufficient?], (Stockholm: Utredning på Uppdrag av Riksdagens Revisorer, 1996).

2. Magnus Löf, *Relationen mellan Miljörörelsen och Skogsbolagen* [The Relationship Between the Environmental Movement and the Forest Companies], (Umeå: Department of Forest Economics, Swedish University of Agricultural Sciences, Working Report 176, 1993); Katarina Eckerberg, "Multiple-Use Forestry Administration, Legislation and Interest Groups," in *Multiple-use Forestry in the Nordic Countries,* ed. Marjatta Hytönen (Helsinki: Finnish Forest Research Centre, 1995), 357-390.

3. The newly elected Swedish Prime Minister, Mr. Göran Persson, emphasized the lead role that Sweden should take in sustainable development world-wide in his inauguration speech in April 1996.

4. Government Bill 1992/93: 226, *En Ny Skogspolitik* [A New Forest Policy], 33; Naturvårdsverket, *Skogsbruk och miljö* [Forestry and Environment], Miljön i Sverige—Tillstånd och Trender, Miljö 93, Rapport 4209 (Solna: Naturvårdsverket, 1993).

5. SOU 1992: 76, *Skogspolitiken inför 2000-talet* [Forest Policy for the 21st Century]. Huvudbetänkande, 1990 års skogspolitiska kommitté (Stockholm: Ministry of Agriculture, 1992), 131.

6. Naturvårdsverket, *Biologisk Mångfald* [Biological Diversity], Miljön i Sverige—Tillstånd och Trender, Miljö 93, Rapport 4138 (Solna: Naturvårdsverket, 1993).

7. Timo Tanninen et al, *Naturskogar i Norden* [Natural Forests in the Nordic Countries], *Nord* (1994), 7 (Köpenhamn: Nordiska Ministerrådet, 1994), 72-75.

8. Skogsstyrelsen, *Biotopskydd* [Protection of Biotopes], Informationsbroshyr om 21 § NVL (Jönköping: Naturvårdsverket, Jordbruksverket och Riksantikvarieämbetet, 1994); Skogsstyrelsen, *Nyckelbiotoper i skogen* [Key Forest Biotopes] (Jönköping: Skogsstyrelsen, 1993).

9. Lars-Erik Liljelund, Börje Pettersson and Olle Zackrisson, "Skogsbruk och Biologisk Mångfald" [Forestry and Biological Diversity], *Svensk Botanisk Tidskrift* 86, No. 3 (1992), 227-232.

10. A recent Nordic report suggests that such reserves should be at least 500 hectares, and in Sweden and Finland maybe 1000 hectares; Tanninen et al, op. cit.

11. Statistiska Centralbyrån, *Skyddad Natur* [Protected Nature], Statistisk rapport, Na 41 SM 9401 (Örebro: SCB, 1994).

12. World Conservation Monitoring Centre, *Global Biodiversity: Status of the Earth's Living Resources* (London: Chapman and Hall, 1992).

13. Lars Kardell and Anders Ekstrand, *Skyddad Skog i Sverige* [Protected Forests in Sweden], 1; Areal och Virkesförråd inom Nationalparker, Naturreservat och Domänreservat (Uppsala: Sveriges lantbruksuniversitet, Institutionen för skoglig landskapsvård, Rapport 48, 1990).

14. The state budget for purchase of nature reserves has increased from 20 million SEK in the beginning of the 1980s to 190 million SEK in 1994-95. For a long period of years, the annual budget was 20 million SEK, thereafter 40 million SEK. Only in 1989-90 was it raised to 100 million SEK. During the last fifteen years, most of this budget has been used to purchase forest land. In 1993-94, 23,500 hectares were preserved to a total cost of 170 million SEK, and in 1994-95, 35,500 hectares to a cost of 174 million SEK. However, only 20,000 hectares of this consists of productive forests.

15. Naturvårdsverket, *Naturvårdsplan för Sverige: En Strategi för Säkerställandearbetet* [Nature Protection Plan for Sweden], (Solna: Naturvårdsverkets förlag, 1991).

16. Tanninen et al., op. cit. In 1997, The Environmental Advisory Council estimated the short-term need for protection to an additional 900,000 hectores, which would mean another 4.2% protected forests. SOU 1997: 97. *Skydd av Skogsmark* [Protection of Forests] (Stockholm: EAC, 1997). However, the financing remains unresolved.

17. For example, the Southern Forest Owners' Association have protected a forest area near Göteborg; in Västerbotten the Vilhelmina Forest Common has been protected awaiting a more permanent solution; the Swedish Association for Nature Protection (SNF) has agreed with the private forest company STORA to protect 10,000 hectares without economic compensation along Dalälven where a threatened woodpecker (*Vitryggig hackspett*) thrives; and in Värmland and Dalsland counties some 1000 hectares of forests owned by municipalities, the diocese, and private individuals, have been set aside without economic compensation.

18. Between 1990 and 1995 some 12.000 more detailed environmental recommendations were issued by the County Forestry Agencies. Of these, only twenty-seven were prohibitions that, if neglected, could be appealed in court. In practice, no legal action has been taken and no forest owner has yet been fined for breaching the law on environmental protection in forest management.

19. Katarina Eckerberg, *Environmental Protection in Swedish Forestry* (Aldershot: Avebury, 1990).

20. Ibid.

21. There is no legal requirement to include environmental concerns into forest planning. Every clear-cutting must, however, be notified to the Forestry Agency prior to commencing the operation. The notification form includes information on environmental values. Henrik Forssblad, *Miljökonsekvensbeskrivningar—Nuvarande och Framtida Tillämpning inom Svenskt Skogsbruk* [EIA—Present and Future Use in Swedish Forestry] (Umeå: Dept. of Forest Economics, Swedish University of Agricultural Sciences, Working Report 195, 1994).

22. The Forest Owner's Association has not accepted the standard. Swedish FSC standard for forest certification, Sept. 24, 1997. http://www.forestry.se.fsc/english/standard/index.htm. *Nordisk Skogscertifiering* [Forest Certification in the Nordic Countries], Rapport nr. 1, February (Stockholm: Nordisk Skogscertifiering, 1996).

23. Forssblad, op. cit.

24. Both the National Environmental Protection Agency and the National Forestry Agency have recently published their Action Programs for Biological Diversity. Naturvårdsverket, *Aktionsplan för Biologisk Mångfald* [Action Plan for Biodiversity], Rapport 4463 (Stockholm: Naturvårdsverket, 1995) and Skogsstyrelsen, *Aktionsplan för Biologisk Mångfald och Uthålligt Skogsbruk* [Action Plan for Biodiversity and Sustainable Forestry], (Jönköping: Skogsstyrelsen, 1995). In both cases, however, these action programs are rather a plan for developing further actions, asking for more inventories and specifications. Previous, more precise, goals for forest preservation have been abandoned, referring to a need to first evaluate the impact of the new forest policy of 1994. In my view, this is merely an excuse for not taking action although sufficient scientific knowledge already exists on how biodiversity goals in Swedish forestry should be attained.

Chapter Eleven

CANADIAN FEDERAL FOREST POLICY

Present Initiatives and Historical Constraints

Joanna M. Beyers, L. Anders Sandberg

Canadian forest policy has largely aspired to the same goals as other northern industrialized countries. Since the Second World War, this has meant the pursuit of the sustained-yield model, which is largely based on promoting an even flow of forest fibre from extensive industrial leases held by large corporations. In this model, even-aged systems predominate, with concomitant clearcutting (or a variation thereof), short rotations, artificial regeneration often using so-called improved seedlings of commercial species, and a reliance on pesticides to control unwanted species. As elsewhere, Canadian forestry has also sought to accommodate other than timber values through a system of multiple use provisions, where such values are viewed as constraints on the central goal of producing forest fibre. More recently, Canadian forest policy has sought to respond to the calls for a more ecologically-sensitive forestry, where the integrity of forest ecosystems takes precedence over the maximum production of forest fibre. Two federal forest policy projects were recently launched to meet these goals: the National Forest Strategy (NFS) of 1992 as articulated in the document *Sustainable Forests—A Canadian Commitment*, and the Model Forest Program (MFP), a nationwide network of ten funded coalitions or partnerships of forest users, charged with the task of setting the Canadian forest sector on a sustainable footing and developed in conjunction with the NFS.

Here we argue that past and present Canadian forestry policy initiatives have had a small impact on forest practices on the ground. Projected fibre shortages and so-called NSRs (not sufficiently restocked areas) suggest that the sustained-yield model has fallen short of its objectives. Even when modified to include values besides timber, the paradigm has been harshly criticized. The sustainable forestry initiatives show similarly that words speak more than action. No doubt, this is in large part a function of the domination of forest capital generally and its more recent search for profits by "logging the globe."[1] Here, however, we are more concerned with exploring the specific and unique factors affecting Canadian forestry. We argue that Canadian forestry has been uniquely affected by four inter-related constraints: the Canadian colonial legacy, federalism, a restricted policy network, and the nature of forestry science and the professional forestry community.

Limiting Factors

The Colonial Legacy

French and English colonialism have left an indelible mark on the modern Canadian state, most obvious in its economy based on the exploitation and production of staples. The establishment of the staples economy has been of critical importance to the development of Canada, its political economy and natural resources policies.

Britain's military requirements for tall lumber for its ships (especially while it was embattled with Napoleon in the Baltic, its preferred timber supply) and its inability to procure it from the United States after independence, was one factor in the development of the Canadian staples economy.[2] The other was the need for European settlers to export products that were valued enough to be shipped profitably across the Atlantic despite high overhead costs.[3] The focus on export staples foreclosed the emergence of an indigenous manufacturing base and instead stimulated the industrial capacity of the mother countries.

The export trade in fur and lumber commanded large outlays of capital and a high degree of organization and, as local resources dwindled, eventually drew all the territories as far as the Pacific into the web of the eastern banking and shipping sectors (located primarily in Montreal), creating the need for a centralized government. As fur gave way to lumber, canals and railroads were built in order to accommodate this bulky product, an expense that reinforced the need for a centralized banking system and government to solve the problem of high overhead costs. Confederation in 1867 reflected this historical pattern. It created an independent country that could attract and administer capital and, by linking east and west, encouraged immigration which stepped up agriculture on the prairies and eventually the development of the mineral and pulp and paper industries. Canada's border with the United States preserved the political and geographical networks established through the fur trade and appropriated by the lumber industry, and their agricultural supply areas in the southern zones.[4]

One condition that the modern Canadian resource economy inherited from colonialism was extensive Crown ownership of non-agricultural lands. Although the lumber industry took on a civilian outlook during the nineteenth century, forests, having been an imperial resource, came to be seen as belonging to the individual British North American administrations (later provinces) in which they were found rather than to private individuals.[5] Crown ownership and the presence of a staples economy have been decisive in the development of Canadian forest policy in the modern era. A related element is the jurisdictional division of powers inaugurated by Confederation.

Federalism

Federalism is the overarching fact of the Canadian political system. The Constitution Act, 1867 (formerly the British North America Act, 1867) gave ownership, legislative authority and consequently undisputed jurisdiction over forest land to the provinces. Over the years the federal role in forestry has been confined to the support of industry through the funding of research and operation of laboratories, the championing and protection of the industry and its products abroad, and the use of the spending power to assist forest management.

Guiding forest policy through these policy instruments has been an exercise in frustration. The provinces have consistently resisted guidance from the federal government. An adversarial federalism has been particularly acute at times of high public salience of environmental issues.[6] The need to cut the federal deficit has further undermined the federal government's desire to be involved in forestry matters. In the Throne Speech of February 1996, Ottawa even announced its intention to bow out of forestry.

The same story applies to the recent attempts to promote sustainable forestry. As member of the CCFM (Canadian Council of Forest Ministers), the group that spearheaded the NFS, Ottawa retains a voice in national forest matters, but it is only one among many. The MFP, the federal government's only other means of exercising some influence over provincial forest affairs, also displays the limitations of the federal position well. For example, as landowners, provincial governments are represented in the partnership that manages each MF, but the Canadian Forest Service is there only *ex officio*. The most important limitation is the fact that whatever a MF achieves, adherence to it is voluntary. This restricts the influence it can have on policy change at the provincial level, since neither the province nor the industrial partner is obliged to implement it. Management plans, which each MF is required to produce, are voluntary because there is in fact only one legal management plan in place, the one negotiated between a province and the industry partner on the MF.

Government-Industry Relationships

The hugely expensive infrastructure associated with the long distances of a very large country and a small population contributed to the typically Canadian situation in which governments are closely involved with industry.[7] Further, Crown ownership of lands has resulted in the establishment of a well-guarded landlord-tenant relationship between the provinces and the forest companies in which the provinces sell the prospects of job creation and revenue for generous concessions in land, low royalties and lax management regulations.[8] Given a staples producing economy that promotes corporate tenures and decision-making control, such ties have over time strengthened.

Public ownership is often viewed as an ideal instrument of resource management in the belief that government will be able to exercise control over it. The Canadian experience shows that it has served instead to undermine government's autonomy and make it a client of the corporate community.[9] Referring to British Columbia, one observer has remarked that the economy "is planned and organized by...controlling privately owned corporations rather than by the State and its institutions."[10] From the perspective of policy community theory, closed policy networks have become the norm. These networks describe a condition in which the policy-making function is exercised by two or three parties: a more or less autonomous state and a well-organized industrial sector, sometimes joined by labour.

One practical outcome of the closed policy networks is that control over access to the forest resource is essentially restricted to large corporations. Pluralistic arrangements imply broader-based access with reduced participation by industry and labour, arrangements which Howlett and Rayner see as prerequisites for the implementation of the new sustainable forestry paradigm but which do not exist.[11] The MFP, where each site is run by a partnership of nominally equal partners drawn from the wider policy community only has the appearance of pluralistic arrangements. In reality, legally mandated restricted access and closed networks continue to direct, if obliquely, the dynamics of resource decision making. A large integrated forest company is a participant in each MF (Table 1). They are normally the only party with legally recognized rights of access and as such hold a disproportionate amount of power.

Table 11.1: Principal Industrial Partners in Canada's Model Forests

MODEL FOREST	INDUSTRIAL PARTNER	AREA UNDER INDUSTRIAL CONTROL (ha)	TOTAL AREA (ha)	%
Une Forêt Habitée, PQ	Abitibi-Price	48,100	112,634	43
Eastern Ontario, ON	Domtar	131,722*	1,534,115	8.6
McGregor, BC	Northwood Pulp & Timber	181,000	181,000	100
Manitoba, MA	Abitibi-Price	728,736**	1,047,069	73
Lake Abitibi, ON	Abitibi-Price	921,294	1,094,690	84
Long Beach, BC	MacMillan Bloedel; Interfor	175,000†	400,000	44
Western Newfoundland, NF	Corner Brook Pulp & Paper;	463,124	707,060	65.5
	Abitibi Price	86,968		12.3
Prince Albert, SK	Weyerhaeuser Canada	152,200	314,649	48
Fundy, NB	JD Irving	134,165	419,266	32
Foothills, AB	Weldwood of Canada	1,012,119	1,218,014	83

* Designated "Crown" land without direct reference to Domtar.
** Designated "Crown unrestricted."
† The figure includes the small Arrowsmith Timber Supply area operated by the BC Ministry of Forests.
Source: Proposals submitted to the Model Forest Program, Ottawa, February 1992.

Experts and Forest Policy

The final constraint in the way of attaining the goal of sustainable development in forestry is the role that professional foresters play in formulating forest policy. Together with government and industry, they represent the decision-making elite in the technocratic tradition.[12]

The professional foresters or experts (those that work within accepted forestry thought) are not just members of the larger policy community, but influence policy decisions at every step. This inclusion dates back to the era of conservation whose dates vary across the provinces but for the majority can be said to have occurred shortly after the turn of the century from seeds sown during the 1880s. During the era of conservation governments set up forestry branches within their administrations which introduced scientific forestry to a sector that had heretofore been structured only by regulations designed to minimize damage, optimize the collection of revenue and prevent monopoly ownership of forest lands.[13]

Steeped in progressive ideology, conservation meant the husbandry of resources through judicious use or, as Gifford Pinchot so famously put it, the "first great fact about conservation is that it stands for development."[14] As was true for the administrators of the French and German forests where scientific forestry was developed, economics, not preservation, was the motivation behind forestry.[15] Canada's staple dependence made rational forest management especially vulnerable to economic paramountcy. The obligation to supply foreign markets with base products pressured foresters to concentrate on cutting trees, quick profit being far more important than the protection of the resource.[16] If, under scientific forestry, efficient use meant a war against waste, in Canada it usually took the form of fire suppression and the classification of forested and agricultural lands, a tactic against settlers who were routinely accused of timber theft and reckless use of fire; a proper land classification scheme would help keep them out of the forests.[17] Small bush operators were also accused of wasteful practices; as a result, large enterprises were favoured by government and by the new breed of scientist, the forester, who looked to the corporate sector for inspiration on how to run the newly formed forestry branches.[18] A third source of waste was the forest itself. The aim of scientific forestry, which Pinchot said was "tree farming" or "handling trees so that one crop follows another," was to impose on forests an economy that nature could not.[19] Not all species were equally usable, so forestry targeted only commercially valuable species. Old and dying trees that do not add wood to their stems or exhibit negative growth through loss of limbs and rot, had to be eliminated and replaced with vigorously growing seedlings. This was to produce a "healthier and more uniform forest."[20] Like a well-run business, a forest had to be made to produce crop after crop in an orderly manner.

We noted that in Canada the conservation movement has been indelibly shaped by business interests. In the past this took the form of conservation rhetoric serving a pure business agenda.[21] Today, it is remarkable how closely the National Forest Strategy and the MFP resemble conservationist teaching in their emphasis on wood fibre and other aspects. A few illustrations will explain the point. With respect to the MFP, the guidelines used to select the ten successful sites from some fifty submissions are indicative of the professional community's resolution of the forestry-sustainability dilemma. Timber was to be the "essential component" in an integrated forest management strategy that supported the other values through, for example, habitat protection for wildlife.[22] Thus forestry is not about sustaining whole but selected features of forest ecosystems. The timber production focus was accentuated by the necessity of having the principal regional timber producer be among a submission's proponents. No provisions were made for experimentation with alternative fibres and ownerships. An emphasis on the use of advanced technology ensured a technocratic bias in the program. Scientific research also featured strongly in the appraisal. In all, the guidelines the experts drafted for the MFP supported rather than challenged the timber-driven, rational and technocratic production paradigm.

Like the MFP, the NFS is to guide the forest policy community towards the goal of sustainable development. In addition to a strong social component the NFS has an extensive ecological content which rests on the two notions of "stewardship of the forest environment" and ecosystem management. Stewardship in the NFS implies ecosystem management, management at the landscape level, expressed through such terms as integrity, resilience and biodiversity. This would be encouraging were it not that the tone of the NFS is permeated with a utilitarian ideology. For example, stewards "ensure intelligent, sensitive use"; an "optimal mix of uses" must be achieved through appropriate management practices; and, in a compromise between preservationist and conservationist sensibilities, old-growth stands can be maintained by setting them aside in preserved areas or, sometimes, by lengthening the rotation age.[23] The repeated emphasis on optimizing a mix of uses implies that enough can be known about forests to produce such "forest benefits baskets" and entrenches the value of professional foresters in designing them.[24] More to the point, it is hard to imagine how the NFS and for that matter the MFP, which takes its philosophy from the NFS, can successfully steer the industry towards a paradigm other than scientific forestry's sustained yield, because the values that initially complemented the focus on timber in this philosophy (for example, care of soil), do not exist in their own right, to sustain "native forest ecosystems," but in order to make forestry, the science of tree farming, more environmentally friendly.[25] In fact, without a hint of irony, the NFS states that "[s]ustainable development in forestry expands the principle of sustained yield…by including wildlife and fish habitats, watersheds and hydrological cycles, as well as gene pools and species diversity."[26] The decision to regard old-growth forests as a natural heritage to be maintained in representative stands rather than as a normal part of the natural cycle of forest ecosystems is also telling.[27]

There are other signs of the technocratic, interventionist tendency embraced in the NFS. Here we note the approval of genetically "improved" seedlings and the fact that the Strategy nowhere indicates that the ultimate aim of Canadian forest management is not to complete the conversion of wild forests to plantations (excepting as museum pieces in protected areas). Rather, the role of ecology or of ecosystem management is to allow us to do a better job of it so that our children's children will still have some timber—not forests—at their disposal.

Thus, Canadian forest policy, under the guidance and with the active participation of scientific foresters, promulgates an approach to forest management that blends a long-standing utilitarian, interventionist and technocratic view of nature with the new ecosystemic notions, giving industrial forestry a more benign, acceptable face.

Summary

The Canadian government has recently become active in the effort to protect the forest sector from losing its markets to damaging environmental campaigns. The most important initiatives are the Model Forest Program and the National Forest Strategy, both dating from the early 1990s and intended to facilitate the sustainable development of forests by leading industry away from the dominant paradigm of sustained-yield timber production. Both are hampered in the speedy attainment of this goal because each is built on the philosophy of sustained yield and envisions sustainable forestry as simply an elaboration of it.[28]

We suggest that four uniquely Canadian constraints further work against a successful conversion. Three are institutional and are directly related to Canada's colonial past while the fourth, which fitted easily into and was enhanced by that institutional framework, is more symptomatic of the turn-of-the-century enthusiasm to improve upon nature (but also owes its industrial character to the colonial legacy). It is our belief that the Canadian approach to forest management can be fully understood only if all four are considered together.

The first constraint is the colonial legacy, apparent in the staples economy and the typically Canadian high incidence of Crown ownership. The second is jurisdiction. Under federalism responsibility for forests lies with the provincial governments whose eyes are on the generation of revenue more than on seeking alternatives to current management structures. There is little room for the federal government to act as a counter force; it can only advise, guide and bring the parties to the table.

The third constraint derives largely from the extensive Crown ownership of forest lands. Although this regime in theory enhances public control over policy, the Canadian case demonstrates that it can also subvert state autonomy by creating a landlord-tenant relationship in which the tenant usurps the dominant position. In such closed policy networks, some practices may change incrementally in response to pressure from an attentive public but they are unlikely to dissolve completely. The MFP indicates that even when all parties appear at the table and are considered equal, control over resource affairs by the provinces and industry means that the most that can be hoped for are incremental adjustments to existing policies. Related to this is the question of access to timber. In a closed policy network, access to the forest resource is in the hands of large corporations who aggressively guard their privilege, aided by the provincial government. Though a few limited experiments to ease access for small operators are underway in British Columbia, they do not threaten the position of the multinationals. On this point too the MFP is impotent, since the only relationship among the partners to have the force of law is that between the province and industry. Besides, the MFP itself is structured to privilege landholders.

Lastly, the dominant social paradigm of sustained-yield timber production is kept in place by the standing of professional foresters. The tenacity of the existing paradigm is shown by the provisions of the NFS which also illustrate the paradigm's roots in the conservation era and its "wise use" philosophy.

These constraints put in doubt the capacity of policy to change beyond minor adjustments in response to agitations by those outside the golden circle of power. The network obtained its tenacity by reason of history and capital, suggesting that a satisfactory transition to the new paradigm of sustainable forestry may only come about as a result of far greater perturbances in Canadian society than the policy community can occasion at present.

Notes

1. M. Patricia Marchak, *Logging the Globe* (Montreal: McGill-Queen's University Press, 1995).

2. Arthur R.M. Lower, *Great Britain's Woodyard: British America and the Timber Trade, 1763-1867* (Toronto: The Ryerson Press, 1973).

3. Harold A. Innis, *The Fur Trade in Canada: An Introduction to Canadian Economic History* (Toronto: University of Toronto Press, 1956, revised edition).

4. Ibid.

5. H. Vivian Nelles, *The Politics of Development: Forests, Mines and Hydro-Electric Power in Ontario, 1849-1941* (Toronto: Macmillan of Canada, 1974).

6. Kathryn Harrison, *Passing the Buck: Federalism and Canadian Environmental Policy* (Vancouver: University of British Columbia Press, 1996).

7. Innis, op. cit.

8. Nelles, op. cit.; R. Peter Gillis and Thomas R. Roach, *Lost Initiatives: Canada's Forest Industries, Forest Policy, and Forest Conservation, 1900-1980* (New York: Greenwood Press, 1986).

9. Nelles, op. cit.

10. O. Ray Travers, "Forest Policy: Rhetoric and Reality," in *Touch Wood: BC Forests at the Crossroads,* eds. Ken Drushka, Bob Nixon and Ray Travers (Madeira Park: Harbour, 1993), 214.

11. Michael Howlett and Jeremy Rayner, "The Framework of Forest Policy in Canada," Chapter 3 in *Forest Management in Canada,* M.M. Ross (Calgary: Canadian Institute of Resources Law, 1995a), 43-107.

12. Alan Miller, "The Role of Citizen Scientist in Nature Resource Decision-Making: Lessons from the Spruce Budworm Problem in Canada," *The Environmentalist* 13, No. 1 (1993): 47.

13. These regulations were not effective; damage to forest lands continued, revenues were low and the anti-monopoly measures weak. Michael Howlett and Jeremy Rayner, "Do Ideas Matter? Policy Network Configurations and Resistance to Policy Change in the Canadian Forest Sector," *Canadian Public Administration* 38 (1995b), 382-410.

14. Gifford Pinchot, *The Fight for Conservation* (Seattle: University of Washington Press, 1910), 42.

15. Henry E. Lowood, "The Calculating Forester: Quantification, Cameral Science, and the Emergence of Scientific Forestry Management in Germany," in *The Quantifying Spirit in the 18th Century*, eds. Tore Frängsmyr, J.L. Heilbron and Robin E. Rider (Berkeley: University of California Press, 1990), 315-342; Gifford Pinchot, *Breaking New Ground* (Washington, DC: Island Press, 1987), 28.

16. L. Anders Sandberg and Peter Clancy, "Forestry in a Staples Economy: The Checkered Career of Otto Schierbeck, Chief Forester, Nova Scotia, Canada, 1926-1933," *Environmental History* 2 (1997): 74-95; Bill Parenteau and L. Anders Sandberg, "Conservation and the Gospel of Economic Nationalism: The Canadian Pulpwood Question in Nova Scotia and New Brunswick, 1918-1925," *Environmental History Review* 19 (1995): 55-83.

17. Gillis and Roach, op. cit.

18. Nelles, op. cit.; R. Peter Gillis, "The Ottawa Lumber Barons and the Conservation Movement, 1880-1914," *Journal of Canadian Studies* 9, No. 1 (1974): 14-31.

19. Pinchot, op. cit., 1987, 31.

20. Ibid., 51.

21. See note 16; also Nelles, op. cit.

22. Canada, *Model Forests: Background Information and Guidelines for Applicants* (Hull: Forestry Canada, 1991), 4.

23. Canadian Council of Forest Ministers, *Sustainable Forests: A Canadian Commitment* (Hull: Canadian Council of Forest Ministers, 1992), 6, 18, 12.

24. Stephen Boyce, "Forest Landscape Management: Fibre Baskets and Much More," *Canadian Forest Industries* (June 1994), 44-46.

25. Howlett and Rayner, op. cit., 1995b, 385.

26. Canadian Council of Forest Ministers, op. cit., 4.

27. Ibid., 12, 4.

28. This may merely point to the inadequacy of the term "sustainable development of forests" since it can be argued that sustainable forests and their sustainable development are incompatible.

CHAPTER TWELVE

THE POLITICS OF STEWARDSHIP

CERTIFICATION FOR SUSTAINABLE FOREST MANAGEMENT IN CANADA

PETER CLANCY

Since 1994, a broad set of forest sector interests including corporations, government agencies and non-governmental organizations, have given increasing attention to the development of certification procedures for sustainable forest management (SFM). The results might be described as a quasi-public political process which, I suggest below, is an apt reflection of a newly emerging forest policy paradigm of the late 1990s. In Canada, the most comprehensive initiative, which remains in the advanced design stages today, is associated with the Canadian Standards Association (CSA). Here the initial proponents were largely corporate, and the process accelerated as federal and provincial government agencies leapt aboard. The CSA was selected as the vehicle for developing an SFM certification process, and efforts were made to include various stakeholder constituencies in the forest sector, who have spent the past three years refining a draft system. Now approved, the CSA will implement "voluntary" certification procedures which will apply only to applicants which are judged, by third party audit, to satisfy the stipulated SFM standards. The fact that this system would bear the imprimatur of the Canadian forest business and government establishment may both enhance and complicate its standing.

Though largely neglected in the discussion of SFM certification to date, there are some fascinating political dimensions to this phenomenon. (Here I understand "political" to refer to the existence of power relationships in public social space, a field which includes both market and governmental realms). They are evident in the conflicting configurations of interest associated with sustainable development debates and SFM certification initiatives.[1] Thus it is important to explore the roots and the evolution of the CSA process, and its proposed certification system (known as the Z808/809 system), against the critiques and the alternative certification options presently in play. Given the substantial differences in conceptualization, sponsorship and delivery, there is much at stake here. Decisions on a certification system denote key political choices, in the sense that their application may benefit or penalize certain affected interests disproportionately.

The Mid-1990s Conjuncture in Forest Politics

The early years of this decade were tumultuous ones in the Canadian forest sector. The policy framework refined over the post-war years, based upon maximum sustained timber yield, was evidently sinking under the weight of political controversy both at home and abroad. The lightning rod for the new environmental campaigns was unquestionably British Columbia, where timber harvesting practices were under trenchant challenge on Vancouver Island, along the Pacific coast, and throughout the massive forest valleys of the provincial interior. The objects of protest included the provincial crown forest tenure system, which parcelled out vast tracts to corporate holders in the form of long-term tree farm licences, and the integrated (often multinational) forest corporations, seen as the direct agents of environmental despoilation through the highly mechanized application of clearcut logging. The battlegrounds for direct action environmental protest included a series of now-legendary landscapes: the Carmanah Valley, the Stein Valley, and most recently Clayoquot Sound. In 1989, British Columbia was included in *The National Geographic*'s profile of de-forestation in the Pacific Northwest,[2] and by 1991 it was being denounced by the environmental public as the "Brazil of the North." Perhaps inevitably, and not without reason, the environmental critique of clearcut logging was generalized to Canadian industrial forestry as a whole. This was followed by international environmental campaigns calling for the commercial consumer boycotts of Canadian pulp and paper products, and strategic pressure on highly visible industrial fibre users in the newspaper, magazine publishing, towel and tissue sectors, to cancel supply contracts in Canada.

The particular alignment of these conflicts had a crucial impact on the Canadian path toward sustainable forest management, which differs from that elsewhere. The European (and to a lesser extent, American) move toward SFM certification was driven strongly by wholesale and retail segments in visible wood-using industries such as building supplies, furniture manufacturing and paper and packaging. Their concern was to preserve domestic market share and offer an expanded product range in response to the heightened "green" sensitivities of European consumers. Large commercial chains, such as B&G in Britain and Home Depot in the United States, made strong commitments toward sustainable sourcing by the mid-1990s.[3] The political economy of Canadian sponsorship was quite different, originating as it did with vertically integrated forest manufacturers of primary and intermediate products such as market pulp and newsprint, destined predominantly for export. Thus for the Canadian firms there were powerful dangers of trade disputes, non-tariff barriers, and export market vulnerability quite distinct from those of green retailing. With the largest Canadian firms facing threats of product boycotts and exclusion from international markets, the possibility of credible third-party certification of sustainable practices clearly represents more than a "green seal" marketing edge (though the latter should not be discounted as a powerful factor which may drive the diffusion of certification in business).

Canadian state authorities have shared the reproach of the newly sensitized public, as crown forest management regimes have been excoriated for failures in protecting the public interest either in allocating commercial rights or in renewing the resource base. By the time the Sierra Club released its illustrated feature volume *Clearcut: The Tragedy of Industrial Forestry*,[4] the new philosophy and discipline of "eco-forestry" had thrown down the gauntlet.[5] Ironically, this criticism mounted as the era of intensive state-funded industrial silviculture (1975-1995) came under increased fiscal challenge. These combined pressures have led state authorities to join the forest products business in an enthusiastic, though also idiosyncratic, embrace of the political discourse of "sustainable development."

Certification as a Political Process

In any dynamic economy, questions pertaining to product standards will constantly arise. Indeed the very definition of a "product" turns on the notion of "like goods or services," implying a cluster of uniform attributes. There are of course many sponsors and many paths for the specification of standards, ranging from the voluntary to the mandatory. Yet the choice of standard-setting strategy is better portrayed by a continuum than a dichotomy. For in addition to the classic cases of voluntary standard setting common to primary and intermediate industry, and the state regulation more typical of retail consumer product standards and health and safety standards, there is a vast middle ground of delegated and collaborative action, on which industry-defined standards are vetted by independent parties or are given legal force by state authorities. The scope of the continuum is portrayed in Table 1 below.

Table 12.1: Continuum of Standard Setting and Enforcement Instruments

Initiators	Type of Standards	Examples
Producer Firms & Associations	Voluntary: -- Self-Labelling (First Party) -- Codes of Conduct (Standards) -- Trade/Industry Agreements	-Product marketing -Forest Accord -Responsible Care
Producer Firms & Associations; Professional Assocs.; Consumers; Public	Third Party Certification: -- Canadian Standards Assoc. -- Forest Stewardship Council -- Pacific Certification Council -- International Standards Association	SFM Mgt. Systems Eco-Labelling programs
National & Provincial Govt's; Public	State Regulation: -- Legislation and regulation -- Tax/Grant Support for SFM -- Model Policies/ Joint Policies	-Forest Mgt. Codes -FRDA - model -CCFM Certification and indicators

At one end of the continuum sit purely "voluntary" standards. These are devised by producer (and sometimes consumer) interests in an effort to differentiate products and confirm product qualities. They may target final commodity attributes, or production process attributes, or both. For example, wood-using firms may claim the mantle of sustainably managed materials for marketing purposes, as "a new pawn in a non-price competition strategy."[6] Alternatively, producers may agree on measures of self-regulation in order to shape the standards of industry oversight and/or avoid more direct state regulation. At the industry association level, many national and provincial bodies have established codes of responsible silviculture or sustainable harvesting practices. At the opposite end of the continuum sit statutory regulations. Over the course of the present decade, several Canadian forest ministries have legislated detailed codes of forest practice to govern the exploitation of crown forests. Here producing firms are obliged to observe the stipulated terms as a condition of access to leased lands.

Between these poles range a variety of hybrids, including voluntary standards with compliance subject to third party verification. This is the traditional ground of the CSA and of other non-governmental standard-setting organizations. A recognized, specialist organization oversees consultations by multiple stake-holders in search of consensual agreement on shared standards. This process extends well beyond the definition of standard criteria to include formal certification procedures and follow-up audits. Another path combines the two, beginning with private standard setting but subsequently extending their enactment into law.

Over the past decade, the Canadian forest industry has traversed the continuum in several directions, most recently in the 1992 policy statement, *Sustainable Forests: A Canadian Commitment.* This spoke firmly of "a new vision" for the next generation of forest management.[7] Nine strategic directions and ninety-six commitments were outlined in a five year work program to "guide the policies and actions of Canada's forest community, which includes governments, industries, non-governmental organizations, communities and concerned individuals..." (viii) The 1992 statement contained several important provisions relating to sustainable standards, including:

Strategic Direction 2: Forest Stewardship: Forest Management Practices
   2.17 By 1994, members of the forest community will co-operate to establish working models of sustainable forest management in the major forest regions of Canada.

Strategic Direction 3: Expanding the Dialogue
   3.5 By 1993, the federal government will develop a system of national indicators to measure and report regularly on progress in achieving sustainable forest management.

Strategic Direction 4: Economic Opportunities: A Changing Framework
   4.12 Industry and governments will work co-operatively to pursue joint technical discussions aimed at internationalizing product standards, codes and certification procedures.

4.13 By 1995, industry and governments will develop and put into operation a means of identifying and promoting Canadian forest products that reflect our commitment to sustainable forests and environmentally sound technologies.[8]

As significant as was this emerging policy discourse on sustainable issues, this 1992 Policy Statement was noteworthy also for its sponsorship. The Canadian Council of Forest Ministers (CCFM) declared itself a trustee of the new strategic program.[9] Furthermore the CCFM invited business and non-governmental organizations to join in endorsing a *Canada Forest Accord,* which re-affirmed the principles and committed the signatories to continuing action. Not only did this inject momentum for follow-up action on the working program, but it also provided a broad political legitimizing umbrella for the entire venture, facilitating the commitment of public funds toward Strategy priorities.[10] While the SFM issue was only one part of the 1992 Strategy, these founding circumstances identified the concept of certification as an important element within a newly emergent policy paradigm enjoying powerful institutional sponsorship.[11]

The CSA and SFM Certification

The Canadian Standards Association is an intriguing organizational heretic which defies easy classification. It is a non-profit, private organization with open and flexible eligibility for membership, welcoming "any individual, company or organization interested in standards activities." Established following the First World War, it boasts over two thousand publications, which have been developed by volunteer committees in some thirty-five technological fields. These documents include product specification documents and guidance documents, as well as formal standards documents. One third of the latter have been referenced into law at the federal or provincial level. Standards may pertain to safety, quality, or performance.[12]

The working unit of the CSA, as distinct from its general membership body, is the volunteer committee assigned to a designated area. Over the years some 7000 committee members have participated. The work of committees is shaped by a "consensus" ethic. That is, agreement is sought by the method of successive approximation, as committee discussions and consultations yield a series of written drafts. For the CSA, consensus is defined as "an attempt to remove all objections and implies much more than the concept of a simple majority, but not necessarily unanimity."[13]

In the case of SFM certification, the CSA became involved at the request of the forest industry. With the Canadian Pulp and Paper Association providing a provisional secretariat, the industry established a Sustainable Forest Certification Task Force in October 1993. It then approached the CSA to develop the standards and procedures for SFM certification. This Task Force also financed the first six months of the SFM exploration. It engaged Dr. Ken Armson, a forestry consultant who served previously as Chief Forester for the Province of Ontario, to produce the first draft of an Overview Document for sustainable forest management (designated Z808).

The Task Force also approached the CCFM early in 1994, seeking support for the CSA certification initiative. In addition, the Task Force requested arrangements for "interim certification" of producing companies during the estimated eighteen months required to complete the CSA process.[14] This would serve to "reassure the world marketplace of Canada's commitment to sustainable forest management."[15]

This intervention was extremely timely. In diplomatic circles, the momentum generated by the Rio Summit and Canada's 1992 Forest Strategy/Accord had carried over to the Montreal Seminar in September 1993, which proposed a set of criteria for sustainable development of boreal and temperate forests. Already the CCFM was sponsoring a Canadian process to formulate both *criteria* (distinguishing characteristics) and *indicators* (measurable variables) for Canada by 1995. As a result, not only did the Task Force win CCFM support for the CSA process, but it was able to graft its preferred vehicle for SFM certification onto wider trends in international forestry diplomacy.[16]

By the time Armson had completed a preliminary draft, the Z808 Committee was assuming a more formal structure. Following normal CSA practice, efforts were made to recruit a cross-section of parties interested in certification for participation on the new Technical Committee. A "balanced matrix" membership was proposed for the Technical Committee, consisting of six to ten representatives of each of the following categories: Producer Interest; Government and Regulatory Authority; Professionals, Academia and Practitioners; and Environmental and General Interest. Beyond this group of voting members, the TC welcomed any other interested members as Associates or Observers. While there was no exact stipulation of numbers, CSA Regulations ensure that no representative group can be larger than the sum of the two smallest groups. In place of the normal category of "user interests," it was agreed to substitute academic representation in this case.

The composition of the Committee is reflected in Table 2 below. While the membership has been circumscribed, with fewer than thirty *voting* members of the Technical Committee and another twenty *associate* members contributing input, the consultative process stipulated an opportunity for public input (and revision) to the advanced draft proposals, prior to a final ballot (by voting members) on the approval of the entire package. Thus the CSA describes its initiative on SFM, as on all other standard-setting questions, as "transparent" to public view.[17]

The ultimate objective of this machinery was to develop an SFM Guideline which would allow the certification of complying organizations across Canada. Two documents would be required for this purpose. The "Overview," or "Guidance," Document (Z808) outlines the context, goals, and approaches to certification in sustainable forest management, while the Specifications Document (Z809) addresses the auditing process. From the outset, the Technical Committee took an aggressive approach to its work, anticipating that the final documents could be approved within one year. While

While the Technical Committee was the main working body to generate proposals, there was also provision for a public review period (soliciting written input) for each document. Ultimately the consensus process would culminate in a ballot of the voting members and (it was hoped) an ultimate decision. If favourable, the Z808/809 documents would be published as a CSA Information Product. The final step, of promulgating the CSA Standard, could follow in as little as six months. Simultaneously, it was hoped that the two documents could be submitted to the International Standards Organization (ISO) Technical Committee 207. The aim here was to have the Canadian document adopted as the "seed document" from which an ultimate ISO standard on sustainable forest management would spring. Furthermore, in order to gain a jump on rival national SFM standards (further discussed below), it was hoped initially to advance Z808/809 at the ISO meeting scheduled for Norway in May 1995.

Table 12.2: Canadian Standards Association, Z808/809 Structure

SUSTAINABLE FOREST MANAGEMENT -- TECHNICAL COMMITTEE			
Producer Interest	**Profess., Academia & Practitioners**	**Environmental & General Interest**	**Government & Regulatory**
Kruger Inc Weldwood of Canada Timberwest Forest Conf. des Co-ops. Forestieres Structural Board Association E.B. Eddy Forest Canadian For. Prods.	UBC For. Faculty (2) Laval U. For. Faculty Can. Inst. Forestry Paprican Feric Ernst and Young	Wildlife Habitat Can. CSN union IWA Canada union Natl Abor For Assoc. WWF Canada Sierra Club Canada Can. Wildlife Fed. CEP union	Nat. Res. Canada (2) Env/Res/Mgt (Sask) Nat/Res (N.S.) Res/Nat (Que.) EcDev/Trade (Alta.) Forests (B.C.) Nat/Res (Ont.)
Associate Members			
Private Consultant External Affairs (Can.) Industry Canada (Can.)	N.B. Fed. of Woodlot Owners Task Force on Churches and Social Responsibility Private Consultant		
Executive Committee		**Editing Committee**	

Ultimately this timetable collapsed as the Technical Committee deliberations unfolded. It became clear that with sustainable forest management, the CSA had taken on a highly visible and politically contested issue.[18] Two examples aptly demonstrate the underlying complexity of the process. One involves the latent conflict between industry and environmental activist agendas on SFM, which constantly threatens to erupt. The second involves the challenge of accommodating a diversity of forest owners and harvesters within a single system, as illustrated by the special position of small private woodlot owners.

During this embryonic phase of SFM design, all certification bodies tended to underestimate the complexity of the task and the time required. The Forest Stewardship Council (FSC), which has been actively certifying products in the United Kingdom for some years, targeted 1995 for a fully operating program but later relaxed the standard from "certified" forest products to "well-managed" products.[19] This allowed more time for the essential work of accrediting certifiers and locating sources. The CSA Committee, still at the design rather than the operating stage, encountered difficulties of a different order.

In a dramatic move, several of the environmental NGO participants (including WWF International, Sierra Club, and Taiga Rescue Network) announced their withdrawal from the process. Arguing that the proposed standards were too weak, that the balance of participating interests was flawed, and that the concept of eco-labelling was being misappropriated to sanction the status quo, some fifty environmental NGO's joined in a public statement.[20] Questioning the political legitimacy of the CSA process, several of the larger groups including Greenpeace called for a new beginning under the (rival) FSC process. The CSA added a series of stakeholder workshops to its SFM agenda during the autumn of 1995. At that point a more detailed critique of the Z808/809 framework was released by the ENGO opposition.[21]

By the end of 1995 the problems created by this schism were well evident. The President of the Canadian Institute of Forestry put the matter succinctly: "without industry participation the FSC will not have anyone to certify; while without environmental activist support, the Canadian process will not have any consumer credibility."[22] Since that time, the Forest Stewardship Council has accelerated its activity in Canada. In January 1996 it upgraded its national presence from a Contact Person to a Working Group, and designated the Acadian Forest as the first forest region in which to design standards. An organizational meeting for the Acadian Forest Working Group occurred in Nova Scotia in April 1996.

For small private forest owners, the emerging CSA model posed a different challenge. The small private segment accounts for nine percent of Canada's forest land, but fourteen percent of the fibre output. However a system premised on vast crown leases to hundreds of thousands of acres, exploited by a single industrial operator over twenty years or more time, made little allowance for owners of small woodlots of 400 acres or less. Active in the CSA process from the outset, a network of woodlot owner and producer organizations pressed for special acknowledgement and adaptations to meet their needs. Some of the particular problems included: the challenge of grouping small producers for purposes of certification, the recognition of new costs required to meet the organizational and documentation needs for small holdings which large industrial counterparts have already met through sunk costs associated with crown lease management; and financial provisions for certification expenses. This prompted extensive revision to the early Z808 drafts, to include explicit equivalency provisions, and an additional (fifth) pilot study on woodlot certification.[23]

From Design to Delivery of SFM Certification Systems

Thus far we have examined the macro-political context and the internal political dynamics of the CSA initiative on sustainable forest management. Since the approval of the Z808/809 draft documents in July 1996, attention has shifted to implementation. For this reason the defining features of this particular certification system deserve close attention.

The objectives of certification have always been more readily grasped than the system's design. Yet the process of specifying, much less implementing, sustainable forest management is far more elusive. As Bruce Doern and Thomas Conway remark of the sustainability concept, "though it has ample constructive ambiguity in its meaning, it has a political and intellectual resonance that is quite genuine."[24] From a commercial point of view, certification can inject a new quality into the commodity which alters both market value and consumer preference. It is expected that the enhanced product can bear a pricing premium commensurate with its production.

Part of the debate turns on differences over what is being certified and by what means. The CSA approach is to graft SFM onto the already existing models for environmental management *systems* or business in general. Certification thus hinges upon the design and implementation of a forest management plan which includes sustainable goal setting-data gathering-monitoring, rather than on the achievement of designated certified sustainable practices on the ground. The intellectual rationale for such systems hinges on the opening premise: a plan which begins with acknowledged sustainable goals and approximates their realization is inherently a SFM plan. Richard Welford has underlined the limitations of this "management system" approach to sustainable business, which emerged from United Kingdom (BSI) and European Community initiatives in the late 1980s and furnishes the conceptual basis of EMAS and ISO standards in the 1990s. They share a focus on "the auditing of the environmental management system and an assessment that the organization is meeting its self-defined policy objectives and targets."[25] Consequently the degree of environmental progress depends on firms setting "targets that are honest and realistic yet challenging and attainable."[26] Ironically, the combination of self-targeting and management process auditing makes it possible (some critics would contend inevitable) for the system to bestow sustainable credentials even upon firms which are engaged (by objective measure) in environmental degradation.

For the proposed CSA system, the consequences are readily apparent. In the initial (preparatory) stage, the sponsor (owner or manager) must designate a set of "values" for a candidate forest area. Relying on the Z808 framework, it is not entirely clear what forest "values" entail. At points they seem to amount to little more than speculative wish-list items, particularly when compared to the more concrete and empirical character of "objectives" and "plans." Indeed values are described in Z808 as "broad" and "dimensionless."[27] Nonetheless, values will be conceptualized on the basis of the six stipulated CCFM criteria (i.e. biological diversity, ecosystem maintenance/enhancement, soil/water conservation, global ecosystem impact, multiple social benefits, and social responsibility). However not all criteria must be addressed as part of the goal-setting stage, if persuasive "local" reasons can be advanced for their omission. Indeed according to Z808 "it is impossible to manage for all forest values individually" so it is better to identify "functional groups of values" and monitor one or more values within the group to assess the quality of management.[28] Thus it would appear that owner/managers can specify the values of their forests from among the CCFM criteria. While owner/managers enjoy the initiative in formulating forest values, this is not exclusive. It should be noted that Z808 also requires an element of "community participation" at this stage. Significantly, however, it is the opportunity for public input, rather than its quality or ultimate impact on value specification, that is measured.

As we have seen, the "values" stage represents the conceptual link to sustainable outputs, and it is from this that management goals and indicators of achievement are derived. In the second (planning) stage, a set of concrete objectives are designated for an intermediate time frame (three to five years) and plans are fashioned to achieve them. At this point, a forest area is eligible for initial evaluation and certification. That is, the existence of a plan is sufficient to achieve initial SFM status. The CSA system calls for an annual verification that the plan is being maintained. Following a third stage interval for implementation, an initial audit occurs after three years and at five year intervals thereafter. Here the benchmark is relative rather than absolute, since even evidence of partial progress can be sufficient for renewal. As Z808 puts it, "the real test of sustainability is comparing the forest that evolves over time with the forest that was forcast, and then assessing the acceptability of any differences."[29] If a forest area is being managed according to the terms of the SFM plan then it will be considered "sustainable." Clearly it is the the quality of the business management system, as distinct from the forest environment *per se*, which is the object of sustainable certification here. Thirty-five years ago this might have been described as "Management By Objectives" for the woodlands sector. Today it is bolstered by the continuous evaluation and improvement ethic adopted from Total Quality Management.

Conclusion

The Canadian experience with SFM certification to date displays many political dimensions. It involves an extension of voluntary third party standard setting, typical of many industry groups, to the primary forest sector where state regulation has more typically applied. A number of political and economic forces have led this shift, including a new public and consumer sensitivity to environmental impacts of forest practices, the threatened loss of key export markets through commercial boycotts and environmental trade rules, and the decline in state fiscal capacity to directly underwrite intensive forest management. This opens the possibility of a significant shift in the policy regime for forest management, which carries important distributional implications.

A functional SFM certification system could revitalize several key elements of the national forest policy network in Canada. The stabilization of forest industry production has already been well addressed. For state authorities, third party certification offers a commercial lever to extend, at the voluntary level, standards which can no longer be publicly financed on so comprehensive a scale. The dangers of lost sales or even entire national markets will create an incentive of a different order than state regulations, and at a far less fiscal outlay. The possibility cannot be discounted, however, that the Canadian state might return to the direct financing of sustainable forest practices through either grant or tax-based instruments, at some future (post-deficit) conjuncture. Finally, the system also creates an extensive permanent demand for technical and professional services to be supplied on a commercial basis by consultants, contractors, auditors, educational institutions, trade and industry associations and owner/managers. Moreover the voluntary nature of the system provides opportunities for a reallocation of market shares and value-added advantages to those producers who successfully meet its terms. In addition, the process of meeting certification standards will prompt a system-wide review of current practices and with an emphasis on deliberation and consistency of commitment. Furthermore, new market segments and opportunities will arise for innovative enterprise to exploit the sustainable value added to presently underutilized forest species.

Yet as the final section suggested, there remain lingering doubts about certain conceptual and operational deficiencies. While these are not unique to the CSA system, they will be manifest first in that setting. Should the incipient cleavage noted within the CSA Technical Committee widen into a formal rift, the future will be further problematic. Indeed should the certification field be perceived to split between "industrial" certifiers (Z808) and "environmentalist" certifiers,[30] much of the potential gain will be lost. It is notable that parallel certification initiatives[31] place far greater emphasis on achieving seamless networks among multiple certifiers, precisely to avoid the danger of incomplete coverage, rival claimants and a consequent loss of commercial and political legitimacy.

SFM Postscript

In the time since this paper was finalized in 1996, the political drive toward sustainable forest management has accelerated. In the race between the contending certification systems, the CSA has taken the lead in 1997. Not only is the Z808 system attracting considerable pulp and paper industry attention, but the first wave of firms is now well advanced in preparations for the eventual certification audits. At the same time, the FSC process has generated a draft technical standard, and a number of state authorities take the view that both processes are consistent with existing policy.

The final drafts of the Z808/809 documents were approved unanimously by the thirty-two voting members of the CSA Technical Committee in July 1996. They were then submitted to the Standards Council of Canada, which gave its approval in October, making Canada the first country to formally accept a set of SFM procedures. Almost immediately the CSA began to mount orientation seminars across the country, a vital step in promoting its system to prospective clients. The Sustainable Forest Certification Task Force, which initiated the process back in 1993, is now vigorously promoting the CSA standards. By the start of 1997 the first wave of corporate forest operators had begun the process of documenting their practices and preparing their submissions. The initial step often involved a "gap analysis" in which the operator gauged the distance between present practices and those required to meet SFM standards. The Coalition estimates that the first wave of prospective applicants account for more than eight million hectares of forest and 10-12 million cubic metres of wood per year. In addition to applicants, an SFM system also requires auditors. The first certification authority, SGS IGS (International Certification Services) was designated early in 1997.

The second track involved deliberations on an international SFM standard. At its Rio Meeting in June 1996, the ISO Technical Committee 207 authorized a Working Group on Forestry. This was charged with preparing a reference document under the auspices of the ISO Environmental Management System (EMS) standards (series 14001-04). Once the Z808/809 standards were accepted, a CSA sub-committee was struck to bring the Canadian case to the Working Group, which began its deliberations in Toronto in November 1996. A Drafting Committee was struck to develop a document to be submitted to TC 207. As 1997 closes this work continues.

The Forest Stewardship Council has also been active during this time. Following its commitment to tapering certification systems to forest regions, the FSC launched an Acadian Forest Region Initiative in April 1996. A Technical Standard Writing Committee produced a draft of "best forest practices" which was released for public consultation in October 1997. After further revision it will be put to a meeting of FSC regional members in 1998, and if approved it will advance to the FSC Board of Directors for final approval.

Notes

1. "Special Issue: Certification in Cascadia," *International Journal of Ecoforestry* 11, No. 4 (1995); Special Issue: "The Certified Forest: What Makes it Green?" *Journal of Forestry* 98, No. 1 (April 1995).

2. Rowe Finlay, "Will We Save Our Own"? *National Geographic* 178, No. 3 (September 1990): 106-36.

3. Christopher Upton and Stephen Bass, *The Forest Certification Handbook* (Delray Beach: St. Lucie Press, 1996).

4. Bill Duvall, ed., *Clearcut: The Tragedy of Industrial Forestry* (San Francisco: Sierra Club/ Earth Island Press, 1993).

5. Michael M'Gonigle and Ben Parfitt, *Forestopia* (Madeira Park, B.C.: Harbour, 1994).

6. Richard Welford, *Environmental Strategy and Sustainable Development* (London: Routledge, 1995), 77.

7. Canadian Council of Forest Ministers (CCFM), *Sustainable Forests: A Canadian Commitment* (Hull: CCFM, 1992).

8. Ibid.

9. This is a federal-provincial ministerial group which has emerged as the co-ordinating body for strategic forest policy direction during the turbulent decade since the Brundtland Report.

10. At the same time, the CCFM recognized its limits as an implementation agency, and chose to fund a continuing multi-sector body known as the National Forest Sector Strategy Coalition. From an initial observational role, the Coalition has progressively assumed monitoring and advocacy functions on behalf of the Strategy.

11. Canadian Council of Forest Ministers (CCFM), *Defining Sustainable Forest Management: A Canadian Approach to Indicators and Criteria* (Ottawa: Natural Resources Canada, CFS, 1995).

12. Canadian Standards Association (CSA) "The Canadian Standards Association's Sustainable Forest Management (SFM) Project," (Toronto: CSA, 1995), 3.

13. Ibid.

14. This envisaged letters from provincial government forestry officials, written on behalf of resident producing firms to their customers, and "attesting to a commitment to the goals of sustainable forestry...and specifically identifying some areas of commitment." G. Lapointe, "Standards for Sustainable Forestry in Canada," *Forestry Chronicle* 70, No. 5 (1994), 514.

15. Ibid.

16. Further weight was added to the CSA process when the Parliamentary Standing Committee on Natural Resources endorsed "the industry-led process, on the basis of cost and the fact that the current drive to develop an international certification process under the auspices of the ISO is well underway." Canada, House of Commons, Standing Committee on Natural Resources, *Canada: A Model Forest Nation in the Making* (Ottawa: The Standing Committee, 1994), 36.

17. Three groups were established within the CSA process. The full TC would serve as the primary working body in discussing and revising the draft documents. A small Executive Committee was struck to include members from all categories. Finally an Editing Committee was established to translate TC deliberations into text.

18. J. S. Tanz and W. L. C. Campbell, "Principles and Perils of Silvicultural Audits," *Forestry Chronicle* 70, No. 1 (January-February 1994).

19. "Forest Products Certification," *Forestry Chronicle* 71, No. 5 (September-October 1995): 580. 1995b, 580.

20. "Statement by Environmental Groups, First Nations, and Unions in Canada on Processes to Develop Eco-Labels for Forest Products and Practices," April 25, 1995, mimeo.

21. Michelle Swenarchuk, "An Environmentalist and First Nations Response to the Canadian Standards Association Proposed Certification System for Sustainable Forest Management," *International Journal of Ecoforestry* 11, No. 4 (1995), 123-27.

22. Steve Tolmie, "To Certify or Not," *Forestry Chronicle* 71, No. 6 (November-December 1995): 683.

23. Canadian Standards Association (1996a) "A Sustainable Forest Management System: Guidance Document," Z808-96, Draft February 6; Canadian Standards Association (1996b), "A Sustainable Forest Management System: Specifications Document," Z809-96, Draft February 6.

24. G. Bruce Doern and Thomas Conway, *The Greening of Canada* (Toronto: University of Toronto Press, 1994), 236.

25. Welford, op. cit., 60.

26. Ibid., 75.

27. CSA, op. cit. (1996a), 8.

28. Ibid., 7.

29. Ibid., 7.

30. Forest Stewardship Council (FSA), Oaxaca, Mexico, Document 1.1, "FSC Statutes"; Document 1.2, "FSC Principles and Criteria for Natural Forest Management"; Document 1.4.2, "FSC Protocol for Endorsing National Initiatives"; Document 1.4.3, "FSC Process Guidelines for Developing Regional Certification Standards."

31. Nordic Forestry Certification Project, "Nordic Forest Certification. Report No.1," February, 1996.

CHAPTER THIRTEEN

THE PUBLIC ACCESS DILEMMA

The Specialization of Landscape and the Challenge of
Sustainability in Outdoor Recreation[1]

Klas Sandell

The *allemansrätt*, the right of everyone to move freely across private land
holdings is a basic element in Swedish and Nordic outdoor recreation. It is a
legacy of pre-industrial society which has become part of public access rights
in modern society. It allows anyone to move about the countryside
undisturbed provided s/he does not disturb or damage the property of local
residents. Generally it prohibits the taking of anything of economic value, such
as trees, crops, birch-bark or acorns (used as animal feed); but the rights "left
over"— picking flowers, berries and mushrooms, or making a camp-fire and
staying overnight—are part of what is now referred to as the *allemansrätt*. As
in other cultures, the *allemansrätt* is a remnant that once recognized and
supported the needs and interests of the landless. Its survival up to the present
day is probably attributable to Sweden's sparse population, and its Germanic
tradition of legislation (as opposed to the Roman) which supports the current
position of the right of public access in the Nordic countries.[2]

In modern times the *allemansrätt* has to some extent been
strengthened by new laws. These include a prohibition to build structures
on sea- and lake-shores that may obstruct public movement; the obligation
of land-owners to, in specific circumstances, make arrangements to let
people pass through their fences; the identification and recognition of areas
of specific interest for outdoor recreation as part of national physical
resource planning; the inclusion of matters of conservancy and responsible
use in legislation concerning agriculture and forestry; and a special law
prohibiting the driving of motor vehicles off-road for recreational purposes
if there is no snow on the ground (which is important for non-mechanized
outdoor recreation). In sum, the right of public access in Sweden is rooted

in the common law and can be seen as a basic right limited by various economic, privacy, and conservation considerations.

Outdoor recreation may result in severe environmental problems, but it may also serve as a vital element in environmental education. It is therefore very important with respect to fostering sustainability. In this chapter, the Swedish *allemansrätt* is used as a point of departure for a discussion of the role, characteristics, needs—and dilemmas—of sustainability in outdoor recreation. Following an introduction on outdoor life in Sweden, the tension between locally-based development and the functional specialization of the landscape is presented. I conclude by exploring some aspects of the relationship between outdoor recreation and sustainability using a conceptual framework of three eco-strategies.

Outdoor Life in Sweden

Around the turn of the century, the rapid industrialization and urbanization of Sweden created a great interest in physical leisure activities. "Swedish nature" and "nature-loving Swedes" became important themes in shaping the modern Swedish nation. The idea of outdoor life and contact with nature was emphasized as fostering a broad range of goals. With rising material standards of living, a gradual shortening of the work week, and the Compulsory Holidays Act of 1938, it became possible for the broad masses to have, and make use of, leisure time. During the twentieth century, parallelling the rise of the welfare State, tourism, recreation and outdoor life established themselves as important economic, regional and professional fields of interests.[3]

The "Swedishness" of this form of dealing with nature must not be over-stated. It is easy to identify various contributions from other countries in what is today labelled *friluftsliv* (outdoor life; literally open-air life) in the Nordic countries. This includes the extensive "back to nature" movement—inspired by individuals such as David Thoreau, John Muir, and Aldo Leopold—that emerged in North America in the late nineteenth and early twentieth centuries, which manifested itself in bird-watching, recreational fishing, camping, and summer cottaging. More recent Swedish trends in recreational activities and equipment come especially from North America.[4]

However, there are also unique features of outdoor recreation in Sweden. The importance of "wilderness" and the emphasis on solitude in North America, for example, contrasts with the broad and popular approach to the out-of-doors in Sweden. It therefore seems relevant to talk about a unique tradition of Nordic outdoor life as found mainly in Norway, Sweden and Finland. I will use the term outdoor life instead of outdoor recreation to characterize this tradition. In an overview of outdoor life during the twentieth century, Tordsson strongly supports the notion that the English and American traditions are different from the Nordic.[5] He especially highlights the differences with regard to identity and ideological context. The Nordic tradition of outdoor life is often characterized by simplicity and mass appeal in contrast to the more commercialized and specialized outdoor recreation activities in

North America and continental Europe. The difference can perhaps be illustrated by two extremes: In the Nordic countries, the out-of-doors typically involves putting on a pair of Wellingtons and taking a walk with the family in the nearby forest, picking some berries, enjoying the scenery and the quietness of nature. In North America, by contrast, the outdoor recreation experience may involve the latest and most expensive equipment, perhaps entering a helicopter for heliskiing in the wilderness or a rubber boat for river-rafting. Frequently, these activities take place once in a life-time.

Looking at current outdoor life in Sweden we note that almost one third (31.2%) of the population between the ages of 16-84 report that they take nature walks once or more a week. If we include the group reporting that they take nature walks at least once a month, we add a further 25.2%. Also, "just over half of the population 16-84 years have access to a summer home...or spent at least one week in one."[6] Vogel says with regard to a comparison of (all five) Nordic countries that:

> The types of leisure activities in the Nordic countries are quite similar due to common traditions, similarities in settlements and climate etc. About 15 activities have been studied. The results show that outdoor life and exercise has a strong position in the Nordic countries.[7]

The Dilemma of a Sustainable Landscape Integration

Today, the need for sustainability is generally unquestioned, though its content has still not been determined. Nevertheless, sustainability is often associated with small-scale local adaptations. Current examples include programs under *Agenda 21* and various discussions on "alternative" development, "bioregionalism" and "eco-regional strategies" aimed at increasing the "capacity of individuals and groups to control their own resources."[8] "Eco-tourism" and "sustainable tourism" are generally also associated with local adaptations and self-reliance.

The importance of public involvement is obvious with regard to sustainability in terms of environmental knowledge forming a viable part of political input and support for laws and regulations. Of special interest seems to be the concrete relation to nature (here understood as what humans—voluntarily or involuntarily—do not control). It is also frequently claimed that a close contact with nature encourages a sense of respect, care and active environmental involvement. Many factors are of course involved in making outdoor recreation a means of attaining greater environmental awareness, for example, the type of activity, the depth of the environmental involvement and other sources of inspiration and information. In any case, it could be argued that the qualities of the landscape and the adaptation of activities to the landscape probably are crucial elements with respect to public environmental awareness and of the attainment of attitudes and life-styles in line with sustainability.[9]

At the same time, the growth of industrialism is causing a global functional specialization of the landscape. The processes of production and consumption are more and more "divorced" from the landscape and regions. Many environmental problems are complex, diffuse, global and unknown, that is, not easy to detect at the local level. With regard to recreation and the out-of-doors, the functional specialization of the landscape is manifested in, for example, the growth of ski-resorts and special areas for summer-homes.

Today Sweden is becoming more and more internationally integrated, and tourism is an important part of this process. The foreign tourists are attracted to the Swedish countryside and the fact that Sweden does not really have a mass tourist industry.[10] The *allemansrätt* is central here. This has led to charges that foreign tourists are misusing it, especially in the most intensely used tourism areas in the southern parts of Sweden. There is also a widespread concern about the right of public access as Sweden is becoming more integrated with the rest of Europe.

This has led to an intense discussion on the future treatment of the right of public access in the Swedish countryside. The discussion revolves around three subjects: the extensive nature of the right of public access[11]; its utilization as a question of judgement and education[12]; and its potential, in an increasingly integrated world, to render Sweden "Europe's open-air recreation area."[13] The discussion of these three subjects has brought to the fore the question of legislating the right of public access. Also, it has been proposed that this right be limited to Swedish citizens and permanent residents.[14] So far, however, no major group has claimed that the right of public access should be defined by law (it is today mentioned but not defined in legislation, besides the "residual" perspective noted above). On the contrary, as this is a question of a tradition, bound by judgement and regional variations, any law would probably limit the right of public access instead of preserving or widening it. Nevertheless, there are good reasons to discuss the need to be more explicit with regard to the traditional basic core of the right, without trying to make clear or absolute demarcations.

It is important to note that the "free space" left for the right of public access is restricted and its value reduced not only by economic, privacy, and conservation concerns, but also by noise, crowding, and landscape exploitation. Also, the increasing "industrialization" of agriculture and forestry makes it physically more complicated to traverse a landscape on foot. Even though counter-strategies are now being developed in order to give greater weight to conservation and aesthetic perspectives, the trend remains consistent with the ongoing process of specialization.[15]

Another aspect of the limitation of the right of public access caused by the specialization of the landscape is the reduced access to "free nature"—the landscape which to a large extent follows natural rhythms in time and space. In addition, the human priorities controlling the landscape are consistent with increased production and consumption levels. This further specialization of the landscape (including special areas set aside and arranged for recreation purposes) will probably form an increasingly important aspect of the right of public access in the future, and therefore also of everyone's perception of nature and environmental issues (Figure 1).

Figure 13.1. Restrictions On The Right Of Public Access To The Countryside

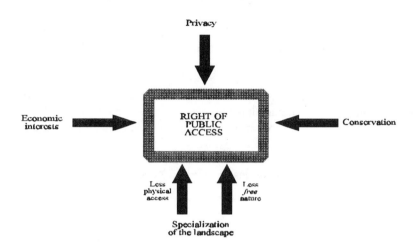

Source: Klas Sandell, "Perceptions of Landscapes: Perspectives on Nature," in *Views of Nature: Report from Two Seminars in Solna and Stockholm, Sweden, October 22-23, 1991* ed. Lars J. Lundgren (Stockholm: The Swedish Environmental Protection Agency and the Swedish Council for Planning and Coordination of Research, 1993), 46-61.

Three Eco-strategies of Outdoor Recreation

It is common to identify a dichotomy of *domination* and *adaptation* with regard to human views and use of nature. A similar division with regard to regional development has been suggested using the concepts of functional and territorial development. An important aspect of the dichotomy between functional domination and territorial adaptation is that various aspects of social integration are brought into focus with the human-ecological issues. Another important aspect of this approach is the tradition of highlighting the time-space dimensions and the landscape perspectives of development and environmental issues.[16] It seems reasonable to conclude that the content of, and potential for, a more territorial development is to a large extent a question of permanence. Three economic development/ecological strategies, or eco-strategies, capture these concepts well.

The eco-strategy of *domination* is understood as the principle of trying to adapt nature to humans as far as possible. With the help of technology and exchange with other regions, society tries to free itself from the local landscape and its resources. The eco-strategy of *adaptation*, by contrast, represents an endeavour to adapt to the local physical and cultural environment. The strategy of adaptation, however, contains features which are quite different, and a division into two sub-categories is appropriate.[17] *Active adaptation* seeks to raise the productivity of local landscapes with the help of technology. It accepts changes in the landscape, but still takes as its point of departure the local territory. The strategy of *passive adaptation*, in contrast, is sceptical of raising the productivity of landscapes and suggests human subordination to nature. All eco-strategies carried out in practice are composed of various elements that more or less could be linked to the three different eco-strategies described above.

Analyzed in the context of the three eco-strategies, the current living situation for most urban residents in the Western industrialized world falls mainly under the domination of nature perspective. Basically, three eco-strategies with regard to outdoor recreation can be identified (Figure 2).

Figure 13.2: Three Eco-strategies of Outdoor Recreation

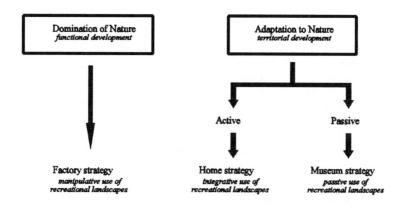

In the eco-strategy guided by the domination of nature theme, the out-of-doors is oriented towards the activities *per se*. Special areas, equipment and organizations are established for specialized outdoor activities. Long distance travelling and heavy use of material resources are often involved. It could be argued that the landscape is looked upon as a *factory* for the production of adventure. In the eco-strategy based on active adaptation, the interest is directed towards the characteristics of the local natural, seasonal and cultural landscape. But the eco-strategy of active adaptation also involves a direct utilization of the landscape, such as collecting firewood, fishing, and hunting. Outdoor recreation is one, among many, locally integrated aspects of a *home district*. Also, in line with this eco-strategy we will find many of the current attempts of eco-tourism and small scale locally-based nature-oriented recreation efforts where the tourist is introduced to a "home district."

In the ecostrategy based on passive adaptation, recreational activities are characterized by passive amusement without any deeper integration in the local nature and culture besides the special feature visited. Typical activities include bird watching and enjoying the sights and smells of wildflowers. The landscape is looked upon as a *museum*—a strategy well-known in the case of national parks and other protected places. If such activities are further detached from local natural features, the eco-strategy may take on the shape of a factory perspective.

Towards Sustainability in Outdoor Recreation?
A public understanding of local traditions and context is probably crucial for the long-term acceptance of an effective environmental policy.[18] Territorial affinity is perhaps a necessary mental prerequisite for environmental engagement and a deep human-ecological understanding (seen as a part of a sustainable attitude towards nature) could to a large extent be a function of living in immediate contact with one's local environment. It seems reasonable to assert that the nature of both public access and physical landscapes play a crucial role in the formation of such values. Using the three eco-strategies, we can assess the dilemma of outdoor recreation, sense of place, public access and sustainability as follows:

A main problem with the *factory* approach—which makes tourism and recreation seem incompatible with sustainability—is its heavy use of fossil fuels. Another problem is its tendency of "delinking" the outdoor activities from their original context of a more or less natural landscape, such as in the case of climbing walls or swimming in wave pools indoors. Looked upon as participation in sports activities, this could perhaps be seen as a positive development. But looked at from the perspective of the human relationship with the environment, this trend promotes a further functional specialization of people's relationship with nature.

The *museum* eco-strategy of passive adaptation poses additional problems for the modern phenomenon of outdoor recreation. Special (recreation) places and special (leisure) time is devoted for the urban population to visit landscape views, historical artefacts and natural beauty. But humans are here only temporary visitors, who do not utilize nature in any active way. This detached perspective of an industrialized society is perhaps a main reason for the following reflection by Gigliotti in his article "Environmental Education: What Went Wrong? What Can Be Done?"

> *What I am proposing is that environmental education has produced ecologically concerned citizens who, armed with ecological myths (e.g., that people are separate from the environment and all human impact on the environment is bad), are willing to fight against environmental misdeeds of others but lack the knowledge and conviction of their own role in the environmental problems.*[19]

The *factory* and *museum* transformations of the landscape for specialized recreation often push aside local popular out-of-doors activities. But here the right of public access tradition probably has had an important moderating role in Sweden. In line with the support of *one's home district,* local populations often oppose landscape exploitation for tourism purposes along the *factory* and *museum* perspectives—unless they are developed "from below." This is often seen as an outdated rural and "backward" perspective in light of the current global specialization process, but it is important to remember the often argued close linkage between local adaptations and sustainability.

Perhaps, then, the Nordic tradition of the right of public access is one of the most sustainable combinations and balances of eco-strategies with regard to outdoor recreation in, and for sustainability. Especially its elements in line with the eco-strategy of *one's home district* involving popular and non-specialized activities in a cultural landscape could be of great importance in the endeavour for sustainability. Indeed, McIntyre has claimed that the challenge for the Swedish community is to maintain and expand "freedom of access" and thereby take an international lead in demonstrating strategies to retain traditional rights of access in these increasingly divisive times.[20]

Notes

1. Financial support from the Swedish Council for Planning and Coordination of Research, and the Royal Swedish Academy of Sciences, is gratefully appreciated. The questions dealt with in this article are also discussed in Klas Sandell, "Access to the 'North'—But to What and for Whom? Public Access in the Swedish Countryside and the Case of a Proposed National Park in the Kiruna Mountains," in *Polar Tourism: Tourism in the Arctic and Antarctic Regions,* eds. Colin Michael Hall and Margaret E. Johnston (Chichester: John Wiley and Sons, 1995), 131-145. All quotations from sources in Swedish have been translated by the author.

2. With regard to the right of public access, see, e.g., Kevin T. Colby, "Public Access to Private Land: Allemansrätt in Sweden," *Landscape and Urban Planning* 15 (1988): 253-264; Tage Wiklund. *Det Tillgjorda Landskapet: En Undersökning av Förutsättningarna för Urban Kultur i Norden* [The Artificial Landscape: An Exploration of the Preconditions for a Urban Culture in the Nordic Countries], (Göteborg: Korpen, 1995); Björn Tordsson, "Friluftslivets Mytologiska Rötter" [The Mythological Roots of the Out-of Doors], in *Naturkontakt och Allemansrätt: Om Alla Människors Rätt till Naturkontakt,* ed. Klas Sandell (Örebro, Sweden: University of Örebro, 1996), 9-25; for current details with regard to the limitations of the right of public access, see Bertil Bengtsson. *Allemansrätten: Vad Säger Lagen?* [The Allemansrätt: What Does the Law Say?] (Stockholm: Naturvårdsverket, 1994); and for examples of the tensions between different interests, see, e.g., Sandell, 1995, op. cit. For an international overview, see e.g., Norman McIntyre, "An International Perspective on Access to Nature," in ed. Sandell, op. cit., 1996, 27-42.

3. With regard to out-of-doors and leisure in twentieth century Sweden, see, e.g., Klas Sandell and Sverker Sörlin, "Naturen som Fostrare: Friluftsliv och Ideologi i Svenskt 1900-tal" [Nature as Fosterer: Outdoor Life and Ideology in Twentieth Century Sweden], *Historisk Tidskrift* No. 1 (1994): 4-43 and Lena Eskilsson, "Fritiden: Om Fritidens Idé och en Utställning i Ystad 1936" [Leisure: The Idea of Leisure and an Exhibition in Ystad 1936], *Tvärsnitt* 17, No. 4 (1995): 16-29.

4. With regard to out-of-doors and wilderness in North America, see, e.g., Peter J. Schmitt, *Back to Nature: The Arcadian Myth in Urban America* (New York: Oxford University Press, 1969); Alan Ewert, and Steve Hollenhorst, "Risking It on Wildlands: The Evolution of Adventure Recreation," *Journal of Environmental Education* 21, No. 3 (1990): 29-35; Max Oelschlaeger, *The Idea of Wilderness: From Prehistory to the Age of Ecology* (New Haven and London: Yale University Press, 1991); Alexander Wilson, *The Culture of Nature: North American Landscape from Disney to the Exxon Valdez* (Oxford: Basil Blackwell, 1992); Mark Blacksell, "Wilderness and Landscape in the United States," in *Leisure and the Environment: Essays in Honour of Professor J. Allan Patmore,* ed. Sue Glyptis (London and New York: Belhaven Press, 1993), 266-276; Donald Worster, *The Wealth of Nature: Environmental History*

and the *Ecological Imagination* (New York and Oxford: Oxford University Press, 1993); but also cf. William M. Denevan, "The Pristine Myth: The Landscape of the Americas in 1492," *Annals of the Association of American Geographers* 82, No. 3 (1992): 369-385.

5. Björn Tordsson, *Perspektiv på Friluftslivets Pedagogik* [Perspectives on the Pedagogy of the Out-of-Doors], (Bø i Telemark, Norge: Telemark Distriktshøgskole, 1993).

6. Statistics Sweden, *Leisure 1976-1991: Living Conditions*, Report No. 85 (summary in English), (Stockholm: Statistics Sweden, 1993, p. 154 and p. 395).

7. Joachim Vogel, *Leva i Norden, Levnadsnivå och Ojämlikhet vid slutet av 80-talet* [Living in the Nordic Countries: Living Standards and Inequality at the end of the 1980s], (København: Nordiska statistiska sekretariatet, Nordisk statistisk skriftserie, No. 54, 1990), 125.

8. Björn Hettne, "The Future of Development Studies," *Forum for Development Studies*, No. 1-2 (1994): 41-71; Dwight Barry, "Looking for Home: Bioregionalism and the Reinhabitation of America," *Trumpeter* 12, No. 2 (1995): 79-83; Gerhard Bahrenberg and Marek Dutkowski, "An Ecoregional Strategy Towards a Fault-tolerant Human—Environment Relationship," in *Human Ecology: Fragments of Anti-fragmentary Views of the World* ed. Dieter Steiner and Markus Nauser (London and New York: Routledge, 1993), 285-295; William M. Adams, *Green Development: Environment and Sustainability in the Third World* (London and New York: Routledge, 1990), xiii.

9. See further about this definition of nature in Klas Sandell, *Ecostrategies in Theory and Practice: Farmers' Perspectives on Water, Nutrients and Sustainability in Low-resource Agriculture in the Dry Zone of Sri Lanka* (diss.) (Linköping, Sweden: Linköping Studies in Arts and Science, No. 19, 1988); and with regard to the relation between contact with nature and environmental engagement; see further, Klas Sandell, "Friluftsliv och Miljöengagemang" [The Out-of-Doors and Engagement in Environmental Issues], in *Natur og Friluftsliv i Byens Nærmiljø* (København: Nordisk ministerråd, Tema Nord, 1996:518), 51-64 and the references given there.

10. Bengt Sahlberg, Halvar Sehlin, Lars Vidén, Anders Wärmark, "Tourism in Sweden," in *The National Atlas of Sweden: Cultural Life, Recreation and Tourism*, ed. Hans Aldskogius (Stockholm: National Atlas of Sweden Publishing, 1993), 80-91.

11. Ingemar Ahlström, *Allemansrätt och Friluftsvett: En Bok för Friluftsfolk om Konsten att Umgås med Natur, Markägare och annat Friluftsfolk* [The Right to Public Access and Environmental Awareness: A Book for Out-of-Doors People about the Art of Relating to Nature, Landowners and other Out-of Doors People], (Stockholm: Liber, 1982), 76.

12. Bo Rosén, *Allemansrätt: Allemansskyldighet* [The Public Right to Access: Public Responsibility], (Stockholm: Rabén & Sjögren, 1979): 13.

13. *För en Rikare Fritid. Ett Diskussionsunderlag* [For a More Rewarding Leisure Time: A Discussion Paper], (Stockholm: Sveriges Turistråd, Landstingsförbundet, Svenska Kommunförbundet, 1990): 16.

14. Staffan Westerlund, *EG:s Miljöregler ur Svenskt Perspektiv* [The Environmental Regulations of EU from a Swedish Perspective], (Stockholm: Naturskyddsföreningen, 1991), 143.

15. Cf. Claes Bernes, *The Nordic Environment: Present State, Trends and Threats* (Copenhagen: Nordic Council of Ministers' Nordic Environment Report Group, Nord, 1993: 12).

16. For examples of parallels and further references, see e.g. Sandell, 1988, op. cit., 47-54.

17. Sandell, 1988, op. cit. Also see further in, e.g. Klas Sandell, "Sustainability in Theory and Practice: A Conceptual Framework of Eco-strategies and a Case-study of Low-resource Agriculture in the Dry Zone of Sri Lanka," in *Approaching Nature from Local Communities: Security Perceived and Achieved*, ed. Anders Hjort af Ornäs (Linköping, Sweden: EPOS, Research Program on Environmental Policy and Society, Institute of Tema Research, Linköping University, 1996), 163-197; and focused on out-of-doors, Klas Sandell, "Ekostrategier, Humanekologi och Friluftsliv," [Ecostrategies, Human Ecology and the Out-of-Doors], *Humanekologi: Meddelande från Nordisk Förening för Humanekologi* 14, No. 3/4 (1995): 11-22.

18. Cf., Robert D. Putnam, *Making Democracy Work: Civic Traditions in Modern Italy* (Princeton, New Jersey: Princeton University Press, 1993).

19. Larry Gigliotti, "Environmental Education: What Went Wrong? What Can Be Done?" *Journal of Environmental Education* 22, No. 1 (1990): 9-12.

20. McIntyre, 1996, op. cit., 41.

CHAPTER FOURTEEN

SOUNDS OF SILENCE?

THE DISPUTE OVER SNOWMOBILING IN THE SWEDISH MOUNTAINS

KURT VIKING ABRAHAMSSON

The Swedish mountain environment is sensitive to the disturbance from the noise of motorized vehicles, especially snowmobiles. The number of registered snowmobiles in Sweden increased from 28,500 in 1975 to 190,000 in 1996, two-thirds of them being registered in the three northernmost counties. During this period, conflicts between skiers and other non-motorized recreation-seekers and the "motorized" population have flared up regularly. This paper is based on the snowmobile traffic in an area in Norrbotten county during Easter, the peak season of the year.

In the fall of 1995 the conflict over environmental disturbances caused by snowmobiles was particularly intense, and their right to use the mountains as an open arena for recreation was questioned seriously. New legislation is now under way which proposes to regulate snowmobile traffic to limited areas and certain routes. These proposals are heavily attacked by the local residents who use their vehicles to get to fishing lakes, and to venture up mountain ridges to socialize over a cup of coffee. The proposals are said to favour people from the outside, i.e., urbanites and recreation seekers from the coastal areas. A central question which follows from this conflict is: who "owns" the mountain environment, and who should control this natural resource—the state or the local community? The paper ends with a proposal for "sound-scaping," the process of delineating and setting aside certain *S-designated areas* (S for Sound and Silence), where silence is to be preserved for the enjoyment of people and wildlife.

Background
Because of government reluctance to impose restrictions when the number of snowmobiles was still manageable, the northern part of Sweden experiences an intensive off-road traffic during the season with a snow

cover. Snowmobiling has grown to be a major source of disturbance to the non-motorized recreation-seekers, especially in the subarctic, high mountain area along the Norwegian border. In 1996 the number of registered snowmobiles had increased to 190,000, which should be compared to 80,000 in Finland and 40,000 in Norway.

Snowmobiles in Sweden have, with some restrictions, free access to privately owned land as well as public land, as long as it is snow covered. Because of the rapid increase in the number of snowmobiles, and a greater awareness of the detrimental effect of noise disturbance upon the environment and other recreation-seekers, a government committe[1] now suggests the establishment, or enlargement, of restricted areas, in which recreational snowmobiling will be forbidden, or allowed only on certain trails. The proposal has been met with firm political opposition, especially in the communities along the mountain range in the northwest. It is fair to say that snowmobiling has become an important part of the rural lifestyle in the interior of northern Sweden. According to one study, "attempts from the central government to restrict the use of snowmobiles is seen by many people in the north as just another imposition in an alleged long history of exploitation and negligence of the region."[2]

The different attitudes towards the right to use the land are at the bottom of the debate over the use of snowmobiles. The Swedish attitude of free access to the land has its roots in the traditional Public Access Right, or the *allemansrätt*, which, translated literally, means "Every Man's Basic Rights." The Public Access Right allows the public usufruct rights to private and public properties for travelling, picking wild berries and mushrooms, and even a few nights of camping, as long as no damage occurs. According to a Government committee report in 1962, the *Naturvårdsutredningen* (the Nature Protection Investigation), travelling is allowed "by foot or by skis, and also by bicycle, horse or kick sleigh," but not on a motorized vehicle. It was thought that public opinion felt that snowmobilers' public access rights be the same as for skiers. In 1975, the Parliament passed a law confirming this interpretation, giving snowmobiles full Public Access Right. The Swedish rules stand in sharp contrast to the more restrictive Norwegian and Finnish legislation. In Norway, off-road motor traffic on ground or on ice-covered water is *prohibited*. Exceptions can only be given to non-recreational traffic. In the northernmost county, Finnmarks fylke, and in some municipalities in Troms fylke, even recreational driving is accepted, but only on routes that have been permitted by the landowners concerned. In Finland, off-road driving with motor vehicles is allowed *only by permission* of the landowner. Thus, while the Swedish legislation emphasizes the rights of motor vehicle drivers, the Finnish legislation stresses the landowners' rights, and the Norwegian legislation gives priority to the rights of third parties (i.e., skiers), even at the expense of the landowners' rights to use their own property for recreational snowmobiling.

The environmental disturbances caused by snowmobiling are considerable. The two-stroke engines used are very inefficient, which means that a large part of the fuel passes directly to the exhaust pipe and the environment. Under heavy use, such as pulling a sleigh uphill, about fifty percent of the fuel passes unused. About thirty percent of the total carbon hydrogen emission (i.e., 7,200 tons of CH, and 9,600 tons of CO) in the three northernmost counties in Sweden is attributed to snowmobiling. This includes the total area of the counties, not just the snowmobile trails in the mountains. Most snowmobiles are noisy, and the vehicles can be heard several kilometres away on mountain slopes and lake ice. This is of serious concern to many recreationists, since the Scandinavian mountain region has until recently been one of the few remaining silent wildernesses in western Europe. In addition to the disturbance to the wildlife—many of the endangered mammal and bird species have their breeding grounds in the mountains—and the reindeer herds, a confrontation with recreation seekers of the non-motorized type is now mounting. This study will concentrate upon noise-related disturbance caused by snowmobiles, and the call for silent areas in the mountains.

Noise Propagation from Snowmobiles

The snowmobiles in use today can be heard over long distances, especially over hard, flat surfaces such as frozen lakes or mountain slopes in spring, when the snow surface is glazed by repeated melting and freezing. A brief discussion regarding noise levels, and especially the spreading and attenuation of sound is needed as a background for a noise disturbance-model and a proposal for noise-free or silent areas. The noise level is commonly expressed in decibel units (dB). The scale is logarithmic, and an increase in the noise level one hundred times is expressed by a 20 dB increase. The current noise limit for a new snowmobile, measured at a point 7.5 metres from the vehicle at acceleration, is 85 dB. A proposal from a Government committee sets the limit at 82 dB starting in 1998, and at 80 dB starting in the year 2000. A study on sound propagation from snowmobiles was made in the Tärna mountains in Västerbotten county at three locations which are quite representative of the average high mountain terrain during the first days of May.[3] The period from Easter to the first week of May is the peak time for snowmobiling in the Swedish mountains. The days are long, the weather often sunny, and the crusty snow freezes during the night and is ideal for snowmobiling during the morning hours, forming perfect conditions for driving out to a fishing lake ten to forty kilometres away!

Sound recordings were made on a ski trail while a snowmobile was driving back and forth at a constant speed at distances between 10 and 300 metres from the trail. There was no wind during the recordings. The peak level drops from over 80 dB at 10 metres to around 50 dB at 300 metres. What is more interesting for the present study is the duration of the peak level. While the peak level lasts for less than 3 seconds at the 10 metre distance, it continues for 35 seconds at 160 metres and stretches out to one minute at the 300 metre distance. It can be said that the sound level *decreases* by 9.5 dB per doubling of distance from the source, but the *duration* of the peak sound level actually *increases* by fifty percent per doubling of distance.

The main contribution to the decrease in peak sound level with increasing distance from the source comes from the divergence of the sound energy, i.e., the spreading out of the sound energy from a point source. The rest of the attenuation (decrease in sound), termed "excess attenuation," depends mainly on weather conditions and ground cover characteristics. For example, loose deep snow absorbs sound, but a hard ice surface deflects sound.

Wind and temperature variation with increasing height above the ground combine to either enhance or inhibit sound propagation. When the receiver is upwind from the source, one may encounter excess attenuations of 30 dB or more (i.e., a large percentage of the sound is lost before it reaches the receiver). When the receiver is downwind from the source, however, sound propagation is improved relative to still conditions, and a greater amount of sound reaches the receiver. Temperature inversions, characterized by increasing temperature with increasing height above the ground, favour sound propagation. During the winter, temperature inversions occur often, especially in mountain valleys, where cold air collects on the valley floor during calm nights.

In summary, the main disturbance from a snowmobile is not from the momentarily high sound peaks heard at a short distance from a passing vehicle, but rather the long duration of sound levels around 50 dB at distances 300 metres or more from a passing snowmobile. Since both snowmobile and cross-country skiing trails usually follow the low, sheltered terrain along valley bottoms, separating the snowmobile trail with its traffic from the skiers by a few hundred metres does not lessen the disturbance or avoid annoyance reactions in the skiers. It is not the peak level at close range that is the problem, but the lingering dull roar of snowmobiles which can echo between the walls of narrow ice-crusted valleys, especially during the morning hours with a temperature inversion, that causes the greatest disturbance.

A Snowmobile Noise Disturbance Model

The annoyance reactions of humans related to sound exposure have been thoroughly investigated in the establishment and enlargement of airports. Investigations show that the extent of annoyance is related to noise level and the overflight frequency. An *annoyance* is defined as a feeling of displeasure associated with a condition which the individual believes has an adverse or negative effect upon his/her well being, momentarily or in the long term. With exposure to a single noise event, such as the passing of a snowmobile while skiing in the absolute silence of a mountain valley many kilometres from the nearest road, the momentary reaction is defined as an *acute annoyance.*[4]

When a group of people is exposed to noise events over a long period of time, a certain part of the population will experience *chronic* annoyance. The acute annoyance due to a single exposure is often directly related to the intensity of the stimulus, whereas the chronic type is more dependent on *extra-expositional factors*, such as the time of the day, expectations of undisturbedness, age and sex. The annoyance reaction, or the response to noise from passing snowmobiles, can be explained through a model (Figure 1). Starting from the noise/sound emitted from the machine, and filtered through the terrain/landscape, the dose evokes a response in the individual, which is related to "built in" personal characteristics.

Figure 14.1 Snowmobile Noise Disturbance Model

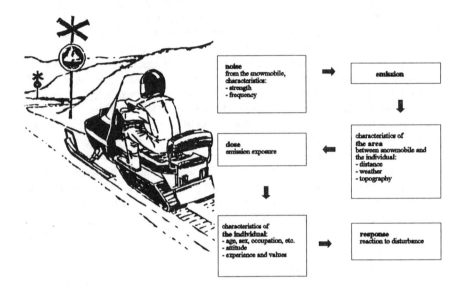

The model has not been tested, but a study on air traffic in the Swedish mountains shows that the first parts in the model, from the noise emitted to the dose received, can be calculated.[5] The *response*, which is related to individual characteristics, is much more difficult to predict. If the exposed population consists of skiers on a mountain-slope far away from roads, the most clearly expressed annoyance reaction will be expected from individuals who reside in large urban areas. They are there to enjoy the open, uncrowded wilderness, where only the mating calls of ravens and the burred sound of a ptarmigan rip through the silence. This group will attain the chronic annoyance level at least for a time, and possibly forever. It is also on these individuals, the "outsiders" with differing attitudes and values, that the snowmobiling groups in the mountain communities turn their anger and frustrations.

It should also be made clear, as has been mentioned before, that it is *not the decibel-levels* that are at stake. The mere presence of a few snowmobiles circling at a distance in a valley or up and down the slopes can provide enough constant noise to seriously annoy individuals who have already established their attitude from previous occasions. However, a high decibel-level does not exactly improve the situation.

How common then is the snowmobile traffic in the Swedish mountains? Is the traffic concentrated to certain parts of the terrain, or along specific trails and valleys? Let us turn next to a rather thorough study that was done in order to find out the geographical extent of snowmobiling in a typical mountain area.

Location and the Extent of Snowmobiling Activity

The snowmobile activity in the Arjeplog mountains in Norrbotten County has been mapped during the peak spring season.[6] The snowmobile owners, mainly from the coast and the nearby communities, were asked to mark on maps the exact routes they used during the Easter holiday. The lines showed the routes followed, and the thickness of the lines indicated the relative intensity of use, i.e., the number of snowmobiles and the number of trips made. The routes were marked from six starting point locations along the so-called "Silver Road," leading from Arjeplog to Bodø in Norway. The centre of the activity was about 25 kilometres east of the Norwegian border. Several hundred snowmobiles were transported to the area on trailers, and the owners, with families and friends, had their sleeping quarters mainly in caravans parked along the main highway and on some secondary roads. Some also rented cottages, or had their own cabins by a lake shore. Every morning the rush was on, since many were competing for the same fishing spots on the lakes, and an early start was necessary. The roaring machines, many of them pulling sleighs with children and older relatives, took off in many directions. Peace settled upon the area for some hours, until in the afternoon the snowmobiles could be heard again, now moving at a somewhat slower pace, heading back for dinner and a social evening at "the base." The pattern of tracks followed valleys and low terrain passes over to fishing lakes in most cases, but other parts of the landscape were also used.

The effect upon a non-snowmobiling skier in the area was obvious. Was the situation described in this study unusual? Is this the ordinary way for people to use the Swedish mountain area during the spring season? Admittedly Silver Road is an area with a heavy concentration of snowmobile activity, but similar activities are found at about a dozen other places along the mountain range. The high mountains areas that are reached by good roads, in some cases the main highways leading across to Norway, experience the heaviest pressure from snowmobiles. The snowmobile season starts in February, the activity increases in March, peaks in April, and continues into May in the northern mountains. The activity is, of course, most intense during the weekends.

Parks of Silence

In 1993, a conference on "acoustic ecology" was held in Banff, western Canada, under the title "The Tuning of the World." The title was taken from Robert Murray Schafer, who also coined the concept of "soundscapes." The idea of developing a soundscape with "S-designated" core areas will be discussed towards the end of this chapter. But let us first look at some facts about noise and silence in the landscape.

Staffan Westerlund, an expert on Swedish environmental law, points out that the public has *no right* to silence.[7] Noise itself is defined by those who are disturbed, and producing sounds that can be regarded as a disturbance, or noise, is allowed as long as it is not forbidden. As has been mentioned earlier, there are regulations on how many decibels a snowmobile is allowed to emit, measured at a distance of 7.5 metres. As long as the level is below 85 dB (in 1996), Swedish citizens are supposed to be satisfied. However, not all are satisfied. As "noise" can be defined as all unwanted sound, there are in principle two ways of solving the problem of being disturbed, or annoyed. Either one teaches people how to love the sound of a snowmobile, or one must do something to reduce or eliminate the noise. The first method might not work very well in Sweden anymore. The number of Swedes who love the sound of a snowmobile may be increasing, but probably not as a percentage of the general population. Rather, the percentage of Swedes who would like to get rid of snowmobiling completely is increasing. (Even the snowmobilers themselves would like to lower the sound level, as it is a nuisance when riding on or behind other snowmobiles).

In nature, creating and emitting sounds have always been used as methods for *demonstrating presence* or for staking out a territory. Who has the right to demonstrate power over a territory in the mountains? Or maybe the question is as follows: is there a social hierarchy in this power struggle, or a struggle between centre and periphery? It appears that the majority of the residents in the northernmost communities feel that a minority living in towns along the coast and in the Stockholm-area are trying to impose their attitudes regarding snowmobiling upon the local residents of northern communities. The outsiders are usually not interested in snowmobiling, but instead in downhill and cross-country skiing. The "downhillers," who tend to stay on the slalom-slopes, close to roads and hotels, are not disturbed by the snowmobile activity. The problem is found among the group of people who go on day trips and longer expeditions between huts along marked ski-trails. The latter group would like to experience the total silence of wilderness, and not be disturbed by convoys of roaring snowmobiles.

As has been pointed out, the basic principle is that the mountains are open to everybody to use. Snowmobiles sharing the area with people opposed to this activity naturally opens the prospects for a land use conflict. We can define this conflict as an *"open-access tragedy-of-the-commons type"* of environmental problem, or a commons-type natural resource problem. The snowmobilers are free to use the land, and they pay no fee to the landowners. However, the third party involved, the silence-loving skiers, are not free to choose *not to hear* the snowmobiling activity. In Norway the sanctity of the rights of the third party, i.e., skiers and wildlife, is given the highest priority. That is why snowmobiling as a general rule is forbidden.

One possibility of at least partly solving the problem would be to set aside sound-disturbance-free areas in the mountains. We already have so-called "K-designated"—"K" as in "*kultur*" (culture)—buildings and parts of the built environment in Sweden. In developing a "soundscape," i.e., planning for zoning towards that goal, some mountain areas could be "*S-designated.*" "S" would stand for Sound and Silence, and indicate that silence must be preserved, not only for the benefit of humans, but also for wildlife. There are today twelve areas in the mountains where unlimited snowmobiling is forbidden, the so-called "*regulation areas.*" The total area included is about 23,000 square kilometres. To this should be added national parks and other nature reserves where snowmobiling is forbidden. The total area with restrictions at present is shown in Figure 2.

Figure 14.2: Parks of Silence or Snowmobile Restrictions

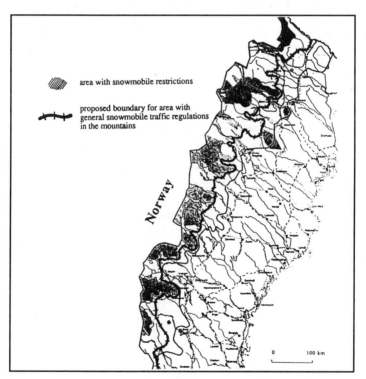

The government committee proposal for sustainable development in the mountains, which during 1996 was circulated for comments to a great number of bodies concerned, is trying to extend the regulation area by another 3,000 square kilometres, including four new "protected" areas. The protected areas are generally located in remote places, far away from roads, and thus they are not much frequented by non-motorized recreationists. However, an important point should be added: snowmobiling is allowed on more than 2,000 kilometres of trails, marked as snowmobile routes, that pass through the regulation areas. These trails are often adjacent to skiing trails. The areas are therefore much more disturbed by snowmobiles than the map would indicate.

S-designated areas should be established within the protected areas on a few localities along the mountains, for example in two areas in each of the three northern counties. S-designation would mean that snowmobile traffic would be totally forbidden (no trails). This would establish silent wilderness areas, where recreationists on foot or skis would be allowed, where wildlife would be better protected, and where reindeer herding would be possible as before. One difficulty in locating these S-designated areas is that they must be located relatively close to a road, in order to be accessible on foot or skis. They cannot be located in the most remote part of the established regulation areas.

The freedom of the local inhabitants in the mountain communities would not be much infringed upon by establishing these S-designated areas, as they would not be located in the most highly frequented areas close to good fishing lakes. But they would have to be large enough to ensure the wilderness experience that more and more people are looking for in the crowded, growing urban areas of Europe.

Notes

1. Department of the Environment, Statens Offentliga Utredningar, *Hållbar Utveckling i Landets Fjällområden* [Sustainable Development in the Mountain Regions] (Stockholm: SOU, 1995), 100.

2. Lars Hultkrantz and R. Mortazavi, "Optimal Institutions for Regulation of Public Access to Private Property: Some Problems in Snowmobiling Regulation," *Umeå Economic Studies No. 396* (1995).

3. Kurt V. Abrahamsson, "Snöskotern och Bullerutbredningen - En Preliminär Studie" [The Snowmobile and the Diffusion of Noise], in *Snöskotern och Människan* [The Snowmobile and People], Report No. 5 (Umeå: Department of Geography, Umeå University, 1974).

4. R. Rylander et al., *Annoyance Reactions from Aircraft Noise Exposure* (Stockholm: Institute of Hygiene, Karolinska Institutet, 1979).

5. Kurt V. Abrahamsson et al., *Flygtrafik i Svenska Fjällen* [Summary: Air Traffic in the Swedish Mountains], Report SNV PM 1285 (Stockholm: Naturvårdsverket, 1980).

6. The raw data of the results of the study are in the possession of the author. Only the general conclusions are reported here.

7. Staffan Westerlund, "Rätten till Naturens Tystnad" [The Right to the Silence of Nature], in *Svenska Ljudlandskap, Om Hörseln, Bullret och Tystnaden* (Stockholm: Institute for Future Studies, 1995).

Part III

Voices from the Margin

CHAPTER FIFTEEN

MEN WITHOUT BOSSES

ENCOUNTERS WITH MODERNITY IN THE LOGGING CAMPS OF NORTHERN SWEDEN, 1860-1940

Ella Johansson

The forest industry in northern Sweden is very closely connected to the rise of nineteenth century industrial capitalism. British free trade and the invention of steam driven saw mills caused a boom in the logging industry which by the 1860s had become Sweden's major industrial branch. Logging was also at the centre of the rapid transformation of Sweden from a peasant society to a modern industrial State, the rural loggers soon representing the largest segment of the Swedish labour force. By 1916, one report estimated that logging employed 150,000 to 200,000 men each winter season. These men lived largely in the sparsely populated rural parts of the North and were usually employed in agriculture when not logging. Workers in other industrial branches numbered at the most 20,000.

Logging thus occupied most men in Northern Sweden, or Norrland, during the winter. They lived in logging camps at varying distances from their homes, isolated for months in very poor living conditions. In these camps, it is possible to study the very direct and sudden encounter of a fairly traditional peasant society with the capitalist world market. This account examines the ways in which some of the features of the modern ideology, such as individualism, freedom, and egalitarianism were articulated in the new everyday practices of the logging camps. The themes explored include the loggers' organization of private and public space in the cabins, their food preparation and consumption, their daily working routines and their story-telling in the evenings.[1]

In the nineteenth century the northern coniferous forest region differed from the south in many geographical, social and cultural respects. In particular, there was an absence of feudalism, which contributed to the emergence of a yeoman-like freeholding peasantry in the narrow river valleys of the north. By the mid-nineteenth century, the northern woods surrounding these valleys were divided into private property, and most of the land was sold or let on long-term lease to various lumber companies. With this development, men's logging became an important source of income.

The logging companies organized the exploitation of the forests through a contracting system. This involved the local peasantry as well as migrant workers. The farmers were the contractors. They were in most cases responsible for housing and provisioning the labour force, as well as hauling the logs to various shipping points. The organization of the huge labour force, within an area comparable to that of a normal European state, was thus left to the local peasantry.

For the felling, each farmer hired a couple of landless men, sometimes his own sons or farmhands, on a piece-work basis. Logging can here be seen as a form of wage labour with hierarchical chains of employers and workers. This represented the paternalistic peasant household organization moving into the forest. The traditional cooperative mechanisms of the households also served the massive capitalist exploitation of the woods. The men of a local community often joined together and travelled to remote hauling jobs for big contracts. The traditional cultural practices, like geographical mobility and economic versatility and adaptability, were thus used to make this massive exploitation a relatively smooth and painless transformation.

Individualism and Autonomy

Yet the workers did not interpret the situation as one of continuity and traditionalism. The cutters saw themselves as free and independent entrepreneurs who were selling their labour power to cut and transport logs for negotiated prices. The demarcation lines between workers and employers were blurred, while the relationship between the amount of work and its monetary value was very clear. The relationship between the sleigh-hauler and the cutters was reduced to the cutters' duty to deliver a sufficient quantity of logs to be transported. A sleigh-hauler had no authority over "his" cutters, nor any power to influence the way they chose to organize their work. The cutters worked individually and on their allotted felling areas, deciding their own working hours. They used their own tools which were sometimes designed or redesigned to suit their own tastes and preferences. Their professional skills and abilities were highly individualized. Personal techniques and deftness were attained over years of practice in a delicate interplay between a man's body and his simple tools. Skill was in no way a shared knowledge which could be transferred between the men. Yet one part of the traditional male social role was the ability to navigate in, interpret and utilize the forest landscape, as well as the ability to use the axe and other tools associated with cutting wood. The working capacity, and thus earnings, varied widely from one logger to another, but also within an individual's life span.

Two central themes which differentiated logging from other jobs were a strong sense of individualism and freedom. These two concepts—which are of course problematic to use—reflect the modern ideology of western individualism. But there was also a basis for this in the traditional society, which was based on self-sufficient and autonomous households, as well as cooperation and claims for absolute fairness in the interaction between households. A competitive work ethic and ruthless self-exploitation was also part of this identity. When industrial logging started, this peasant society was in many ways altered by an increase in population and mounting competition for land. This increased the social stratification and cultural hierarchies of the *bygd*, and in this respect modernity made local peasant communities seem feudal in a way that had little historical precedent. The egalitarian, atomized and competitive culture of the winter camps thus made for a sharp contrast to the populated and cultivated open landscape of the *bygd* in the river valleys, whose social hierarchies and cultural complexities the men returned to during the summers.

Money and Commodities

Agricultural work in the *bygd* was partly paid for in clothes and food. When times were bad, the payment was arbitrarily set by the farmers who often saw it as charity. In logging, by contrast, the payment was set, at least for the season, and the idea of a fixed price per piece was seen as very just, making the cutters feel more like entrepreneurs than wage labourers. The landless felt that with logging came a long-desired liberation from the oppressive paternalistic hierarchy of the *bygd*. This view was shaped out of people's creative blend of everyday experience and the symbolism of the forest.

The loggers' memoirs are in part texts packed with figures. Many loggers had an amazing memory of the payments (or prices, as they called them) from different seasons and also the measures and quantities of the logs they cut. Much effort was put into understanding and judging different systems for turning logs into money. During work and evenings in the cabin the men were constantly occupied with calculating, extrapolating and estimating their expected incomes, the cost of the provisions and the use of the final income. The "prices" and the passbooks of the contracting system were important in creating a culture of rationalization and calculation. Furthermore, money was the pattern for forms of thought creating commensurability between what were previously not comparable categories. Money as a measure of value gave rise to a new paradigm of abstract, quantifying and universalizing thought. Money in the form of the contracting system was seen as creating social relations which were more neutral and less arbitrary than those of the late peasant society of the *bygd*.

The wealthy farmers, however, were perturbed by these new possibilities for the small farmers and the landless. They criticized them for living in greed and luxury, having sold their souls to Mammon or the devil. The food the landless consumed in the forest was one cause of the accusations that they wallowed in luxury and money.[2] Owing to the structures of production and distribution, the only accessible food at the haulings—for those who could not bring their own domestically-produced food—were the imported world market commodities of wheat flour, bacon, sugar and coffee, all purchased at high prices. In the *bygd* this was food reserved for holy days and feasts, and it appeared very annoying and immoral in the eyes of the farmers that the poorer a person was, the more of these products he would consume at the haulings. The criticism had religious dimensions, and logging was in some areas done by migrant workers as the local population believed that a logger could not go to heaven.

In most cases the landless people's answer to these accusations was an intrepid affirmation. They cheerfully took on the role of defendants of modernity from the attacks of people they felt to be backward peasants of a petty *bygd*. The landless "saw nothing sinful in making honest money and keeping the family with American pork and bread, coffee and sugar." The wheat flour dumplings the loggers fried in the pork dripping became the symbol of commodification. The religiously coloured battle over the wheat flour can be interpreted as the symbolic expression of a change in "belief system." This was not only a process of secularization, but one of new beliefs in money "making the world go round" and the blessings of commodification with its clarification of social relations.

Alienation as Utopia

The most dramatic sides of the social conflict were, however, reserved for life in the *bygd*. In the everyday life of the haulings, where farmers and landless lived very close in cramped cabins, conflicts and differences in status were understated for the benefit of an egalitarian spirit. The strong headed and authoritative male camp cooks characteristic of the Canadian logging camps were absent in the Swedish cabins.[3] The cabin, however small and crowded, was invisibly divided into small private areas or one-man households, each conceptually forming a complete unit of production and consumption. Each man not only had his own food supply, but also his own coffee pot and cast-iron pan. The pattern was one of no exchange or sharing. There was one prominent exception to this: the storytelling in the evenings. In spite of the great economic inequality and social tension among the inhabitants, a strong cohesion could prevail in the log cabin, and this seems somehow connected to the practice of exchanging stories.[4]

At the haulings the acknowledged good qualities of a person was the ability to produce plenty of logs and to be entertaining in the small talk and storytelling of the evenings. A farmer or farmer's son could thus easily find himself in a lower position to a stranger or tramp who owned nothing but a deft hand and a sharp tongue. The storytelling tradition of the loggers was focused on this inversion of the social order. The heroes of the stories were precisely those tramps who were of the lowest kind in the social classification of the *bygd*. Although they were often dirty and homeless alcoholics dressed in rags, they could still turn out to be the ones who cut the largest number of trees, made the most money, and were the most skilful at storytelling and answering back to the foresters with witty repartee.

A moral code concerning what human beings truly are and how the relationships between them should be, was communicated in the stories. The stories identifying "tramps" as ideal workers can be interpreted as statements emphasizing the inner human qualities hidden under a coarse surface, repelling those who judged humans only by their external appearance. The image of the farmer, on the other hand, illustrated the superficiality of ascribed status and accumulated wealth. In the life of the *bygd* during the summers, people were different in terms of social position. In the forest, they were all the same, regardless of whether they were farmers or landless. This moral and political ideology of equality, autonomy and tolerance communicated in the stories and in the performance situation, was perhaps the most important aspect of the praised freedom of the forests, which made the landless see wage labour as liberating.

The work processes and organization of everyday life were, as we have seen, extremely atomized and individualized. Anthropologists tend to look for specific phenomena for clues to cultural unity: food sharing, rituals, initiations, rules of order and cleanliness. In all these aspects of life, however, the logger managed to organize themselves in such a way as to deny the meaning of culture and collective community. By this I do not wish to claim that the loggers' world was not culturally organized, but rather that it was done as if it wanted to deny the existence and relevance of culture. Thus loggers differ from many other egalitarian cultures in their avoidance of sharing and cooperation. The most striking part of their culture was their consistent avoidance of anything that could contribute to the formation of a hierarchy among them. The forest's traditional "meaning" could in some ways be a background for this ideology of individualism and freedom.[5] Even if forest use was strictly regulated and a scarce good with respect to grazing and haymaking for cattle, in most other aspects it was a free resource, open to individuals self interest. With respect to hunting and tree felling, for example, one can find attitudes very far removed from an ecological concern or humble reverence. Hunters seem to have seen it as a duty to shoot at anything they found. Some evidence indicate that they believed that neglecting to take whatever prey they found would be to challenge the exuberance of nature. An informant of the 1930s stated: "In no way did we bother to save the females and the young. There was total war against everything. And because of that, the forest was full of life. Ever since they started with game management and such devilry, game has started to go extinct."[6] The felling of trees was also an easy-going enterprise. Logging increased grazing and haymaking resources. Forest fires were sometimes lit in order to promote livestock breeding. It seems that in contrast to the thoroughly organized and well kept *bygd*, the forest was more of a *res nullis* space, open to individual projects.[7]

In the forest, the modern culture provided a breathing space from the increasingly stratified rural societies where the loggers spent their summers. The actual content of the egalitarian log cabin spirit was of course constantly negotiated, and it seems that the landless had the best bargaining position, the forest being "their" territory, historically associated with equality and "wealth through work." As the loggers perceived it, the men in a camp were not connected to each other through any economic, hierarchical or other organizing device except the shared shelter. They were in the camps on an egalitarian and autonomous basis and they were also temporarily disengaged from their households. This meant not only the absence of women, but also the old patriarchal structure.

To understand the role of the forest as breathing space, one has to reconsider the division of private and public spheres that exist in modern society. In northern Sweden, a home was not a private space. Anyone could enter at anytime, without knocking, and spend a few hours sitting in the kitchen. The farm kitchens were the places where people met for a chat and a game of cards in the evenings. And even if the family was alone in the house there was no place for individual privacy. If there was any need for this—and some people seems to have felt that need—the solution was to stroll in the forest, poaching or trapping, and this is another way in which the forest symbolized freedom and individualism. The lonesome poacher is also a character which stories are told about, and whether heroic or awkward, he is a person who has turned his back to society and its demands.

The loss of quality and enchantment—which is often seen as the deplorable products of capitalist society—was in the loggers' case a utopian project moulded in the everyday culture of the log cabins. The simplicity and transparency of monetary relations set the paradigm for the culture. Like money, men were basically of the same value. Just as money could buy anything, so men had the right to put any personal content into their individuality. Even the complex multi-purpose forest of traditional society was turned into an industrial forest of trees, to be standardized into logs of certain dimensions and price. The trees and allotments were thus a form of currency.

At the haulings men shared and communicated the juvenile—men without women—masculinity, in which the values of modernity were embedded, where property was neglected in favour of inner personal qualities, where men were singular atoms with a simple form of social organization. In the *bygd* during the summers, by contrast, the married men's form of masculinity dominated, with the desire for head-of-household and landowning respectability.[8] Yet these values met in the idea of freedom in the forest: freedom from paternalistic domination, freedom to build up an economic base so as to become one's own boss and a head of a household.

The disembeddedness of the uniform and pure dimensions of tree-production and monetary relations contrasted with the more complex relations of the traditional society but was not seen as destituting and alienating. The formalized and atomized social relations at the haulings formed a kind of free zone or breathing space from the increasing pressures of modernity on the *bygd*.

Modernity or Tradition?

The division of society where the landless were connected with the forest and farmers with the *bygd* was thus negotiated through logging. The forest came to be connected with modernity and "modern" phenomena such as money, rational calculation, achieved status, men's equal value, tolerance, individualism, and romanticism, while the *bygd*, from the logger's point of view, was associated with traditionalism, paternalism, prejudice, ignorance, inherited status, and the suffocating backwardness of rural life. Still this did not correspond in a simple way to disparate class values held by two social groups. It seems that in many cases the same small farming people shifted between the two value systems as the winter and the haulings annually gave way to summer and agriculture.

The capitalist exploitation of the woods, and even modernization itself, were in fact such a rapid and effective success because they happened to fit so well with the traditional values and ambitions that the *bygd* held towards the forest. This applies to what perhaps can be described as a Northern Swedish version of the "frontier spirit," where the forest was a vast resource which in different ways was exploited and colonized in the formation of new households. The ruthless self-exploitation and the harsh living conditions to which the workers subjected themselves is perhaps another aspect of this frontier spirit of traditional society. Logging was seen more or less as a hunting expedition, an occasional and profitable excursion, the prey of which was brought back to the *bygd* and used to produce or reproduce the household. Life at the haulings was never looked upon as a permanent part of the real and continuous life, and thus the harsh conditions prevailed year after year as a permanent makeshift.

The road to modernity taken through the Norrland forest presents a highly complex process of adaptation, resistance and change, very different from the grand narrative often used to describe the industrial transformation of Sweden from peasant villages to factory towns. In the contracting system, modern citizens were very efficiently cultivated out of the soil of a peasant society, which was well suited for such a crop. Yet, in the local system, logging and modernity were merely used to reproduce the traditional values of the household's self-sufficiency and the small farmers' life-world.

Notes

1. This article is based on Ella Johansson, *Skogarnas Fria Söner. Maskulinitet och Modernitet i Norrländskt Skogsarbete* [with a summary in English: Free Sons of the Forest: Masculinity, Modernity and Forest Work in Northern Sweden] (Stockholm: Nordiska Museets Förlag, 1994). The empirical contextualization, which is an important feature of the study from which this chapter is taken, cannot be given justice here. For articles in English elaborating parts of the thesis in greater detail, see Ella Johansson, "Beautiful Men, Fine Women and Good Workpeople: Gender and Skill in Northern Sweden, 1850-1950," *Gender and History* 1, No. 2 (1989); "Free Sons of the Forest: Storytelling and Construction of Identity Among Swedish Lumberjacks," in *The Myths We Live By*, eds. Raphael Samuel and Paul Thompson (London: Routledge, 1990); and "Flat as a Pancake: Consumption, Commodification and Cosmology in 19th Century Swedish Logging," Paper presented at the 5th Interdisciplinary Conference on Consumption, 1820, August 1995, Lund, Sweden. The major source for the everyday life of the loggers of this study was the Collection of Loggers' Memoirs at the Nordic Museum, Stockholm. This collection consists of about 200 autobiographies or recorded life stories of loggers based on a list of questions posed in the late 1940s. The sources also include various other life story interviews, autobiographical material, state records and surveys of the loggers' living conditions.

2. Johansson, 1995, op. cit.

3. Ian Radforth, *Bushworkers and Bosses: Logging in Northern Ontario 1900-1980* (Toronto: University of Toronto Press, 1987), 99-102.

4. Johansson, 1990, op. cit.

5. Sverker Sörlin, "Frihetens Hemman på Jorden," *Skogsforskning* 2, No. 8 (1992).

6. From the Ethnological Archives, the Nordic Museum, Stockholm, EU 19800.

7. Hans Marks, "Elkhunting and Household Production: Images of Equality and the Right to Animals," mimeographed paper presented at the Conference "Man and the Animal World," Nijmegen (1988); Ella Johansson, "*Bygd och Obygd: Landskapstillägelse och Social Skiktning*' [Countryside and Wilderness: Landscape Appropriation and Social Stratification], in *Moderna Landskap: Identifikation och Tradition i Vardagen*, eds. Katarina Salzman and Birgitta Svensson (Stockholm: Natur och Kultur, 1997).

8. Johansson, 1989, op. cit.; AnnKristin Ekman, *Community, Carnival and Campaign: Expressions of Belonging in a Swedish Region* (Stockholm: Almqvist and Wiksell, 1991).

Chapter Sixteen

HEGEMONY AND GENEALOGY
Managerialist Discourse in the Forests of British Columbia

Russell Janzen

In casual conversation with environmentalists or trade unionists, one is likely to hear that forestry workers have a "natural interest" in sustainable forestry or that the two movements are "natural allies."[1] Yet in British Columbia (B.C.) since the early seventies a series of high profile disputes over logging and wilderness preservation indicate that affinities are more problematic than natural. There are differences that seem intractable enough that a cease-fire in the "war in the woods" may appear to be the best that can be hoped for.

I will argue, however, that while there are clearly ways in which forestry workers and their unions reproduce a managerialist discourse of "clearcut culture"[2]—which includes opposition to wilderness preservation and alternative forms of logging—it does not entail an indifferent assimilation of a forest industry agenda. The genealogy of forestry workers' resistance in the workplace may be read as a neglect of "nature" and an acquiescence to technology, but forestry workers also retain an ambivalence about the forest. Although they supported the predominant role of the forest industry in the postwar B.C. political economy, the hegemony of clearcut culture thus constructed is neither uncontradictory nor complete. It might be difficult to anticipate, but a common labour-environmental politics of sustainable forestry is not ruled out simply by virtue of forestry workers' role in the industry.

The Forest as Work Place
Spatial practices structure the forest as simultaneously "natural" and "social." For loggers the forest is a "working forest," a workplace. Spatial practices in which forestry workers are engaged enable and constrain their "common sense" of how things are done and what are the limits to and possibilities of doing things differently. Loggers in particular, and forestry workers in general, participate in a process that embodies a partial perspective on

forest ecology. The labour process in which they are engaged is essentially limited to "harvesting" (and processing) what in this context is simply a resource differentiated in type and scale not only from the ecological processes that make up a forest but also from the social processes that constitute timber as a "resource."

Loggers on their own cannot change the nature of the forest landscape and their inhabitation or inscription in it inasmuch as it is defined also by their relation to their employers, i.e., to forest capital. The issue is about class, not in the usual sense that environmentalists are accused of being middle-class but in the sense that it is about the relationship between workers and the forests *and* that between workers and forest capital. No analysis of forestry workers' interpretations and representations of "the forest" would be complete without an understanding of this class dimension.[3]

This double encounter occurs at the level of "relations *in* production" and "relations *of* production."[4] In this I am relying on the Marxian interpretation of capitalist production. The labour process is the means by which "nature" is transformed through human action and a valorization process through which capitalist social relations operate to define forests as a "resource," a commodity for "exchange value." It is the equivocal character of these simultaneous scales and processes that permits us to see how forestry workers might reproduce the hegemony of clearcut culture while continuing to resist domination by forest capital at the genealogical level.

Genealogy and the Labour Process

Clearcut or managerialist discourse is not unequivocally about the control of nature: it is also about the control of labour. It is in this genealogy of control and resistance by workers that we find the resistance and ambivalence of forestry workers.

For forest capital there is an incentive to structure the labour process so that the extraction of timber is less susceptible to the variability of natural conditions. According to Richard Rajala, early logging operators in B.C. were dependent, especially in yarding, "on the physical and conceptual skills of loggers to cope with the variable conditions of the coastal environment." He argues that "Timber capital sought domination over nature not as an end in itself, but to secure control over the activities of those they employed."[5]

Rajala argues that the forest became a factory with the introduction of overhead logging systems in which the "fundamental advantage...lay in their capacity to restructure timber capital's relationship to the environment, and in consequence, with workers." The adoption of overhead logging methods permitted the elimination of positions, deskilling and, with other developments, speed-ups.[6]

The consequences were destructive. Not only did overhead systems permit the extension of clearcutting beyond the previous technical and capital cost limits of other methods of skidding and yarding, but it damaged or destroyed younger growth.[7] Moreover, the "high speed at which the logs and rigging now travelled not only brought greater regimentation to the labour process, but also made logging one of the most hazardous of industrial operations."[8] Dangerous conditions were only made worse by the competition between crews encouraged by managers.[9]

Rajala reports that the Industrial Workers of the World (IWW) was critical of the job displacement effects of technology, but resistance by the IWW and later industrial unions in the inter-war period was unsuccessful. There were several reasons, but largely due to the transience of the workforce and the open shop.[10] By the time that the International Woodworkers of America-Canada (IWA) had managed to secure industry-wide representation and collective agreements, technological change was not an issue causing conflict of any particular scale.[11]

There are several respects in which it might be seen that loggers were being incorporated into the commodified version of forestry. First, the competition between crews in which they would seek to out-produce each other, and gain more pay, might be regarded as an example of the kinds of work floor games that Michael Burawoy argues reinforce the capitalist forms of hegemony in the workplace—facilitating the mutual reinforcement of relations *in* and *of* production.[12] Second, such conditions can easily be imagined as being of the type that would foster interpretations of the forest as a hostile entity, harbouring danger at every turn. The IWA continues to maintain that the choice between clearcutting and selection methods of logging is a question of occupational health and safety.[13] Third, the introduction of newer more sophisticated mechanical methods of production, while they permitted the replacement of skilled positions with others that could be paid at a lower rate, nevertheless did not eliminate skill but recomposed it and the hierarchy of logging positions. Perversely, some positions owed their status to the initiatives of forest capital.[14] Finally, Ken Drushka suggests that the increasing mechanization of the inter-war period also required a more stable crew and workforce.[15]

Clearly what is at stake is equally a question of the social relations *in* and *of* production, but one can easily see a kind of displacement in which relations with the employer become displaced into the realm of relations with the forest.[16] The clearest example here is the way in which the danger of the job of logging is reduced to dangers represented by the forest. But the organization of work and the introduction of new technologies are themselves contributors to the safety or danger of the job, and these are management decisions that are contested or negotiated with workers, i.e., a question of social relations.

Even so, the loggers' apparent acquiescence is more ambivalent and provisional than all of this would indicate. First, struggles over control of the labour process are also about skill. Interests in preserving skill may be less about worker control over the forest than about forestry worker relations with the forest. Despite recomposition of the labour process and skill, forest capital's goal of complete control over nature is never quite complete. For example, one logger interviewed for *Battle for the Trees* claimed that over a thousand decisions a day had to be made independently by the workers.[17] That is, the labour process was *still* dependent on workers' intimate knowledge of complex forest conditions.

Second, there is some sense in which the ecological complexity of forests is recognized. Loggers also express regret at destructive forestry practices that foul salmon-bearing streams, reduce the capacity of regeneration and squander valuable timber, even if they may be hesitant to criticize the ugliness of clearcutting itself.[18]

Third, forestry workers are not without their aesthetic sentiments too. There may be discerned some sense of awe and respect for the impressiveness of the trees and forests being cut down. That would seem to extend to what forestry workers seemed to see as the use of the extracted wood—for use value rather than exchange value. There is also a sense in which the forestry workers recognize in the decline of the impressive stands of trees of old growth a decline also of loggers as a breed.[19] And living close to wilderness is part of the appeal of being a forestry worker for many.[20]

I have been referring to loggers, but they cannot stand in for all forestry workers and the IWA membership is not all loggers. The common interests of functionally different occupational categories of union members are articulated "dialogically" through the union.[21] Even were loggers to be conscientious worker-ecologists, the forest as a workplace is not a matter articulated by them alone. Even aside from the role played by forest managers, the union membership includes sawmill workers whose relation with the forest is different from that of the loggers. This does not make the union a pernicious influence, but it does produce unintended consequences in which the sin, if such there is, is one of omission rather than of commission.

Hegemony and the Sustained Yield Policy

According to Myrtle Bergren, efforts to organize in the logging industry (she devotes little attention to milling) were up until the mid-thirties based on grievances over specific issues like working and living conditions. In an open shop, and apart even from the hostility of employers, organizations were hard to maintain, localized, and tended to ebb and flow with the business cycle. In the middle to latter thirties there was a movement away from organising on the basis of grievances to one based on policy—an organising policy and a policy for the entire industry. That is, the genealogical scale of struggle in the workplace was more explicitly linked to the scale of hegemony and the character of the provincial forest industry and economy.

In 1936 the first attempt to establish a presence across the woodworking industry occurred when the Lumber Workers Industrial Union joined forces with the Carpenters and Joiners to establish the Lumber and Sawmill Workers Union, AFL. In 1937 it was granted a charter as District 1 of the IWA-CIO. The type of policy advocated for the IWA (by local 1-80, Lake Cowichan) included an economic, social and political program for the lumbering industry, labour relations legislation, social programs and, notably, a forestry program. In 1937, the provincial government passed the Industrial Conciliation and Arbitration Act, which recognized unions and set the stage for the IWA to play a role in a postwar compromise over forestry and economic development.

Coincidentally perhaps, but certainly fortuitously for later developments, a 1937 B.C. Forest Service report from F.D. Mulholland indicated that the rate of reforestation was insufficient to keep pace with the rate of exploitation.[22] The eventual response, the British Columbia Royal Commission on Forest Resources, issued its report on forest tenure and forest policy in 1945. The commission endorsed a "sustained yield" policy and recommended new forms of tenure that were presumed to ensure that the forests would be better "managed." Tree Farm Licences with longer tenures (twenty-five years with virtually automatic renewal) were to enable private planning that corresponded to the new policy (planning for sustained yield on Public Sustained Yield Units was to be administered by the Forest Service). The favoured agents were integrated companies with substantial holdings already and mills for which they wished to assure adequate supply.

Whether or not the IWA endorsed consolidation and centralization, it has supported the predominance of large integrated firms. For example, the IWA supported the 1978 Forest Act because the union assumed that large integrated firms provided job security, high wages and better working conditions, as well as being easier to organize.[23] Rajala suggests that a kind of "social contract" was constructed around the sustained yield policy. In return for long-term access to timber supplies, forest companies were to adopt the principles of sustained yield, reinvest their money and assure long term employment and community stability, as well as adding to the provincial treasury.[24] Resource rents were distributed to forestry workers, making them and their unions "partners with industry."[25]

There are two respects in which this would prove problematic to forestry workers and their unions. First, the condition under which gains from greater productivity would be shared out to forestry workers also meant more intensive use of capital—and labour shedding, and more intensive and extensive exploitation of the forests. On the one hand, new technologies in milling that permitted "closer utilization" meant that forests could be exploited more intensively, extracting more material from the same quantity of timber. On the other hand, other technologies in yarding and transportation made previously "inaccessible" stands of forest fair game. The implication of these trends for forestry workers is that workplace specific job loss would obtain if there were not a continuous expansion of supply and production. As well, regional job loss occurs as economies of scale are sought by centralizing or consolidating milling.

Second, the advantages of the quality of B.C. wood eventually would be lost as the rate of logging exceeded the calculated rate of regeneration: it would force the reduction in the annual allowable cut. Closer utilization standards and greater accessibility provided an increase in inventory that would be used to justify increasing levels of harvesting. The problem is that policy was essentially based on a hewers of wood model in which intensive growth is based on the combination of extensive and intensive harvesting rather than on the reinvestment of profits and rent into value-added manufacturing. Any kind of interruption of that version of intensive growth would itself result in a decline of employment in the forest industry.

The success of the sustained yield policy was, as Rajala suggests, dependent on the willingness of the State to enforce it. Yet forest companies were able to convince the government and forest service to raise the annual allowable cut to unsustainable levels.[26] And, as environmentalists point out, there was an unwillingness to apply or enforce rigorous standards of practice and performance. In fact, one may interpret the complicity of the government and the forest service as simply another way of ensuring the goals of its development and employment policies were met: by ensuring that the full costs of production were not borne by the forest industry, their share of the rent on resources was assured.

It is a rather messy dilemma for the IWA. While it has been critical of the industry and the government for bad management and for failing to foster the development of added-value manufacture, its dilemma is in important respects self-made. Having endorsed the utilization of technology to increase productivity and thereby the living standards of its membership, the IWA coincidentally endorsed the continued expansion of the harvest by virtue of the fact the political economy of forestry in B.C. in the post-war period did not include investment in value-added production. To maintain a stable, much less increasing, number of members the level of the harvest had to increase. But clearly the IWA cannot today opt for continued expansion or a simple perpetuation of the logic which will eventually exhaust the forests. And it is not clear that second growth plantations are adequate replacement sources or that even closer utilization standards will supply surrogate forms of growth.

What has the IWA done? Essentially, I think it has tried to defend what is left of the "social contract" of sustained yield. It fought a strike in 1986 against contracting out, and since then sectoral bargaining has been under attack as members of the employers' association have opted out. Likewise, Share B.C. is a community-based attempt to preserve the social conditions of sustained yield policy. It isn't necessary to argue that the IWA has "bought" the industry line about having changed its stripes and that it is now diversifying into value-added manufacturing to realize that in some respects the IWA can't afford not to maintain the line. But, as both environmentalists and former IWA members alike argue, the IWA policy has unwittingly pitted its members against each other and, in the name of solidarity, directed internal contradictions outward.

Conclusion

The social and ecological conditions that underwrote the hegemony of sustained yield policy, or clearcut culture, no longer exist. As Ernesto Laclau and Chantal Mouffe have argued,[27] hegemony is at best provisional and the task of articulating common themes or purpose from among a number of discourses fraught with uncertainty. Stuart Hall has stated that the working class can have contradictory interests and pulls. And while this kind of contradictory positioning imposes limits on the possibility of framing a discourse that incorporates those that may be deployed by the labour and environmental movements, "there is no prescriptive law as to which will prevail."[28] It is an open question whether or how forestry workers could be assimilated to either an alternative environmental discourse or to a redefined version of sustained yield.

There are in B.C. indications that differences between labour and environmentalists are not intractable. Environmentalists no longer as a rule argue simply for preservation. From the early eighties there has been a steady movement to extend the critique of forestry in B.C. to include forest practices and tenure and the structure of the industry. And whatever its limitations the attention to jobs displays a broader perspective on issues of land use and sustainability. Environmental organizations have also endeavoured to undertake more practical displays, by negotiating the South Island Accord with an IWA local, joining with labour and First Nations in the Tin-Wis coalition, and more recently by showing solidarity with striking workers at MacMillan Bloedel's Port Alberni mill.

If the IWA were taken as the "paradigm" of the labour movement, the move towards an accord on environmental issues would be less than auspicious. But other forest unions in B.C., the Pulp and Paper Workers Union and the former Canadian Paperworkers Union, have been more progressive on environmental issues and both have participated with environmental organizations in campaigns like the Georgia Strait Alliance. Perhaps the distinguishing feature about these two unions and what I perceive as a not-yet-prominent trend among trade unions is the move to disassemble the boundaries between workplace and community and workplace and environment. This is largely on the basis of the relationship between occupational health and safety and community health issues. As yet a similar "deconstruction" is not to be discerned within the IWA, except perhaps in the local environment committees that have not been coopted as forms of enterprise corporatism.

Whether any of this is cause to be hopeful of a convergence is difficult to say. In any case, it is less likely that alternative discourses of sustainability will emerge as the result of a convergence. As Roger Keil and Laurie Adkin have argued, the articulation of such a discourse through dialogue and debate between the labour and environmental movements will entail change not only for their respective discourses, but in the movements themselves.[29] Such a process could hardly be easy; frequently it is a matter of fumbling around in the dark. Some of the darkness has been due to hasty or sweeping generalizations. This paper is a small contribution towards shedding some light.

Notes

1. With forestry workers I here mean those who work in all sectors of the forest sector, such as harvesting, silviculture, and wood processing.

2. Michael M'Gonigle distinguishes between "wilderness-as-clearcut" and "wilderness-as-cathedral" paradigms, see, "The Stein River: Wilderness, Culture and Human Survival," Alternatives 15, No. 3 (1988), 12-21.

3. Cf. John Bellamy Foster, "The Limits of Environmentalism Without Class," *Capitalism, Nature, Socialism* 4, No. 1 (1993), 11-41.

4. Michael Burawoy, *The Politics of Production* (London: Verso, 1985), 29.

5. Richard Rajala, "Forest as Factory: Technological Change and Worker Control in the West Coast Logging Industry, 1880-1930," *Labour/Le Travail* 32 (1993a), 79-80.

6. Ibid., 94-95.

7. Richard Rajala, "The Receding Timber Line: Forest Practice, State Regulation, and the Decline of the Cowichan Lake Timber Industry, 1880-1992," *Canadian Papers in Business History, Volume 2* (Victoria: Public History Group, University of Victoria, 1993b), 184, 186.

8. Rajala, op. cit., 1993a, 101; See also Ken Drushka, *Working in the Woods: A History of Logging on the West Coast* (Madeira Park: Harbour, 1992), 129.

9. Rajala, ibid., 99.

10. See Rajala, op. cit., 1993a, 90, 101; Drushka, op. cit., 102; Myrtle Bergren, *Tough Timber: The Loggers of British Columbia—Their Story* (Vancouver; Elgin, 1979), 30ff; Gordon Hak, "British Columbia Loggers and the Lumber Workers Industrial Union, 1919-1922," *Labour/Le Travail* 23 (1989), 67-90.

11. Rajala, op. cit., 1993a, 78.

12. Michael Burawoy, *Manufacturing Consent: Changes in the Labour Process under Monopoly Capitalism* (Chicago: University of Chicago Press, 1979).

13. See "International Woodworkers of America," *Forest Policy* (1989), 8.

14. Rajala, op. cit., 1993a, 98.

15. Drushka, op. cit., 99.

16. Cf. Thomas Dunk, "Talking About Trees: Environment and Society in Forest Workers' Culture," *Canadian Review of Sociology and Anthropology* 31, No. 1 (1994), 14-34.

17. John Edginton, director/producer, "Battle for the Trees," (Gillian Darling, Jack Silberman, George Johnson, producers) (Montreal: National Film Board of Canada, 1993).

18. Ibid.; For a look at how forestry workers in Northern Ontario address the problematic character of "natural," see Thomas Dunk, "'Is it only Forest Fires that are Natural?': Boundaries of Nature and Culture in White Working Class Culture," in this volume.

19. Dunk, op. cit., 1994, 21-22.

20. Dunk, op. cit., 1994, 20; Patricia Marchak, *Green Gold: The Forest Industry in British Columbia* (Vancouver: University of British Columbia Press, 1983), 298; Jamie Swift, *Cut and Run: The Assault on Canada's Forests* (Toronto: Between the Lines, 1983), 205.

21. Claus Offe and Helmut Wiesenthal, "Two Logics of Collective Action," in *Disorganized Capitalism: Contemporary Transformations of Work and Politics*, ed. John Keane (Cambridge, MA: MIT Press, 1985).

22. Rajala, op. cit., 1993b, 192.

23. Marchak, op. cit., 61.

24. Rajala, op. cit., 1993b, 194.

25. James Lawson calls this "socred fordism"; "Triumph of the Mill: The Disruption of US Trade Law and 'Socred Fordism' in the Canada-US Softwood Lumber Dispute," paper presented to the Canadian Political Science Association Annual Meeting, 1993. See also Marchak, op. cit., 71-73.

26. Rajala, op. cit., 1993b, 194, 200-203.

27. Ernesto Laclau and Chantal Mouffe, *Hegemony and Socialist Strategy* (London: Verso, 1985).

28. Stuart Hall, "The Toad in the Garden: Thatcherism Among the Theorists," in *Marxism and the Interpretation of Culture*, eds. Cary Nelson and Lawrence Grossberg (Urbana: University of Illinois Press, 1988), 45.

29. Roger Keil, "Green Work Alliances: The Political Economy of Social Ecology," *Studies in Political Economy* 44 (1994), 7-38; Laurie Adkin, "Ecology and Labour: Towards a New Societal Paradigm," in *Culture and Social Change*, eds. Colin Leys and Margaret Mendell (Montreal: Black Rose Books, 1992).

Chapter Seventeen

"IS IT ONLY FOREST FIRES THAT ARE NATURAL?"

Boundaries of Nature and Culture in White Working Class Culture

Thomas Dunk

Culture and nature are two of the most ideologically-loaded concepts in contemporary Western discourse. It is common to perceive of the relationship between culture and nature as corresponding to the relationship between social categories; hence, the practice of thinking that culture is to nature as men are to women, or as the West is to "others."[1] Of course, the ethical and political implications of this relationship depend upon the context and the speaker. At the height of European colonial expansion the idea that indigenous people in newly discovered (from a European perspective) lands were "more natural" (or less cultured) than Europeans provided the rationale for the destruction of these cultures in the name of human progress. In post-colonial white-settler societies such as contemporary Canada, the idea that indigenous people have a special relationship to nature carries, among many whites as well as the First Nations, a positive moral and ethical connotation. European culture stands condemned for the way in which it represents and ultimately treats other cultures and the natural world. In other words, both domination and resistance utilize ideas about the natural and the cultural for ideological purposes.

An obvious example of a current dominant discourse is that which presents "market forces" as natural laws that individuals, social groups, and nations must learn to accept and adapt to. Attempts to resist or mitigate the consequences of market forces are said to be naively foolish at best and harmful at worst. According to this line of reasoning, economic and social inequality is simply the result of dispassionate economic laws, a process of natural selection which sorts and ranks us all according to our innate abilities.[2] The counter arguments invoke the concept of culture. Racial, ethnic, gender, and class distinctions, as well as the concept of market forces are viewed as cultural constructs; that is they are objects that are of human making and thus open to change.[3]

In other contexts, the concepts of culture and nature may be used to the opposite effect. Environmentalists, for example, employ ideas such as natural processes and natural limits to critique modern capitalism. We must learn to recognize and adapt to immutable natural forces to save ourselves from the baleful consequences of modern economic activities and lifestyles and/or to protect the rights of other living creatures.[4] Of course, this kind of argument is often met with one that says that we ought to use our culture, in the form of knowledge and material technology, to transform nature to meet our economic needs and desires.

All of these examples operate according to a dualistic logic. The social world is divided into two parts which are figuratively or sometimes explicitly elided to one or the other term of the nature/culture couplet. There are, however, many social groupings which do not objectively or subjectively fit neatly into these dualistic models. The way members of these groups represent how they relate to these categories reflects their ambivalence about the nature of the discourse within which debates take place and, perhaps, a way of transcending these categories. In this paper, I discuss one of these groups: the working-class in a hinterland region within Canada. Although, many of these workers are "white" and thus part of the dominant Euro-Canadian society in a region with a significant indigenous population, in terms of class and regional experiences they are not part of the urban, middle-class society which is usually intended by glosses such as "Euro-Canadian," "white" or "mainstream" society. Thus, even though at times they insist upon their difference from the local First Nations, they also frequently insist upon their difference from the so-called mainstream.[5]

I seek to illustrate the role the category of nature plays in the discursive efforts of these workers to forge a subject position in the context of current debates over land and resources. The dominant figurative associations which the culture-nature dichotomy is commonly said to carry in Western culture are questioned and, perhaps, transcended. Certainly, the idea that there is a radical distinction between at least some human intentional practices and natural processes is seen to be problematic by these workers.

Nature, Culture and Workers

The concepts of nature and culture have both been invoked to explain what dominant groups in society have perceived to be "problematic" features of the working class.[6] In the nineteenth and early twentieth centuries in Europe, workers were often seen to be lacking in culture. Debates around extending the franchise, public education, and public health all involved the idea that in some respects workers, and other subaltern groups, were "too natural." They did not exhibit the level of self-control, decorum, rationality and, more recently, political correctness that bourgeois elements (of both a left and a right political persuasion) of society considered to be desirable and indeed necessary for an orderly, productive, democratic and/or "just" society. On the other hand, workers have frequently been seen as having too much culture, especially when they attempt to resist economic transformations such as corporate restructuring, rationalization, and downsizing, or resource conservation strategies that threaten their livelihoods and communities. In these contexts, workers are said to be too wedded to outmoded lifestyles, labour practices, and expectations. They are told they must adapt to reality, cast aside their culture, so they can be reborn as flexible workers in the new leaner and meaner or more-environmentally-friendly economy. In other words, the working class is trapped in a matrix of meaning whereby no matter how the discourse goes they are indicted by it. They are either too lacking in culture to do the right thing, or they are too saturated in culture to do the right thing.

Of course, workers, like all subaltern groups, in trying to resist the forces impinging upon them often employ similar terms. Their discourse of resistance frequently reflects the influence of the hegemonic discourse which sets the parameters within which debate and contestation occurs. The contradictory ways in which the concepts of nature and culture structure dominant discourse are also evident in the way workers employ them to represent their perspective on various issues. However, they also at times refuse the dichotomies the dualistic logic of the hegemonic discourse tries to force them into.

Fire = Nature, Labour = Culture?

I want to illustrate this with a short section from a conversation I had a few days before Christmas in 1991 with a logger from a small community in northwestern Ontario. I was carrying out research on the issue of loggers' images of the environment and environmentalists. Jim (a pseudonym), a unionized logger, was driving me to see the environmental mess left in an area that had been cut over by one of the independent owner-operators who work on contract for a company well known in the region for its virulently anti-union attitudes. We were having a free-ranging discussion about environmental issues that I was recording. At one point, Jim pointedly asked me the following:

> Remember the Yellowstone Park fire? The environmentalists were all clapping because everything burned and that was natural. Why is that more natural than if it had been cut? If it burns it's wilderness but if it is cut it isn't. I just don't get it—why that one is natural and another one isn't.

In the course of my research, both in the year that I was involved in intensive interviewing and observation and since then, similar sentiments have been expressed many times, both about the specific example of the Yellowstone Park fire, and more generally about environmental policies whose goal is to "let nature take its course." In other words, from the workers' perspective a feature of environmental discourse is the idea that human intervention in natural processes should be curtailed or stopped altogether. They frequently question the dichotomy between the human and the natural that this involves.

Of course, there are a variety of ways of interpreting Jim's comments. One may simply put them down to ignorance or simplicity. It is widely understood that one of the meanings of the term natural is, in the words of Arthur O. Lovejoy, "the part of empirical reality that has not been transformed (or corrupted) by human art."[7] Thus, a forest fire, at least one not started by humans, is natural because humans had no hand in it; whereas logging consists of human intentional practice. One may want to say, then, that Jim just doesn't understand the meaning of the term nature.

It also is possible to interpret this question more cynically, as an attempt to muddy the waters by someone who, although concerned about a variety of environmental issues, is profoundly opposed to what he perceives to be the philosophy and actions of environmentalists.[8] In other words, one might read Jim's question as a coy response to those who demand greater respect for natural processes by pushing them to justify their conceptual categories. If one can push the point that there is no such thing as nature independent of some human construction of it, then one can argue that it is illogical to argue in defence of nature as if it was an objective, independent object or phenomenon. In other words, one may read this as an intelligent discursive strategy in the ongoing ideological debates about land use.

There is no doubt that loggers from forest-dependent communities have indeed established discursive strategies for use in debates about forest use. But it would be overly simplistic to explain their defence of logging as natural only in such narrowly instrumental terms. As I have discussed elsewhere, loggers in northern Ontario express many concerns about the environment including forestry practices.[9] However concerned they may be about employment and income, they do not have the mind set of the archetypal "calculating forester"[10] or working-class red-necked bigot. The environment around their communities is imbued with cultural significance that goes far beyond the fact it provides jobs and incomes. Moreover, as others have shown, the common idea that loggers and other rural dwellers are necessarily opposed to environmentalist concerns is not well supported by empirical research.[11]

Many of my informants lamented the disappearance of what they referred to as the "natural" forest. To cut a tree was said to be "a natural act" but clear-cutting was said to be unnatural. Thus, they also were willing to draw distinctions between natural acts and unnatural acts, but they did not necessarily see this division as equivalent to a dichotomy between actions carried out by humans and those in which humans played no role.

How we do and should conceptualize the relationship between the "natural" and the "cultural" is a fundamental issue, both in terms of theorizing about political ecology and in terms of the practical issues involved in resource use and conservation.[12] The Yellowstone Park fire is a well-known example that illustrates how tightly bound together are the theoretical and practical issues.

The handling of the fires was an extremely controversial issue in the summer and fall of 1988. The initial fires were ignited by lightning in June of that year. Since 1972 park officials had pursued a policy of letting "prescribed natural fires" burn themselves out as part of an attempt to reintroduce natural processes into the park ecosystem. Prescribed natural fires were fires that had been started by lightning and which posed no threat to human life or property. Between 1972 and 1988 the natural-fire program was perceived to be successful. Between 1976 and 1987 an average of about 15 lightning-caused fires a year were allowed to burn without interference. The majority burned no more than 100 acres.[13] But in the summer of 1988 a combination of drought, high temperatures, windy conditions, and, perhaps, a build up of fuel, caused either by the normal process of forest succession or the earlier practice of suppressing forest fires, led to a series of massive fires. Even though by mid-July a massive campaign to extinguish the fires was underway, close to 1,000,000 acres burned and the fires were not completely dead until November 13, thanks to autumn rains and snow.

Of course, if the fires had not been in Yellowstone Park they may not have become the media event that they did. As one of the most famous "wilderness" areas in the world, it is the focus of intense scrutiny by those concerned about the use of the environment in the U.S. Two million acres of forest were burned in the rest of the continental U.S. and some 2.2 million in Alaska that same summer. But because it was Yellowstone the policies and practices surrounding forest fires became the subject of intense interest and political significance. They also became a metaphor for the struggles between environmentalists and their opponents and these arguments condensed some of the key issues involved in the debates about the connection between nature and natural processes and human intentional action, that is the application of labour power to the natural environment.[14]

Many other environmental issues were elided with the fire controversy. One of the most contentious of these was the issue of whether or not wolves should be reintroduced into the park to help control the populations of elk and bison which had become too large. This pitted environmentalists, ecologists and park managers against ranchers. Indeed, when William Penn Mott was forced out of his position as National Park Service director because of his supposed mishandling of the fire situation, commentators interpreted this as a cover for the fact that many Western members of Congress were angry with him for his support of the wolf re-introduction scheme.[15] Other issues were involved as well. For example, the exclusion of hunters from the park. Why not, after all, let them cull the elk and bison herds if they were too large? And why not solve the problem of a build up of old forest growth and the concomitant fire threat through logging within the park? Thus, the debate over the handling of the forest fires reflected the basic issues at play in a variety of environmental controversies.

One of the central issues of debate was natural versus human regulation of the park's ecosystem. The natural-fire program in Yellowstone Park was developed in the wake of a growing awareness of the dynamic nature of ecosystems and of the role fire played within forest environments in terms of the maintenance of biodiversity and normal patterns of forest succession. The 1963 "Leopold Report" recommended that within national parks in the U.S. the ecosystems be maintained or if necessary recreated as near as possible to the condition they were in when whites arrived. In other words, parks were to be maintained or returned to what was considered their natural state and natural processes, such as fire, were to be allowed to regulate the environment. Such policies clearly reflected a wider and growing sense that human intervention into nature is not necessarily wise, if only because often we are not aware of the consequences of our actions.

These policies were always controversial, both in terms of overall philosophy and in terms of their implementation. In the case of the Yellowstone fires one of the specific criticisms was that the natural-fire policy was foolish unless human-controlled prescribed burns were carried out to remove excessive fuel build up from the first 100 years of the park's existence when all fires were supposed to be suppressed.[16] At a more general level, and the one I am more concerned with here, questions were raised about just what it means for an object or process to be natural. Several issues are relevant here.

Firstly, there is the question of how natural it is to create islands of wilderness such as Yellowstone, surrounded by environments where "development" is pretty much allowed to proceed according to the dictates of the human economy. These islands of wilderness are artificial. Indeed, it seems that the elk and bison that now live in the park were much rarer when the park was established in 1872. The large herds, especially of elk, that had built up by the 1980s, were the result of the development of the prairies and other surrounding areas, the elimination of wolves, and protection from hunters afforded by the park.

A second element of the debate surrounds the question of what is considered a natural environment and what is considered a natural fire. Some commentators pointed out that the aboriginal people who inhabited the park area prior to their expulsion by whites had already altered the natural environment both by their hunting and gathering activities and by the use of fire to drive game or to create environments more favourable to their prey. Wilbur Wood in *The Nation* asked: "Are fires set by prepark people 'natural' and fires set by Park Service people 'unnatural'?" Another critic of park policy posed the question thus:

...how 'natural' were the fires of 1988? They had burned after a century of unprecedented human activity at Yellowstone—not only the

installation of a new set of practices but also the abolition of ancient practices, including anthropogenic fire [fire set by humans], that had occurred for millennia.[17]

Similar concerns were raised around the issue of the reintroduction of wolves into the park. "Most of those favoring the reintroduction of wolves would be appalled at opening a hunting season in a national park. But are human beings any less 'natural' than wolves?"[18]

Workers, Identity and the Nature/Culture Dichotomy

These issues were debated in all the media in the summer of 1988 and well into 1989. Thus, the Yellowstone Park fire became a well-known example of the problems caused by what loggers in northwestern Ontario considered to be the naive ideas of environmentalists who, mistakenly in the eyes of my informants, imagine natural processes as relatively benign and gentle forces, and exclusive of any human element. Their interpretation of the events was, to be sure, coloured by their anti-environmentalist sentiments. However, it also hints at the fact that the radical gulf and opposition between nature and culture which is of such significance in Western culture as a whole may not have the same kind or extent of resonance among workers, at least among workers such as loggers whose labour power is expended in the primary appropriation of the product of natural forces.

The question about what is and what is not natural in the context of northern Ontario is not only a philosophical or practical question relating to environmental practice. It also resonates with issues related to the construction and defence of subject positions and group identities. The question about pre-park inhabitant's use of fire reminds us that arguments about a special relationship to the natural world are integral elements in debates about land use throughout Canada. Indigenous people's land claims struggles involve a legal element that to a certain extent is beyond the realm of everyday discourse in so far as the arguments take place in the court system and involve the seemingly arcane language and rhetoric of that venue. Outside the courts, however, the political and ideological battles have involved the argument that not only do Native people have legal rights to the land, they also have moral and ethical rights in view of their special relationship to nature. In northern Ontario, this fact is not missed by the local workers and other members of the so-called white community. They, like whites in analogous situations in other "white-settler" nations, have begun to adopt the language of tradition and of special relationships to place and the natural world to construct an identity that is outside the hegemonic understanding of the affinities between nature, culture and the identities of social groups.[19]

In presenting logging as a natural thing to do, loggers in northern Ontario not only invert the usual meanings of the categories natural and cultural. They also seek to rearrange what they perceive to be the boundaries of these categories and the figurative associations that they connote in the dominant discourse. Indeed, although they are not aware of it, my informants are thinking along lines similar to various theoreticians who are trying to achieve an accommodation between "red" and "green" thought. Much of this work has taken the form of an attempt to bridge the chasm between various environmentalist theories and Marxism. This involves several dichotomies. Firstly, Marxism's alleged Promethean disposition towards nature is juxtaposed to the arguments of deep ecologists and animal rights activists that nature has intrinsic value and rights independent of any human needs or desires. Secondly, Marxism's social constructionist perspective with regard to the concept of natural limits, as in Marx's critique of Malthus, contrasts with the idea that there are natural laws that function independently of human societies and to which human societies are or will be subjected. Another key feature of these debates is the question of how we should conceive labour power and whether there is such a thing as naturally produced value. It is worth remembering that Marx recognized that, while human labour power can be differentiated from that of animals in terms of its consciously purposeful character, it is still a matter of setting "in motion the natural forces which belong to his [sic] own body."[20] In other words, actual living labour cannot be separated into distinct realms of the cultural and the natural, despite the efforts of managerial experts to separate hand and brain. The phenomenological experience of this fact may no longer be a feature of many kinds of occupations but for at least some forest workers, and perhaps others involved in the primary appropriation of nature, it still registers.

In the last two decades or so there have been many efforts to bridge the differences between socialism and environmentalism mainly by reinterpreting Marxism so as to generate a more environmentally-friendly version.[21] The emphasis in these analyses is to think of the society/nature relationship as a dialectic; each of the terms being dependent upon and influencing the other. In Noel Castree's words, these efforts have generated,

> ...a conceptual edifice, albeit a very general one, through which Marxist theory can take nature seriously as a material entity and actor in history, without hypostatizing it as a fixed, unchangeable, universal given separate from society. In other words, it allows us to think of nature as simultaneously produced and real and active in the history and geography of capitalist societies.[22]

Of course, the loggers' discourse on nature does not have such lofty theoretical goals. Rather, the loggers are reacting to a variety of pressures acting upon them and in so doing they constitute themselves against indigenous cultures, whose "naturalness" and "traditionalism" they profoundly question, against corporate and state bureaucratic processes whose rigid and technological bent threatens their employment, and against what is perceived to be urban-based environmentalism. They do this by inscribing some of the fundamental dualisms of western culture with a new meaning. In the process, they may also open up new possibilities for rethinking key cultural concepts and for forming various social and political alliances, even if they are not aware of it.

Notes

1. For discussion of this practice see, for example, Sherry B. Ortner, "Is Female to Male as Nature Is to Culture?" in *Women, Culture and Society*, eds. Renata Rosaldo and Louise Lamphere (Stanford: Stanford University Press, 1974); Terry Goldie, *Fear and Temptation: The Image of the Indigene in Canadian, Australian, and New Zealand Literatures* (Montreal: McGill-Queen's University Press, 1989), especially pages 19-40.

2. The reification of the market is a cornerstone of neo-liberal economics. For a thought-provoking discussion of contemporary social biology see Andrew Ross, *The Chicago Gangster Theory of Life: Nature's Debt to Society* (New York: Verso, 1994), 237-273.

3. There is now a huge literature on this subject. See, for example, Ross, ibid.; Ortner, op.cit.; Edward Said, *Orientalism* (New York: Pantheon, 1978) and *Culture and Imperialism* (New York: Random House, 1994); Homi Bhabba, *The Location of Culture* (New York: Routledge, 1994); Ruth Frankenberg, *White Women, Race Matters: The Social Construction of Whiteness* (New York: Praeger, 1993); David Roediger, *The Wages of Whiteness* (New York: Verso, 1991) and *Towards the Abolition of Whiteness* (New York: Verso, 1994); Steven Maynard, "Rough Work and Rugged Men: The Social Construction of Masculinity in Working-Class History," *Labour/Le Travail* 23 (Spring 1989), 159-69; Thomas Dunk, "Culture, Skill, Masculinity and Whiteness: Training and the Politics of Identity," in *The Training Trap: Ideology, Training, and the Labour Market*, eds. Thomas Dunk, Stephen McBride, and Randle W. Nelson (Halifax: Fernwood, 1996).

4. For a recent insightful discussion of these issues see the exchange between Ted Benton and Reiner Grundmann. Ted Benton, "Marxism and Natural Limits," *New Left Review* 178 (September/October 1989), 51-86; Reiner Grundmann, "The Ecological Challenge to Marxism," *New Left Review* 187 (May/June 1991): 103-21; Ted Benton, "Ecology, Socialism and the Mastery of Nature: A Reply to Reiner Grundmann," *New Left Review* 194 (July/August 1992), 55-74.

5. This paper extends the analysis of white male working-class culture in northern Ontario presented in my *It's a Working Man's Town: Male Working-Class Culture* (Montreal: McGill-Queen's University, 1991) and "Talking About Trees: Environment and Society in Forest Workers' Culture," *The Canadian Review of Sociology and Anthropology* 31, No.1 (February 1994), 14-34.

6. There is a huge literature on these debates. I have been most influenced by the following works: Helmut Gruber, *Red Vienna: Experiment in Working-Class Culture 1919-1934* (Oxford: Oxford University Press, 1991), gives a revealing description and analysis of a left-wing attempt to improve and uplift workers; Phillip Corrigan and Derek Sayer, *The Great Arch* (Oxford: Basil Blackwell, 1985), especially the chapter on the "working class question"; and Jonas Frykman and Orvar Löfgren, *The Culture Builders* (New Brunswick: Cornell University Press, 1987), which contains an excellent analysis of how Swedish bourgeois culture was constituted in relationship to the bourgeois perception of workers and peasants.

7. Arthur O. Lovejoy, "'Nature' as an Aesthetic Norm," *Capitalism, Nature, Socialism* 7, No. 1 (March 1996, original 1927), 107.

8. See my "Talking About Trees" for a fuller discussion of northern Ontario loggers' environmental concerns, especially pages 19-24.

9. Ibid.

10. For a discussion of the origins of professional forestry's way of representing the forest see Henry E. Lowood, "The Calculating Forester: Quantification, Cameral Science, and the Emergence of Scientific Forestry Management in Germany," in *The Quantifying Spirit in the 18th Century*, eds. Tore Frangsmyr, J.L. Heilbron, and Robin E. Rider (Berkeley: University of California Press, 1990).

11. Louise Fortmann and Jonathan Kusel, "New Voices, Old Beliefs: Forest Environmentalism Among New and Long-Standing Rural Residents," *Rural Sociology* 55, No. 2 (1990), 214-232. With regard to loggers' opposition to environmentalism they say:

> *Although forest workers might be expected to hold procommodity attitudes, this effect [experience in a forestry occupation] is actually minimal because...forestry workers do not necessarily have a reasonably uniform experience. For example, some people work as casual labourers planting trees and fighting fires in order to finance an alternative lifestyle. Such temporary work does not necessarily involve or engender commitment to commodity values. In addition, some loggers oppose extensive clearcutting because they feel it threatens the*

sustainability of their livelihood. They stand with environmentalists in this opinion against others in forestry occupations, such as mill owners and timber industry executives. (p. 223)

In the region where I have conducted my research there appears to be few living an alternative lifestyle (to my knowledge this has not been studied, my comment is simply based on personal experience). However, Fortmann's and Kusel's comments on the attitudes of loggers is consistent with my findings reported in my "Talking About Trees" article. The loggers I have dealt with are anti-environmentalist but, as I have argued there, this "attitude" must be understood in the context of regional and class grievances not as a defence of industry or capital. As Foster has argued, because environmentalists have ignored the class issues a void has opened up and industry has sometimes put itself forward as the defender of workers. In the absence of any other voices speaking on their behalf, workers may at times be interpellated by this discourse. This is not inevitable, however, especially in the context of a more class-conscious environmental movement. See John Bellamy Foster, "The Limits of Environmentalism Without Class: Lessons from the Ancient Forest Struggle in the Pacific Northwest," *Capitalism, Nature, Socialism* 4, No. 1 (1993), 11-41.

12. A useful recent review of the theoretical attempts to transcend this nature/culture dichotomy is Noel Castree, "The Nature of Produced Nature: Materiality and Knowledge Construction in Marxism," *Antipode* 27, No. 1 (1995), 12-48.

13. William H. Romme and Don G. Despain, "The Yellowstone Fires," *Scientific American* 261 No. 5 (1989), 39.

14. It is also a significant statement on the cultural environment in Canada and the impact of globalization on perceptions and experiences of space and place that Canadian loggers in a small forest-dependent community would employ the Yellowstone Park fires as an example in a discussion about the environment and environmentalism.

15. For example see Wilbur Wood, "Political Fires Still Smoulder," *The Nation* (August 7/14, 1989), 162.

16. Romme and Despain, op.cit., point out that until the postwar era the policy of suppressing all fires within the park's boundaries may not have had much effect because the technology to detect and effectively fight forest fires, especially in remote regions, was lacking.

17. Stephen J. Pyne, "The Summer We Let Fire Loose," *Natural History* (August 1989), 49. Another element in this debate is that, although the initial fires of June were started by lightning, of the ten fires that consumed 40 percent of Yellowstone that summer some were started by humans. The North Fork Fire, one of the largest, was started by a woodcutter's cigarette.

18. Wood, op.cit., 163.

19. See, for example, Michele D. Dominy, "White Settler Assertions of Native Status," *American Ethnologist* 22 (1995), 358-74.

20. Karl Marx, *Capital,* Volume 1 (Harmondsworth: Penguin, 1990), 283.

21. See the articles by Benton, Castree and Grundmann previously referred to. See also David Pepper, *Eco-Socialism* (London: Routledge, 1993). Another key article, although one that comes at the issues from the perspective of a critique of eco-feminism is Donna Haraway, "A Manifesto for Cyborgs: Science, Technology, and Socialist Feminism in the 1980s," *Socialist Review* 15 (March/April 1985), 65-107.

22. Castree, op.cit., 25.

Chapter Eighteen

GREENING THE CANADIAN WORKPLACE

Unions and the Environment

Laurel Sefton MacDowell

Over the last two decades, it has been common for the media to focus on the conflict between workers and environmentalists. The "war in the woods" in British Columbia over the future of old growth forests, and the confrontations in the Temagami forest in Ontario, made national and international news. Typically, the media has portrayed land-use issues as a choice between jobs or the environment, conveying the tension between the social equity objectives of trade unionists and environmentalists' ecological goals.[1] In this chapter, I will argue that this picture is too simple. Workers are not only interested in jobs and job security. They also share a common experience with environmental groups of being pressure groups, sometimes marginalized, in a society which historically and currently has placed priority on development and often ignored both workers' needs for a secure, healthy workplace and environmental issues like biodiversity and a clean atmosphere.[2] The media stories, in focussing on workers' interest in job security, have thus ignored the labour movement's environmental policies, its experience with environmental problems in the workplace, and its occasional cooperation with community groups concerning broader environmental issues. It is these environmental struggles that I document here. I conclude, however, that while substantial gains have been made, Canadian workers face formidable obstacles in a resource dependent economy, where jobs and revenue are tied closely to resource extractive and polluting industries.

Linking Occupational Health and Safety with Broader Environmental Concerns

The Canadian labour movement has long been concerned about environmental hazards on the job which threaten the health and safety of workers. Since the 1960s, unions have called for improvements in occupational health and safety legislation, and their experience in trying to achieve a cleaner and safer work environment has led the labour movement at all levels to broaden its concern, develop policies for a healthier environment, and work with community groups to achieve such ends. Throughout the 1970s and 1980s, as unions increasingly brought occupational health and safety matters to the bargaining table, the number of strikes over such issues increased, and unions allocated more staff, time and money to reducing workplace hazards and disease.[3]

There are many examples of union action regarding occupational health and safety. One of the more significant was a strike in June 1971 by the International Chemical Workers Union against the Canadian Johns-Manville Co. Ltd. in east Toronto. It was unique in that the main issue was unsafe plant air. Several workers had developed asbestosis, and provincial safety inspectors ordered the company to install a new ventilation system to exhaust asbestos-soaked air.[4] In 1973 the Energy and Chemical Workers Union (ECWU) struck Shell Chemical in Sarnia and won recognition of joint health and safety committees and full disclosure of the chemicals used in the workplace.[5] In September 1981, the United Steel Workers of America (USWA) negotiated a contract provision with Denison Mines Ltd. and Rio Algom Ltd. to allow inspectors access to company health and safety records and the authority to shut down workplaces they deemed unsafe. The union pushed for this breakthrough on health and safety issues as uranium mine workers were exposed "to significantly higher amounts of silica dust than in other mines, as well as several types of radiation and potentially cancer-causing uranium dust."[6]

Union action has often resulted from exploitive employers who have ignored both workers' health and the environment. One spectacular case was the Robson-Lang tannery, operating for fifty years in Barrie, Ontario, before closing in 1986. Here, half the workforce (87 of 165 people), all members of the United Food and Chemical Workers' Union, had died of lung or throat cancer by 1990 from exposure to lethal substances like chromium dust. While working at the plant, the workers were unaware and the union apparently uninformed of the dangers. At the same time, the company discharged waste in excess of the legal limit into Kempenfelt Bay, on which it was located. This was in spite of municipal and provincial environment ministry officials frequently warning and threatening to lay charges against the company between 1969 and 1977. After the plant closed, and a condominium was to be built on the site, the soil proved so contaminated with chromium that it had to be removed to a landfill site before the construction could proceed. It was at this stage that the Simcoe County Injured Workers' Association finally took up the employees' cause at the Workers' Compensation Board and the case became public.[7] Through such events, unions have learned of employers past abuse of their employees' health and their similar neglect of the natural environment.

Unions have also expanded their lobbying activities for better protective legislation, tougher regulations, more information about toxic substances in the workplace and financial aid to train their members about workplace hazards to improve work environments.[8] Governments have responded by setting up inquiries like the Ontario Royal Commission on Matters of Health and Safety to which, for example, the Ontario Federation of Labour (OFL) and the ECWU have presented briefs advocating an immediate reduced exposure to asbestos, a ban on its future use and rapid action to regulate new hazardous chemicals in the workplace.[9] As such occupational health and safety issues have gained publicity and government attention, new legislation has been introduced which recognizes the worker's right to refuse unsafe work without reprisal, the right to information about work hazards, and the right to participate through joint worksite health and safety committees in resolving problems. The 1972, Saskatchewan legislation set the precedent and by the end of the 1970s, Ontario, Quebec, Alberta, Manitoba, New Brunswick and Newfoundland had passed similar legislation. In 1978, for example, Ontario amended its Occupational Health and Safety Act, and workers won the right to refuse unsafe work and to be part of mandatory joint health and safety committees. In the following three years, 435 workers exercised their rights to refuse dangerous work.[10]

In 1988, Ontario adopted the Workplace Hazardous Materials Information System agreement, a national standard for testing and labelling substances, and disclosing information and educating workers about them.[11] In 1989-90, Bill 208 introduced closer scrutiny of workplaces by the joint committees. It placed the onus for responsible occupational health and safety decisions on workers and their employers and strengthened the requirement that workers or unions select their own representatives. Joint workplace committees became mandatory in more places of work and were given new powers "to obtain information about tests of any equipment, biological, chemical or physical agent in the workplace," to consult with the employer concerning tests and testing procedures, and the controversial right to "bilaterally shut down operations under dangerous circumstances."[12] Monthly inspections of the workplace were required by the joint committees and employers had to respond promptly in writing to joint committee recommendations and provide a timetable for implementing recommendations to which it agreed. Employers in specified industries "wherever workers could be exposed to hazardous biological, chemical or physical agents" were required to establish workplace medical surveillance programs with medical examinations and tests. The bill increased the powers of government inspectors; employers were required to share more information with workers and to pay for more occupational health and safety related services. Enacted in January 1991 after intense debate inside and outside the legislature over issues like the right of certified joint committee members to stop work, expanded grounds for work refusals, and mandatory pay for workers investigating work refusals, the legislation meant that virtually all Ontario employers were required to implement and enforce an open occupational health and safety policy for their particular businesses. It ensured adequate training and better informed worker representatives and allowed "workers to act meaningfully in the workplace to protect their own health and safety."[13]

Despite improved legislation, more empowered government inspectors and joint health and safety committees in workplaces across the country, the Canadian labour movement has continued to view collective bargaining as its preferred route to achieve ongoing, lasting occupational health and safety improvements. Once a law is established, labour has used it as a basis for further negotiation because "what has been achieved in health and safety laws has resulted from breakthroughs by strong unions and sometimes by strike action," as in the 1980s when there were many walkouts and wildcat strikes over issues of occupational disease and safety.[14] The reason for Canadian unions resorting to the collective bargaining approach is not only because it works at the local level of the job. It is also because it protects unions from the effects of negative changes in legislation or loss of rights enacted by newly elected provincial governments. When, for example, workers became discouraged that the Ontario government might weaken Bill 208 and drop the work-stoppage provision, Local 1000 Canadian Union of Public Employees (CUPE) negotiated and won a stoppage provision in its contract, and this strategy was adopted in many steelworkers' bargaining sessions as well.[15] Joint occupational health and safety committees can range from small local groups without any authority to make policy or spending decisions, to larger committees with real clout. In the former case, collective bargaining supplements their work. In cases where the law is broken, and inspectors are slow or negligent, workers fall back on union negotiations.

Some unions have also gone beyond legislative lobbying by establishing their own health and occupational centres. In 1984, the Manitoba Federation of Labour established and ran an Occupational Health Centre in Winnipeg and Hamilton. Unions set up a Workers' Occupational Health Clinic for both union and non-union workers.[16] In 1993 the OFL began to broaden its focus when it pushed for protection of workers who refused to perform work that would damage the environment and the Ontario NDP government responded with an Environmental Bill of Rights which protected workers who blew the whistle on polluting employers.[17] Thus the experience gained by unions fighting occupational health and safety issues in work environments in the 1970s and 1980s, broadened to include community health and safety issues in the environment as a whole in the 1990s.

As workers linked environmental problems on the job to broader community issues, union conventions in the late 1980s adopted new policy positions. In 1988 the Canadian Labour Congress (CLC) established an Environmental Committee to educate trade unionists and forge links with environmental groups.[18] In 1989, the USWA National Policy Conference adopted a comprehensive environmental policy called "the Steelworkers' Environmental Action Plan." In 1990, the CLC convention passed a statement entitled "A New Decade: Our Future." It contained a section on "sustainable prosperity" which stated that Canadian workers were no strangers to environmental problems as "in our workplaces, the health and safety problems our members face are on the front lines of the fight for a cleaner environment" and workers in their communities have joined other Canadians in reacting to problems of air pollution, waste disposal, and degradation of public recreational resources. It recommended tougher environmental standards and penalties for their violation, as well as protection and compensation for workers whose jobs were affected by environmental reforms.[19]

In 1991, the first Canadian Auto Workers (CAW) conference on the environment[20] established an Environment Fund, and Local 636 in Woodstock Ontario negotiated a contract clause whereby the company paid an amount into the fund equal to pay for a minute per month per employee, and this agreement also resulted in the establishment of a joint union-management environment committee to discuss issues and develop educational materials. Another CAW local in Coquitlam B.C. extended its health and safety committee at Co-Van International to include the environment. It was mandated to eliminate or reduce pollutants, promote recycling and employees were given "whistleblower protection" if they reported releases of hazardous materials into the air, earth or water systems, to the authorities.[21]

In 1991, the Pulp, Paper and Woodworkers of Canada demanded laws to eliminate chlorine based products in Canada by 1995 as "chlorine dioxide is harmful to workers and the environment, and organochlorines threaten the fisheries and public health."[22] In June 1991, Local 6500 USWA and Inco created an Environmental Awareness Committee to review environmental issues and enlarge the focus of the existing safety and health committee. A joint press release stated that "for the first time in Canadian industrial labour relations," concern about the environment has led to the establishment of a senior level union-management committee "whose purpose is to identify environmental problems in the workplace and recommend solutions."[23] In 1989, Inco committed $500 million to contain ninety percent of its sulphur dioxide emissions by 1994. The company also increased its efforts to clean up conditions both inside and outside the workplace, after being "hounded" by the union to "clean up its act" and attacked by environmentalists as a major producer of pollutants which caused acid rain.[24] In Manitoba, the Government Employees Association developed an environmental strategy to evaluate the health and safety of government offices but also provided its members with information to improve the environmental standards in their homes.[25]

At the national level in 1993, the CLC (with government, company and environmental representatives) participated in the Accelerated Reduction and Elimination of Toxic Substances program, which aimed to establish a national standard for pollution prevention. The labour congress explicitly linked the use of toxic substances in the workplace to the destruction of the community environment and stated that it was concerned for "the health and safety of workers who must use pollutants on the job. Its other [concern] was to secure income and job protection for anyone displaced from work as a result of pollution elimination programs."[26]

Union/Community Cooperation

In the 1990s, the connection between occupational health and safety issues on the job and broader environmental concerns in the community has been made more frequently in labour circles. Some examples of union/community cooperation have emerged but not as many as might be expected, given the labour movement's record of working to improve health and safety standards. In the early 1980s, unions like the steelworkers and paperworkers worked with grassroots organizations such as Great Lakes United and Acid Rain Coalition to fight toxic pollutants in the air and water systems in eastern Canada.[27] The Green Work Alliance (GWA) in Toronto led by Nick de Carlo of Brampton Local 1967 CAW and Stan Gray of Greenpeace, worked towards a green future by promoting environmentally friendly industries. Formed as traditional manufacturing plants in Toronto and Mississauga closed, the GWA worked under the banner "Green Jobs not Pink Slips" and sought to retrain workers for jobs in green industries organized to conserve energy and water supplies. In 1993, however, Greenpeace management left GWA after the unions attempted unsuccessfully to organize its office staff, an episode which reflected the class tensions which sometimes prevent greater union/environmentalist cooperation.[28]

A more successful example of cooperation is the non-profit Suzuki Environmental Foundation, created in 1981 by the United Fishermen and Allied Workers' Union, named after an early trade unionist and environmentalist. Most of its initial funding came from the sale of herring, caught and donated by members. In the 1990s, as the B.C. fishery was threatened with pollution, the Suzuki Foundation fought back by organizing campaigns to stop pulp mill pollution, the destruction of estuaries, dam projects, fish farms, poor logging practices and other actions that endangered fish stocks and habitat. It also planned to "conduct workshops that teach loggers about the biology of the salmon stream, which logging practices are a violation of the Federal Fisheries Act and how we can work together to stop the damage."[29] Rank and file union members with the help of federal government money cleaned up the marshlands around the Fraser River which provide oxygen and resting spots for salmon as they go down the river to the ocean.

In its work, Foundation members have sat on government advisory committees and joined forces with First Nations councils, community organizations, environmental groups, as well as other unions. One such coalition—the Georgia Strait Alliance—took the Greater Vancouver Regional District to court for several pollution infractions under the Federal Fisheries Act to prevent water from a sewage overflow pipe, which was lethal to fish, from being spewed into the waterfront.[30]

The Suzuki Foundation represents people whose jobs depend on a healthy environment, and who do not approach environmental issues simply as preservationists. Through coalitions of groups, activists like Miranda Holmes learned that "it's really important for unions and environmental groups to join forces" and stress their mutual interests but it is made more difficult when business and the mainstream media perpetuate a jobs-versus-environment approach.[31]

Conclusion

Labour has a vested interest in resolving health and safety problems in the workplace as many of today's most pressing environmental issues like exposure to toxic substances such as asbestos and PCBs began as on-the-job health and safety issues. The advantage to environmentalists of having unions engaged in cleaning up the environment is that often they can work on preventing problems at the source—on job sites. As a CLC policy statement put it, "as trade unionists we understand instinctively the conflicts between the corporate bottom line and the public interest that underlie much of the environmental debate." From the environmentalist side, Paul Muldoon of Pollution Probe has acknowledged the need for labour's expertise in workplace safety and trade issues in relation to toxic substances.[32] "Often," as Reg Basken of the ECWU has noted, "trade unionist action to protect their members from...industry-based hazards is the first and most essential step towards ensuring public safety," as they contribute their organizing skills to assist community-based initiatives to confront broader environmental issues.

Cooperation between workers and environmentalists, however, remains difficult and the gulf partly reflects class tension, cultural differences and a different perspective of the work process.[33] Workers, it is often assumed by middle class environmentalists, are only interested in keeping their jobs at any cost while some workers, who feel frustrated at environmentalists' apparent lack of concern about disappearing employment, stereotype environmentalists as hopeless romantics bent on preserving wilderness for the sake of a few owls.[34] Greater dialogue and cooperation between the two groups might lead to workable policies including short-term "workers' environmental compensation funds" and the longer term development and promotion of green industries.

There is thus a link between social equity and ecology, as the power imbalance in society has created both socio-economic injustices and environmental damage,[35] but groups concerned about the environment often have different priorities depending on their vulnerability in a rapidly changing economy. In its Statement on the Environment 1990, the CAW recognized that the battle for a healthier environment must be fought on several fronts, that "the interests of the union and the environmental movements largely coincide" and that they must work together.[36] But the issues remain complex. The CAW appeared to be protecting jobs over the environment when it complained about the Ontario NDP government's proposed tax on "gas guzzling" cars, yet the union has developed pro-environment policies, recognized the damage of cars' emissions to the environment, and supported more public transit, tighter emission controls for cars and the manufacturing of vehicles which run on alternative fuels.[37] In 1991, Keith Newman of the Canadian Paperworkers' Union expressed the belief that regulations in the pulp and paper industry need not harm employment security and environmental protection, but added that there may be instances of "job blackmail" whereby workers might be convinced by employers that their support of pollution controls could lead to layoffs. David Bennett of the CLC believes that strategies to improve on ecology can succeed if they are combined with an industrial strategy, which must involve "transition measures for workers caught up in environmental change."[38]

Both labour and environmental groups consist of citizens who reside in communities where cleaning up pollution and maintaining biodiversity is essential to future public health.[39] Clearly, in the context of the global environmental issues looming in the twenty-first century, current class divisions between workers and environmentalists must be overcome for "the pollution that poisons workers also ruins communities and leads us to demand that the clean-up be both inside and outside the workplace at the same time."[40] Better communication can be facilitated by a more tolerant appreciation of the complexity of the issues, by environmentalists becoming more sensitized to how class relates to ecological issues and by workers developing more consciousness of the environmental and social consequences of their actions. Such an approach will hopefully transcend the polarized slogan "Jobs or the Environment" so often used in the mainstream media.

The greatest problem confronting both workers and environmentalists, however, is the strength of the industrial community and its pursuit of growth at the expense of the environment.[41] This challenge is reflected in labour's many efforts to rely on direct action and collective bargaining rather than safety legislation and government enforcement of regulations. This is no doubt a global trend as governments are cutting spending and services by relaxing work safety legislation or making safety regulations meaningless as monies for enforcement are cut. This may be particularly acute in Canada, where the dominant resource industries have been particularly destructive to the environment, and where 'job-blackmail' of workers and governments by resource corporations figure prominently. In Ontario, the internationally-renown Occupational Disease Panel, an independent agency providing objective information on workers' compensation claims, was recently closed by the Ontario government after intense lobbying by the provincial mining industry.[42] In Nova Scotia, twenty-six coal miners lost their lives in the Westray coal mine explosion in 1992 because of the province's blinkered pursuit of resource revenue at the expense of workers' safety.[43] And in Quebec, which harbours the world's second largest chrysolite asbestos industry, "the danger of asbestos is almost a forbidden subject" as the government and the union leadership see only "jobs, jobs, jobs."[44]

Notes

1. Elaine Bernard, "Labour and the Environment: A Look at B.C.'s 'War in the Woods,'" in *Getting on Track: Social Democratic Strategies for Ontario*, ed. Daniel Drache (Montreal and Kingston: McGill-Queen's University Press, 1992), 202; Robert Paehlke and Pauline Vaillancourt Roseneau, "Environment/Equity Tensions in North American Politics," *Policy Studies Journal* 21, No. 4 (1993), 672.

2. H.V. Nelles, *The Politics of Development: Forests, Mines, and Hydro-Electric Power in Ontario 1849-1941* (Toronto: Macmillan, 1974); Eric Tucker, *Administering Danger in the Workplace: The Law and Politics of Occupational Health and Safety Regulation in Ontario 1850-1914* (Toronto: University of Toronto Press, 1990).

3. *The Facts* February (1985), 40; this trend was also true of the United States. Daniel Faber and James O'Connor, "The Struggle for Nature: Environmental Crises and the Crisis of Environmentalism in the United States," *Capitalism, Nature, Socialism* 2 (1989), 12-21.

4. *Toronto Telegram* June 30, 1971.

5. *At the Source* 14, No. 1 (1993), 6.

6. *Globe and Mail* September 7, 1981.

7. Julian Zuckerbrot, "A Tale from the Dark Side: What Went Wrong at Robson-Lang," *Occupational Health and Safety Canada* 6, No. 5 (1990), 70-76.

8. *The Facts* February (1988), 40.

9. *Globe and Mail* February 6, 1978.

10. Stan Gray, "The Squeaky Wheel," *Occupational Health and Safety Canada* 6, No. 4 (1991), 114; "Workers have more and more used their right to refuse unsafe work. At times they have also engaged in massive shop action—exacting an economic penalty in order to force employers to clean-up." The vast majority—97 per cent in Quebec between 1981 and 1988—of right-to-refuse cases have been carried out by unionized workers, as non-union workers either did not know their rights or were afraid of employer reprisals. Scott Williams, "The Right to Refuse Unsafe Work," *Occupational Health and Safety Canada* 4, No. 1 (1988), 25. By the time this legislation was introduced, 48 percent of unionized workplaces already had such committees in place and the right to refuse dangerous work had also been won by many union negotiators before it was entrenched in law. Thus such legislation was often based on concessions already won in union contracts. Peter Kenter, "Paradise Lost," *Occupational Health and Safety Canada* 4, No. 5 (1988).

11. David Bennett, "Environmental Contaminants: Legal Protection," *Canadian Labour* (February 1987), 13.

12. Lee-Anne Jack, "Behind the Headlines," *Occupational Health and Safety Canada* 6, No. 5 (1990), 79-80.

13. William R. Watson, "Ontario's Bill 208: What You May Have Missed," *Occupational Health and Safety Canada*, 7, No. 2 (1991), 108.

14. Kenter, op. cit.

15. *At the Source* 11, No. 1 (1990).

16. *Steel Shots* November 29, 1984.

17. *CALM/CLC* (1993), 2; Glen William, "Legislating Rights and Responsibilities," *Occupational Health and Safety Canada* (Sept/Oct 1992), 37-39; see also OPSEU's Proposal for An Environmental Bill of Rights, March 1, 1991, file-Pollution and the Environment 1991, Centre for Industrial Relations Library, University of Toronto.

18. In 1993 the CLC collaborated with the National Round Table on the Environment and the Economy to publish a handbook for union environment committees and joint labour-management environment committees. Ted Schrecker, *Sustainable Development: Getting There From Here* (Ottawa: CLC and the National Roundtable on the Environment and Economy, 1993)

19. CLC Convention 1990, Document #14, "A New Decade: Our Future," Pollution file, Centre for Industrial Relations Library, University of Toronto; Michelle Walsh, "Safety and Health: Cleaning Up Our Act," *Canadian Labour* (Spring 1988), 29.

20. *CAW Memo*, 21, No. 9 (March 15, 1991).

21. *CAW Health and Safety Newsletter* (August 1993), 7.

22. *CCU Bulletin* (May 1991).

23. *Steel Labor* 54, No. 2 (1991).

24. *Globe and Mail* January 5, 1989.

25. *Contact* 21, No. 3 (1991).

26. *CALM/CLC Today* (1993).

27. *Labour Times* (April 1994), 8.

28. *Labour Times* (June 1993); Stan Gray, "Labour's Environmental Challenge," *Canadian Dimension* 28, No. 4 (1994); Roger Keil, "Green Work Alliance: The Political Economy of Social Ecology," *Studies in Political Economy* 44 (1994), 36.

29. *Our Times* 13, No. 1 (1994).

30. The Canadian Paperworkers Union and PPWC also participated with environmental organizations in the Save the Georgia Strait coalition.

31. *Our Times* 13, No. 1 (1994)

32. "A New Decade: Our Future," op. cit.; *Our Times* (April 1994).

33. Bill Megalli, "Jobs Versus the Environment: Difficult Decisions Ahead," *Labour Gazette* (June 1978), 228-32. The cultural gulf between environmentalists and loggers has been analysed as a distinction between "clearcut culture" and "cathedral culture" by Michael M'Gonigle, "The Stein River: Wilderness, Culture and Human Survival," *Alternatives* 5, No. 3 (1988), 12-21.

34. *Daily Labour Report* (The Bureau of National Affairs, Washington D.C.), 62 (April 2, 1993). The natural resource conflict in the western United States over the fate of old-growth forests became a lightning rod of the Endangered Species Act (ESA) as environmentalists argued in court that the northern spotted owl was threatened. They won several injunctions from 1989 to cease logging on federal lands and challenged federal timber sales and management plans. Nine million acres of federal timberland in Oregon, Washington and California were closed to logging resulting in the loss of 150 lumber and plywood mills and the layoff of 15,000 workers, which the Sierra Club argued were a small fraction of jobs in the regional economy of the States affected by the issue. The owl became a symbol of balancing species preservation with economic considerations.

35. Stan Gray, "Double Exposure: The Environment as a Worker's Issue," *Our Times* (June 1992), 28-29; Stan Gray, "Democracy, Jobs and the Environment," *Canadian Dimension* 26, No. 8 (1992), 17.

36. *CAW Contact* 20, No. 33 (1990).

37. *Labour Times* (April 1994).

38. *Labour Research Exchange* (April 1992), 8.

39. Stan Gray, "Labour's Environmental Challenge," *Canadian Dimension* 28, No. 4 (1994). He advocates that unions bring more environmental issues to the bargaining table, even as they deal with the effects of recession and global economic restructuring because of the alarming 1994 report of the IJC which showed ecological damage harming fish, plants, water and people.

40. David Bennet, "How Will Labour Handle Environmental Issues," *Our Times* (November 1990), 11.

41. Glen Williams, "Greening the Canadian Political Economy," *Studies in Political Economy* 37 (Spring 1992): 5-30.

42. *Canadian Broadcasting Corporation Radio 740 AM.* April 13, 1997.

43. *Globe and Mail* December 2, 1997. The report of the disaster is entitled: "The Westray Story: A Predictable Path to Disaster."

44. *Globe and Mail* November 25, 1997.

CHAPTER NINETEEN

LEARNING A BIOREGION
TRENT UNIVERSITY AND THE HALIBURTON HIGHLANDS[1]

John H. Wadland, Anna Gibson

The impact of free trade and economic globalization on nation states and local communities has been political, economic and social fragmentation. This is expressed in several ways. Multinational capital moves wherever its interests are best served while nation States compete for such investment, dismantling environmental regulations, labour protections, social safety nets and other "encumbrances." Deprived of their tax bases, "uncompetitive" nations are threatened by collapse while the international placeless bourgeoisie gains greater power. Within nations, the steady marginalization of small communities is the unavoidable result of globalization. Many such communities simply abandon themselves to marginalization, and get lost in the "limitless abstraction" of the global market.[2]

In this paper we explore one such region in the central parts of Ontario, the Haliburton Highlands, and an attempt by a project at the local university, Trent University in Peterborough, to assist in reversing this trend (Figure 1). For eight years, two faculty members have conducted a course on Bioregionalism, and four years ago began working on a Bioregional Atlas project in cooperation with the local community, to promote local community development in harmony with the natural environment.[3] We here describe the concept of bioregionalism, then introduce the Haliburton Highlands, and conclude by exploring the limits and potential of such projects to create tools for resisting globalization.

Figure 19.1: Haliburton Highlands Bioregion, Ontario

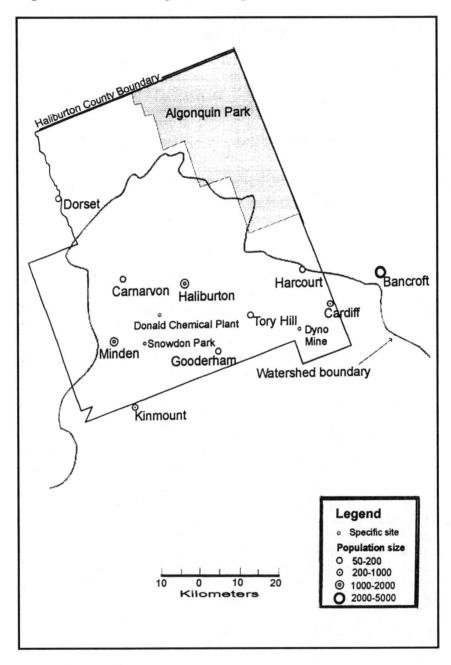

The Concept of Bioregionalism

The concept of bioregionalism is rooted in the land. The term "bioregion" means, literally, "life territory," from the Greek *bios* and the Latin *regere*. Bioregionalism is interdisciplinary. It examines interconnections and context, striving to form a "whole" or "complete" picture of a geographically specific region. Ecology, politics, society, culture, geology, economics, history—all are fundamental aspects of place and integral to bioregional analysis.[4] The relationships that exist between these aspects and their interplay are crucial to understanding and expressing the story of community. A region is recognized not only as a community, but as a "home place." "The bioregional undertaking," as Gary Snyder explains it, "is to learn our region; to stay here and be at home in it; and to take responsibility for it, and treat it right. And then to take pleasure in that."[5]

Bioregionalism recognizes the human place within, not outside of or above the environment. Bioregionalism demands that we ask many questions about the appropriateness of established behaviours, and about external issues which impact upon the community or which measure the impact of a local community on its adjacent communities and the world at large. This kind of understanding of the place in which we live is necessary for creating a sustainable future. We are all—animals, plants, soils, fish, humans—part of ecosystems, and therefore in relationship. Bioregionalism is a holistic and integrative concept. It is utopian in the sense that we are far from being able to achieve its vision.[6] There are many challenging obstacles along the path, but the concept provides an important framework and direction for understanding and action.

Bioregionalism can be employed to shape realistic, sustainable and appropriate development designed to be in harmony with the region, and therefore with the nation as a whole. As a method of analysis it aspires to explore such factors as the economic base of the community. Does it degrade the environment? How can this be remedied? Is it a long-term, viable and sustainable economic base? Does it make effective use of the skills within the community? Does the historical culture of the community reflect its economy and relationship with the land? Are the majority of the people working within or outside the community? Can the people tell the stories of their community? Do they define themselves by the work they do or by the things they buy? How are issues of class and race addressed by and within the community?

A central project of bioregionalism is to restore humans' understanding of their integration with the natural world. The social construction placing humans above nature, of which western language and history are a reflection, ignores the relationship, the context, which bioregionalism seeks to rehabilitate. Watersheds, mountain ranges, coasts, or valleys are likely measures, "on a scale which is meaningful to regularly interacting groups of reinhabitant communities."[7] Peter Berg defines bioregions as "geographic areas having common characteristics of soil, watershed, climate, native plants and animals that exist within the whole planetary biosphere as unique and intrinsic contributing parts."[8] Progressive planners use "physiographic determinism" to define boundaries. This approach, which uses overlays of watershed information, animal communities and vegetation types, does not, however, provide human scale to the territories defined.[9] Bioregions evolve and alter; overlapping boundaries exist. Nothing is neat and tidy. "A bioregion refers both to geographic terrain and a terrain of consciousness—to a place and the ideas that have developed about how to live in that place."[10]

Economy, cultural pluralism, ecology, ecosystem, biodiversity—all are fundamental elements of bioregionalism. Ecology, which favours a language of pattern and system, does not privilege a dominant culture. It favours the maintenance, defense and evolution of the relationship. Bioregionalism recognizes that change is a normal, necessary and desirable feature of any region. It also understands that humans have become the central agents of change, that humans have a responsibility to the places they inhabit to live sustainably and to develop strategies to achieve that purpose in the long term. Bioregionalism builds upon the connection that individuals feel to "home," extending it to encompass the wider social and ecological community.

The Setting

The Haliburton Highlands contain the headwaters of the Trent watershed. Sitting on the Canadian Shield, it is blessed with a vast quantity of pristine lakes and rivers, surrounded by dense, mixed deciduous and coniferous forest. The bioregion is a rural community with a resident population numbering approximately 16,000. There are several small villages within the Highlands: Haliburton, Minden, Dorset, Wilberforce, Gooderham, Bancroft, and Kinmount. Immigration to the area began in the 1860s by means of colonization roads, after all of the good farm land had been taken up in Southern Ontario. There remain a number of working farms, but thin, acidic and poorly drained soils render few of these sufficiently prosperous to support the families who own them.

The logging industry was favoured in the early years, with the Mossom Boyd, Gilmour and other lumber companies virtually clearing the area of its merchantable white pine timber. The annual log drive required the manipulation of the water courses. Dams were built at the exit points on many lakes to control water levels and to facilitate the movement of logs to sawmills further south. Most of these dam sites are now used to regulate flows to downstream hydroelectric generating facilities and the Trent Severn Waterway (TSW). Both the Trent system and the dams that feed it are federally controlled. In the eyes of those who manage the TSW, Haliburton County is essentially a series of "reservoir lakes." Water levels in these lakes are altered dramatically to meet the needs of luxury boat owners far to the south. Water quality is also an issue. The impacts of raising and lowering water levels on the habitats of spawning game fish, and the inadequacy of septic fields on many cottage properties, are matters of considerable concern to tourist operators and biologists.

Mining and other industrial activity has been pronounced over the years. The Donald chemical plant, a short distance from the village of Haliburton, supplied acetone, antifreeze and wood alcohol to the Canadian military in two world wars. It began as a charcoal producer, extracting and processing all the maple trees in ever-expanding concentric circles out from the plant, to supply the coke ovens of steel companies in the urban south. This huge plant, eventually rendered obsolete by the petrochemical industry, is now sinking slowly back into the ground. It employed upwards of 500 people at one time, many of them Finnish and Italian immigrants. Its legacy can be partially ascertained from a careful analysis of aerial photographs. But detailed research is needed to find out what it has left behind underground and in the soils, and to determine the ways in which its toxic residues may be affecting, for example, the adjacent river.

Near Bancroft there has been a long history of uranium mining. All of the mines have been decommissioned, but the "Keep Out" signs surrounding collapsing infrastructure and tailings ponds remind the children of the miners that their isolated community was once a major player in the Cold War. Are statistical indicators of heightened cancer rates in the Bancroft area related to the mines, or possibly, to the fact that tailings have been used for landfill, sometimes at construction sites for new housing? Or, are they simply a reflection of the age of the residents?

Good highways from nearby Toronto make the Highlands natural cottage country—with the result that the summer population swells to about 40,000. Chronic unemployment and underemployment are serious problems. Tourism is now heavily dependent on servicing the cottage and related tourist industries. The tourist industry capitalizes on a seasonal round of recreational activities—from snowmobiling and cross-country skiing in winter, to hiking and canoe-tripping in summer. The autumn colours draw many visitors and, because the panhandle of Algonquin Park penetrates deeply into Haliburton County, the Highlands benefit from Ontario government literature promoting this internationally recognized wilderness reserve. The countryside is sprinkled with lodges, summer camps, small resorts and bed and breakfast establishments, all of which are at the mercy of weather conditions. Wet summers and snowless winters can have devastating impacts.

The population of the Haliburton Highlands is diverse. Although very few Native people actually live in the region today, the archaeological record indicates that an extraordinarily rich indigenous culture flourished here, before and after contact. Minden is named for a place in Prussia. English, Irish, Scottish, Chinese, French, Indian, German and Vietnamese names punctuate the pages of the telephone book. In every hamlet and at many crossroads one can find churches whose cemeteries and registers record the complex genealogy of the surrounding area.

Of recent interest has been the demographic change dictated by an aging population. As older people retire many have sold their city homes and taken up permanent residence at the family cottage. The retrofitting (sometimes the demolition and rebuilding) of cottages has provided a great deal of work in the community. But rural intensification is a many headed hydra. An aging population also requires more extensive health care. Medical facilities have never been adequate in the Highlands, but the pressure for change is now outdistancing even anticipated need. Many retirees had planned to live at cottage retreats as long as they were capable of maintaining their independence. The intention, then, was to sell the cottage and return to the city. The economic recession has, however, undermined the real estate market. Cottage properties are not moving—and cottage properties which have been upgraded at great expense are often priced beyond the means of potential buyers. As a result, some retirees have in a sense become trapped in the community. Urban retirees are active in the membership of many local service clubs—the Lions, Rotary, Kiwanis, etc—and they tend also to be vocal (and articulate) in representing their needs to the District Health Council and to the newly formed Haliburton Highlands Health Services Corporation. Municipal (township and county) governments are frequently controlled by generations-old local families whose priorities are not necessarily those of the retirees. Health-related issues, however, seem to foster unanimity of purpose, by degrees proving the need for co-operation in related sectors.

It should be clear from these examples that environmental, social, economic and cultural questions cross-pollinate the Trent bioregional case study of the Haliburton Highlands. In ways that even Raymond Williams[11] could not have imagined, the transforming power of urban economic imperatives has rendered the "nature" of 1998 far different from the "nature" of 1668. The aboriginal presence is erased. The borders, shapes and constituent species of lakes, rivers and forests have been altered irrevocably by human agency. The Minden Wild Water Preserve, a world class canoe and kayak slalom course, was created on the Gull River by the Ontario Wild Water Affiliation (OWWA) using a thirty-seven tonne bulldozer.

The river was diverted, the bottom was blasted to make it narrower and deeper, and a series of deflectors fanning out from the shore on either side were built to give it a twisting, serpentine course. When the changes were completed, they had a course 800 meters long that dropped ten meters from start to finish...The river was then about a third as wide from shore to shore as it had been...It's now a regular stop on the national circuit, and well respected around the world as a tough, interesting slalom course—one of the three best in the world according to the promotional literature.[12]

The "wilderness" marketed to nostalgic cottagers and weekend motorists is accessible on roadbeds mined from local eskers, some of them formerly home to aquifers. The scenic traverse of highways through drained wetlands and dynamited granite rock cuts encourages speeding, yet without threatening the safety of the passengers who, from their climate-controlled, bug-resistant insulation, rejoice in the abstracted autumn colour of the second growth forest.

Problems and Prospects

No local issue exists in a vacuum. The health of all bioregions requires that locally derived evaluations be pooled in the interests of expanding the analytical equipment of others, while understanding that no single blueprint will serve all bioregions. The variety of relationships to be teased out of oral narratives, census data, aerial photographs, secchi disk readings, community economic development statistics, municipal archives and mental maps depends upon the willingness of people, a community, to take ownership of and responsibility for their place. This process involves more than casting ballots on election day. Representative democracy creates a psychology of assigning responsibility to others. Bioregionalism is participatory democracy which lays less emphasis on voting and more on what John Ralston Saul calls citizenship—individuals acting in community in the interest of the public good.[13]

The dynamics of a university course conceived as a ten year research project can be daunting. The classroom pedagogy of the Trent bioregionalism course is directed by a historian and a biologist for whom fostering and protecting the interdisciplinary integrity of the process is vital. The quality of student research, and the comprehension of bioregional theory informing its interpretation, are essential to meeting the goals of the project and the Atlas. Approximately sixteen undergraduate and graduate students begin each academic year grappling with the concept of bioregionalism, reading and discussing a rapidly expanding body of literature. A field trip in the first term introduces students to the Haliburton region, its historical sites and some of its citizens. Students are exposed to the work of the previous year's classes and select a general area of interest. Further exploratory research helps to narrow projects, some of which are chosen from a list provided by Haliburton residents, some of which continue the work of previous students, some of which branch off in wholly new directions. For the rest of the course students pursue research on and discuss their projects, visiting Haliburton, selected libraries, archives and government offices, conducting interviews and gathering information. At the conclusion of each year students invite the people from the community with whom they have worked to a presentation open house showcasing the final products of their research. The press and general public are also invited to attend and to question the researchers. Duplicate copies of all student papers are stored and made available through the Haliburton Highlands Museum and the Trent University Archives.

In addition to the collection of papers, a Bioregional Atlas is being produced as a main product of this research project. A student of the bioregional course took on the task of designing the framework for and coordinating the Atlas project. She has been its Coordinator since its beginning in 1994. This Atlas will include approximately thirty map plates, complete with text, and will be available in both digital and printed formats. The digital database development is to be directed by the Atlas team and the faculty and students in the GIS Program at neighbouring Sir Sandford Fleming College with whom a formal partnership has been developed. Other institutional partners include the Haliburton, Kawartha, Pine Ridge-District Health Council (HKPR-DHC) and the Haliburton County Development Corporation. The process of partnering with other institutional members of the community ensures that the project is under constant scrutiny by those whose interests it is intended to meet. It also enhances the interdisciplinary process.

The project is governed by a framework which includes a five year production strategy for the completion of the Atlas, a working list of map plates, a Steering Committee made up of Haliburton residents, an "Adopt-A-Map" program through which community members take responsibility for co-ordinating work on each of the thirty plates, and a budget. Continuing work includes maintaining and raising awareness of the project, involving more volunteers in the "Adopt-A-Map" program, keeping volunteers and student researchers engaged, making public presentations about the Atlas, informing the local news media about problems, successes and needs, and securing funding sources which will keep the project glued to its timelines. The project to date has been funded by the Environmental Youth Corps, Trent University's Canadian Studies and Environmental Studies Programs and with the assistance of faculty Social Sciences and Humanities Research Council grants. Despite this funding, the project has been able to secure funds for little more than basic wages in the summer. There are also problems in acquiring appropriate digital data (in terms of scale, information and cost and copyright agreements) that have caused numerous refinements in the original timeline. It is typical in using Geographic Information Systems (GIS) to face these challenges. We chose to use GIS for its high potential for advanced query and analysis of the database, which can include not only geographic map data, but also quantities of attribute data like rainfall, census and pollution level information—all of which can be analyzed in exciting ways. This Atlas has the potential to be a powerful tool for planning, environmental monitoring, data storage and education. Being a high-technology mapping process, GIS does pose challenges like those listed above that would not be an issue with a less technologically intensive process. At the same time, a less technologically intensive process would not be capable of the same type of built-in query and analysis functions, though it would be possible to collect the same data and do the analysis in other ways.

As in any major undertaking, there are obstacles in this process. The Map Designers are dedicated, but work out of their own interest, on their own time and as volunteers. Without their commitment, this project could not move forward. Because so much of the data collection and research is being done by community volunteers, the project proceeds at its own pace. The Atlas team can only work full-time during the non-academic year. The collection of data across boundaries (2 Universe Transverse Mercator zones, 3 Ministry of Natural Resources districts, 5 counties)[14] and the high cost of acquiring or entering digital data also present recurrent difficulties.

The challenges faced by the Atlas project are indicative of the effects of globalization on rural communities. Lack of funding (for research projects like this as well as for the communities themselves), and a suffering local economy based on resource extraction and tourism, demonstrate the very dependency on outside capital which must be overcome through greater self-reliance.[15]

Despite these challenges the bioregionalism project and the Atlas are consistently moving forward. Where globalizing forces are pulling communities apart and contributing to a neutralization of place,[16] the bioregionalism course and Atlas are specifically focused on learning about place, creating a strong understanding of the relationships within that place and how it is connected to other places, the global ecosystem and the global economy. From this basis of increased local knowledge and understanding can come better informed long-term planning.

The work done so far in these projects has already had significant positive impacts. The collection of student research papers at the Museum in Haliburton is routinely accessed by local reporters, teachers and citizens looking for detailed information on matters of interest to the region. The extensive network being built in the development of the Atlas has fostered many community projects and partnerships that may previously have been unlikely or impossible. Through this network, for example, Stanhope Township has connected with the HKPR-DHC and the Trent Conservation Coalition (TCC), an amalgam of conservation authorities in the Trent region. Their combined Rural Intensification Project has secured funds to undertake community projects within the HKPR-DHC district. The initiative is concentrated on developing a GIS for Stanhope that will aid in the planning and development of emergency services. The Otonabee Region Conservation Authority is currently working on developing the digital basemap, preparing it to meet the Bell Canada 911 addressing specifications. A new museum which has recently opened in the Highlands has entered into a partnership with the Atlas project to develop a historical map of the local region. This will be available for sale with the profits assisting both the Atlas and the museum. Several undertakings from the bioregionalism course stand out in particular: a paper about Snowdon park[17] was used by the community in the development of the park itself; two papers on the Donald Chemical Plant[18] have been used on several occasions by local schools, residents and even by one of the local newspapers; and one student prepared her Master's thesis[19] around the Dyno uranium mine in Bicroft, building on research originally done for the course.[20]

This thesis clearly demonstrates the ways in which the Haliburton Highlands became a vital link in the machinery of the Cold War. One of the map plates in the Atlas focuses on a particular aggregate mine that is located in a sensitive wetland complex, depicting ongoing years of struggle with the Ontario Municipal Board around the issue. This map plate will illustrate the ways in which aggregate extraction can devastate wetlands, demonstrating the relationships between lack of adequate wetland inventory, designation and protection.

All of these projects contribute to the increased knowledge and understanding of the Haliburton Highlands, not only compiling important and interesting information, but making it available and accessible, collected by community members for the community. In this effort the university is merely a partner, a citizen of the community with particular skills to contribute to the analysis.

The Atlas is an innovative project that will constitute a valuable resource for community-based regional planning and for sustainable community economic and social development, contributing to the continuing dialogue around Local *Agenda 21*, a centrepiece of the UNCED Conference at Rio in 1992. Their basis in partnerships and resource sharing and their foundation in bioregional principles make of the bioregionalism course and the Atlas project real adventures in exploratory learning which help to answer the appeal by a growing number of educators for a responsible examination of possibilities alternative to the received wisdom of consumer-driven globalization.[21]

Paradoxically, the fate of the Canadian nation lies in the health of the communities which, together, constitute the relationship of which it is the expression. Bioregionalism places responsibility for the well-being of the nation where it belongs, in the hands of the people who understand that "economic growth and development is no longer the overriding social and political objective, but merely one objective that has to be balanced with other objectives such as sustainability, equity, livability, social cohesion and environmental quality."[22] Bioregionalism exists within an established Canadian tradition of communitarian, decentralist thought.

The course and Atlas project we have described acknowledge this tradition and its marriage to the evolving paradigm of ecology. Through the integration of teaching, research and community service they concentrate on problem solving at a local level while understanding that the local is a referent of the national, the national of the international. They teach respect for the analytical and critical perspectives of others, and what it means to generate new knowledge. Above all, they privilege a co-operative community of scholars, sharing responsibility, and the belief that the ultimate object of citizenship is to defend, through real democracy, the relationships which sustain life.

Notes

1. The authors wish to recognize, with thanks, the generous support of this project by the Social Sciences and Humanities Research Council of Canada, by the Ministry of Natural Resources of Ontario and by the Canadian Studies and Environmental Studies Programs of Trent University.

2. John Ralston Saul, *The Unconscious Civilization* (Toronto: Anansi, 1995), 186.

3. The project of understanding the complex set of relationships within a bioregion requires a marriage of the humanities, social sciences and sciences. Attracting students from a wide variety of subject areas including economics, comparative development studies, Canadian studies, biology, environmental studies, geography, anthropology, women's studies, and cultural studies, the Trent Bioregionalism course embodies interdisciplinary study. Conceived as a ten year research project, its goal is to create a database of easily accessible information collected and interpreted by students conducting primary research in the Haliburton Highlands. The Atlas Project has grown out of this bioregional course and involves community members on the Steering Committee and as volunteer Map Designers.

4. Discussion of bioregionalism can be found in *Home: A Bioregional Reader* ed. Van Andruss (Gabriola Island, B.C.: New Society Publishers, 1990); John Cartwright, "Bioregionalism vs. Globalization," in *Growth, Trade and Environmental Values,* eds. Ted Schrecker and Jean Dalgleish (London, ON: Westminster Institute for Ethics and Human Values, 1994), 203-213; Jim Cheney, "Postmodern Environmental Ethics: Ethics as Bioregional Narrative," *Environmental Ethics* 11, No. 2 (Summer, 1989), 117-134; David McCloskey, "On Bioregional Boundaries," *Raise the Stakes* 14 (Winter, 1988-89), 5; Donald W. McTaggart, "Bioregionalism and Regional Geography: Place, People and Networks," *Canadian Geographer* 37, No. 4 (1993), 307-319; Allen Van Newkirk, "Bioregions: Towards Bioregional Strategies for Human Cultures," *Environmental Conservation* 2, No. 2 (Spring, 1975), 108.

5. Gary Snyder, "Regenerate Culture," in *Turtle Talk: Voices for a Sustainable Future,* eds. Christopher Plant and Judith Plant (Lillooet, B.C.: New Society Publishers, 1990), 14.

6. The "bioregional vision" was first written about in Kirkpatrick Sale's *Dweller's in the Land: A Bioregional Vision* (San Francisco: Sierra Club Books, 1985). There is no blueprint or recipe for a bioregional world, but it is clear that it would involve living within the means of nature, the limits of place, and the ecological carrying capacity.

7. Doug Aberley, "How to Map Your Bioregion: A Primer for Community Activists," in *Boundaries of Home: Mapping for Local Empowerment,* ed. Doug Aberley (Gabriola Island, B.C.: New Society Publishers, 1993), 75.

8. Peter Berg, "What is Bioregionalism?" *Trumpeter* 8, No. 1 (Winter 1991), 6-8.

9. Aberley, op. cit., 74.

10. Berg, op. cit., 6.

11. Raymond Williams, *The Country and the City* (New York: Oxford University Press, 1973).

12. Andrew Milne, "Wild Water," *Minden Summer Times,* May 15, 1995, 14-17.

13. John Ralston Saul, *The Unconscious Civilization* (Toronto: Anansi, 1995).

14. The collection of data across boundaries is a significant issue in mapping. In digital maps, UTM grid zones are seven digit numbers, the first digit of which is generally omitted to keep the data volume smaller. This causes problems when using data from two adjacent UTM zones. The data must all be altered to reflect the appropriate first digit, or the data from the two zones will not match up. This process is relatively simple, but time consuming and takes much more data storage space. Working across MNR and county boundaries poses problems in collecting data for a bioregion which does not have the same boundaries. The bioregion may only encompass a small piece of a county, municipality or MNR district. The challenge then becomes how to make the data collected by that unit fit into the section of the bioregion. If the deer population for the Bancroft MNR district (only a piece of which is in the Haliburton Highlands bioregion) is known, how is the deer population for the piece in the Highlands to be determined? A calculation could be made based on the relative area, but that assumes that the deer are equally distributed, which is not the case.

15. Self-reliance is used here as opposed to self-sufficiency. "Self-reliance implies the reduction of dependence on other places but does not deny the desirability or necessity of external trade relationships." Jack Kloppenburg et al, "Coming into the Foodshed," in *Rooted*

in the Land: Essays on Community and Place, eds. William Vitek and Wes Jackson (London: Yale University Press, 1996), 113-123.

16. Saskia Sassen, "The Spatial Organization of Information Industries: Implications for the Role of the State," in *Globalization: Critical Reflections,* ed. James H. Mittelman (Boulder, Colorado: Lynne Rienner, 1996), 33-52.

17. Sandra Stoddart, "Snowdon Park: Getting to Know Your Bioregion," Unpublished Paper, Trent University, 1994.

18. Andrew Hamilton, "Modernity, Metaphor and Maples: The Landscape Created by the Wood Chemical Plant in Donald, A Study Concerning the Interrelations of Technology, Community and Land," Unpublished Paper, Trent University, 1992; Maggie Julian, "Bioregional Education in Action: Lessons of the Donald Chemical Plant," Unpublished Paper, Trent University, 1997.

19. Michèle Proulx, "The Uranium Industry in Haliburton County," Trent University, Unpublished Paper, 1995.

20. Michèle Proulx, "The Uranium Industry of the Bancroft Area: An Environmental History and Heritage Assessment," Unpublished M.A. Thesis, Trent University, 1997.

21. Malcolm Plant, "The Riddle of Sustainable Development and the Role of Environmental Education," *Environmental Education Research* 1, No. 3 (October 1995), 253-266.

22. Trevor Hancock, "Healthy, Sustainable Communities: Concept, Fledgling Practice and Implications for Governance," *Alternatives* 22, No. 2 (April-May 1996), 18-23.

Chapter Twenty

NASTAWGAN OR NOT?

First Nations' Land Management in Temagami and Algonquin Park[1]

Jamie Lawson

Since the Second World War, First Nations in Canada have acquired new strategic resources to deal with land rights. Legalized and finally publicly-assisted national organizations grew up in the 1950s through the 1970s.[2] Since 1973, courts have shown a new understanding and recognition of First Nations' land rights. In the late 1980s, nonviolent resistance was widely used to confront Canadian authority and legal administration.[3] This paper is about two peaceful confrontations over forest use in the Temagami and Algonquin Park regions of Ontario (see Figure 1). During 1988 and 1989, the Teme-Augama Anishnabai (TAA) led two lengthy blockades of a logging road, and participated in a third led by non-aboriginal wilderness advocates. At stake were rare old pines, but also jurisdiction over N'Daki Menan ("our land"). On Labour Day weekend 1988, Golden Lake Algonquins (GLA) conducted an information blockade over their rights in the Park. In 1989 and again in 1990-91, deliberate hunting in the park pressed their position, shocking parks and wilderness advocates. The two cases are differentiated by the First Nations' relations with wilderness advocates, and the relative success of their strategies in obtaining various land rights.

The TAA[4] and the GLA[5] are both small aboriginal communities, centred in Ontario on single reserve villages created outside regional treaty processes. Both have long claimed that larger traditional territories, never transferred to the Crown,[6] remain under their stewardship.[7] Their tiny reserves offer few economic resources in themselves, but both First Nations still make distinctive use of off-reserve Crown land. In the 1970s and 1980s, they used their new political resources to influence the key sectors affecting them—logging, tourism, and mining.

Figure 20.1: Temagami and Algonquin Park, Central Ontario

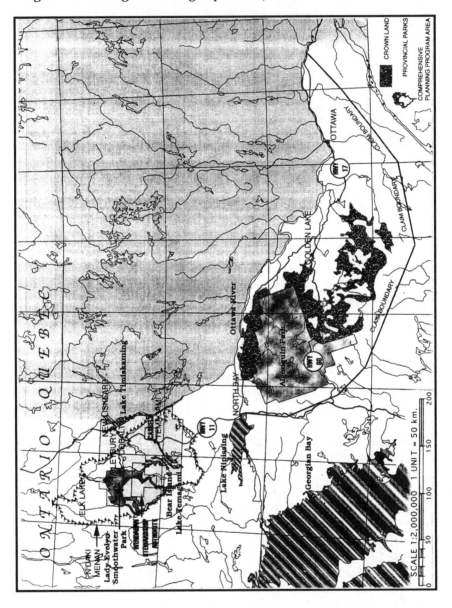

Both regions represent the "northern wilderness" to many Americans and southern Ontarians. These visitors enjoy forest land in different ways, which is especially noticeable in tourism. Tourist subsectors, their suppliers and consumers, enjoy surprisingly ambiguous local relations with the traditionally better-paid resource sectors. Local non-aboriginal residents share a distinct northern identity, combining real affection for nature with genuine pride in a heritage of resource extraction.[8] As in many "protected places," First Nations' hunting, trapping, and gathering have been forbidden or reordered in the course of the century, as extraction has intensified and wilderness advocates have mobilized.[9]

Canadian provinces have an unusually direct role in forestry.[10] Forests—unlike most mines and tourist facilities—remain overwhelmingly provincial property. Timber production has been prioritized by the Ontario Ministry of Natural Resources. But both the "Timagami" Forest Reserve (1901-61) and Algonquin Park (1893 to the present) were to be provincial showcases for conservation. These arrangements set higher public expectations that government should "save" these forests in the Upper Ottawa Valley. In comparison with southern Ontarian conservation initiatives, these northern initiatives involved local people much less.[11]

The Upper Ottawa has become a relatively depressed region, and by provincial standards private timber firms have been less able to resist government initiatives or assume forest management functions. Small cutting blocks, small and mid-sized firms, a high reliance on logging sub-contractors, an enduring role for seasonal operations, and low unionization are all related historically to the enduring regional role of lumber and other wood products, when compared with the pulp and paper predominance in the northwestern Ontario forest sector.[12]

However, recent phases of aboriginal resistance in the two areas have unfolded quite differently. In Temagami, legal action began quietly during a phase of community revitalization in the early 1970s. In 1973, the First Nation filed for land cautions over their entire traditional territory. The cautions made the bounds of the TAA homeland enforceable against many other interests, including state land-use planners. The TAA even clashed with tendencies in the apparently sympathetic environmental movement over their resource rights in "wilderness" areas.[13] The TAA refused to accept prior conditions restricting types of land-use in a land settlement. Their campaign was thus a fight for land-use rights and against existing land-use, but also against confining all their future land rights to particular zones within N'Daki Menan.

The most recent legal challenges by the GLA began in the early 1970s against a significantly more complex, militant land politics in the nine Quebec Algonquin reserve communities. Firstly, unlike the TAA and N'Daki Menan, the GLA stood largely outside a stable array of non-aboriginal interests. They thus confronted a well-established negotiating forum for zoning the parklands. Secondly, the boundaries of Algonquins' traditional lands were never enforced by cautions. Paradoxically, however, a court defeat on treaty rights in 1983 redirected and arguably strengthened their legal claim for land rights beyond existing treaties. Petitions for a negotiated settlement were subsequently ignored. In 1988, the GLA responded by issuing a negotiating position which included jurisdiction over Algonquin Park. In support of their demands, the controversial hunts were started.[14]

Temagami

In 1973, two issues provoked the First Nation in Temagami to legal action. Firstly, regional pressure for year-round tourist jobs had led the Ministry of Industry and Tourism to plan a large, four-season resort at Maple Mountain, a First Nation spiritual site. Secondly, the Ministry of Natural Resources produced Lake Temagami's first comprehensive land-use plan. These policy initiatives were part of a postwar trend of dividing and coordinating activities spatially.[15] Before the Second World War, many land uses had coexisted in Temagami, partly by virtue of their seasonality. This pluralism broke down after the war in part because resource activities became more capital-intensive, less seasonal or mobile, and thus more dependent on monopolising particular plots of land.[16] Logging, for instance, resorted to heavier equipment and to faster, more comprehensive clearances incompatible with many renewable resource activities. Winter school schedules on Bear Island were also introduced, making the island a year-round home for many families. Non-aboriginal activities declined on Bear Island before it became a tiny Indian reserve in 1971.[17]

This "spatialization" trend ran against deep traditions common to many northern Ontario First Nations: winter dispersal into the family territories of N'Daki Menan and summer gathering at common sites.[18] Over time, other activities and their organization of space had grown in importance for the First Nation. But aspects of many TAA members' daily lives, knowledge, memories, and traditions, having first grown up around this seasonal round, continued to generate a unique kind of space. New uses emerged alongside traditional ones for seasonal portages, canoe routes, and pathways, collectively known as *nastawgan.*[19] A latecomer to life under the Indian Act's reserve system and precluded by soil and climate from a southern-style agriculture, the TAA never lived its whole collective life in the kind of highly zoned space more typical of southern Ontario. The non-aboriginal dominant culture, by contrast, had emerged generating the latter kind of space, and state agencies, business pressures, and even some deeply committed wilderness advocates saw it as means of advancing interests and resolving disputes. But spatialization itself—the increased coordination of activities by year-round monopolies in space rather than in seasonal alternations—disrupted the patterns of peripatetic living that underlie *nastawgan. Nastawgan* space was watershed- and path-centred, rather than plot- and road-centred. It was maintained by periodic population dispersions, an adaptive culture, and community consensus rather than by centralized or sovereign institutions.[20]

Seen from the *nastawgan,* N'Daki Menan was a logical unit; seen from roads in heavily-zoned space it was not.[21] Significantly, the *nastawgan* survived partly because it was shared by the newcomers. For example, the area's oldest youth camps specialized in long white-water canoe trips, often hiring First Nation staff. This distinctive camping tradition was then publicized and taken up by independent campers. This camping tradition was revitalized in the 1970s, but threatened in Temagami by the spatialization process. Regular canoeing fostered awareness of the impact on *nastawgan* space by the spatializing activities.[22]

Previously, *nastawgan* and its users had co-existed relatively well with most introduced activities and populations. Most of the latter hugged capital-intensive transportation corridors and the limited severances from Crown land nearby. The Lake Temagami Plan and the Maple Mountain resort signalled a potentially epochal reorganization of N'Daki Menan, an extension and systematization of spatialization. In reaction, a century-long cultural exchange bore political fruit. The cottagers' and campers' Temagami Lakes Association (TLA) and the First Nation radicalized in tandem. Out of the former arose the Save Maple Mountain Committee and later the Temagami Wilderness Society.[23] Out of the latter came the 1973 land cautions under Chief Gary Potts and lawyer Bruce Clark, which successfully blocked both plans, and laid the basis for a land claims court case.

Land cautions normally notify registered owners and potential buyers that land-registry entries are in dispute. Only after filing a caution does a cautioner have to justify the claim. Until that is legally resolved, the cautioner retains a state-enforced veto over land transfers. An administrative tribunal normally handles the process, but appeals may go to the regular courts.[24] The land cautions the TAA registered, based on anthropological and other records, encompassed provincial lands in 110 geographic townships.[25]

Temagami was probably unique in linking the caution process to aboriginal title. Like many land disputes in the 1970s, it held that the original aboriginal title had not been extinguished. Unlike most others, it impaired the Crown's ownership, management, and vending rights through cautions.[26] The cautions froze land patents for mining which led to a provincial freeze of mineral exploration and staking, as well as many tourist development projects. As a land settlement neared, industry and government planners later feared major transfers to TAA jurisdiction would occur, without knowing the scale, location, or governance of the lands involved. Under prevailing company financing norms and provincial forestry regimes, reliable business plans and annual cutting rates were left in doubt.[27]

Cautions do not impose accommodation or a negotiation process. They only create conditions that are normally intolerable to all parties, which in turn provokes a resolution.[28] Common land-use planning techniques had evolved to resolve private conflicts in which the State can arbitrate a negotiated spatialization. But in this case, the relevant boundaries and the very process of spatialization were in dispute. The State itself was party to the central dispute.[29]

By May 1978, Ontario officials opted to appeal the cautions rather than negotiate. The First Nation reorganized as the TAA, transferring most negotiating authority from the federally recognized band, and confirmed N'Daki Menan's boundaries with neighbouring First Nations. Then trilateral negotiations were launched with the federal government, raising hopes for a settlement.[30] But in 1982, Ontario, pressured to expand its parks system, announced a considerable wilderness park. Lady Evelyn-Smoothwater Park doomed the Maple Mountain resort, but it also exercised provincial authority over the land the First Nation claimed to be in dispute. For a time, the courts seemed to be the First Nation's obvious recourse. But the first court decision in 1984 put the TAA on the legal defensive. Thereafter, it was far from evident what the preferred TAA strategy should be. A more accommodating Liberal government offered a settlement in 1986, restarting negotiations, but by February 1987, the TAA refocused on regaining its legal leverage through an appeal.[31]

Then, suddenly, a third TAA option opened up: Ontario authorized a critical logging road extension. During repairs in the late 1970s, MNR planners had seen new economic potential there, and the Liberals were under pressure to save local jobs. This was not "pristine wilderness," but Milne and Sons, Temagami village's sawmill, would reach hitherto uncut pockets of "old-growth" forest.[32] This exercise of provincial authority mildly reduced the local economic impact from the cautions, but threatened the TAA position as well as the rare stands. The 1988 TAA blockade was launched, eventually to be enjoined in court. The Temagami Wilderness Society (TWS) led more publicized blockades in the summer of 1989 until the TAA lost a further appeal. Freed by the loss from the injunction, the TAA assumed leadership of the logging road blockade.[33]

Together, these actions provoked a political seachange that lifted the blockade in favour of primarily bilateral negotiations. A preliminary Ontario/TAA accord in April 1990 announced four main points: negotiations for a "treaty of coexistence"; a bilateral Wendaban Stewardship Authority (WSA) to pioneer land-use planning around the road extension; TAA consultations over MNR's local resource management; and the purchase and closure of Milne and Sons.[34] (Cutting resumed in the area amongst remaining user companies based in the surrounding areas.)

This bilateral path appealed to the NDP government elected in the fall of 1990. The premier-elect had been arrested at the blockades, and aboriginal matters were a policy priority. But multilateral structures which treated the First Nation as one stakeholder among many soon grew up alongside the accord process. From 1989, the MNR-led Comprehensive Planning Program (CPP) was advised by a multilateral, effectively non-aboriginal forum, revised and expanded after 1991 as the Comprehensive Planning Council (CPC). The CPP and CPC were to draft and negotiate model land-use planning. Their jurisdiction included only an MNR administrative district that included the Tri-Towns (Cobalt, Haileybury, and New Liskeard) to the east, and central N'Daki Menan.[35]

In August 1991, the Supreme Court of Canada rejected the TAA claim. This further undermined the bilateral approach, though it confirmed regular treaty benefits were owing to the First Nation.[36] From 1991 to 1993, the TAA negotiated, its leverage now based largely on the case's notoriety and the NDP's commitment to find a precedent-setting compromise. The TAA's 1992 Vision of Coexistence proposal insisted on some ongoing authority throughout N'Daki Menan. Ontario apparently favoured a more traditional land-for-cash arrangement. The TAA ultimately accepted provincial pre-eminence and renewed resource development in northern N'Daki Menan, lifting cautions there in stages. In return, the CPC was reorganized in 1993 introducing more bilateral elements, including TAA representation and a co-chair.[37] These concessions damaged TAA unity (the province insisted on split First Nation representation in final negotiations) and alarmed environmentalists. But they heartened the anti-caution lobby of local municipalities and resource businesses, long since unwilling to have the government represent their interests.

The TAA/Ontario agreement-in-principle in 1993 was more conventional than the TAA Vision: a limited joint management area, reserve lands, and money for land. It was a significant offer, worth some $30 million, especially given the new bargaining situation.[38] But ratification failed twice in last-minute double-voting arrangements recognising both the TAA and a new grouping centred on the Temagami Indian Band.[39] This failure marked the end of an era. TAA negotiating funds were cut soon thereafter; its research facilities burned in September 1995, and Gary Potts retired as chief.[40]

The north of N'Daki Menan has resumed a distinct institutional path. Mineral exploration reopened in 1995, and a provincially funded Elk Lake Community Forest was launched with a broad-based, populist commitment to sustainable forestry.[41] Meanwhile, the WSA lands were rolled into the CPP process in 1995.[42] The remaining cautions there were finally removed, and the radically neo-conservative government that replaced the NDP reopened Crown land sales. By 1995, the TAA was boycotting the CPP/CPC, but the latter concluded its work. The new government then revised the plan, and consolidated stripped-down MNR operations at North Bay.[43] All this angered environmentalists, but blockades in the fall of 1996, though well-planned, were sparsely attended.[44]

Golden Lake Algonquins
In the short-term, GLA hunting in Algonquin was less well received than the TAA road blockade. But from 1974, Temagami strategy initially emphasized autonomy from other aboriginal organizations; land cautions there chilled relations with local industry and with Ontario. GLA legal research drew from the start on the wider Ontario leadership, and the GLA cultivated government and inter-Algonquin discussions.[45] This seems consistent with a distinctive aim, integration of the GLA in an existing, relatively elaborate forum of interests.[46]

Algonquin history has been shaped by invasion and displacement.[47] The Ottawa Valley has been successively a war zone off-limits to Europeans, a contested trading route, a logging and settlement frontier, and a relatively depressed rural region. Written documentation of Algonquin history is greater in quantity and age, if not in consistency. Driven out by the Iroquois in the 1640s, ultimately reaching a base near Montreal, a large body of Algonquins significantly altered their traditional seasonal rounds. Survivors in the tributary headwaters are poorly documented. Unfortunately for later legal work, seventeenth- and eighteenth-century Europeans rarely travelled the Ottawa, particularly the more remote area around the present park. At least two other First Nations the British needed as allies signed treaties that included Algonquin lands.

Permanent Algonquin resettlements sprang up upstream in the nineteenth century, just ahead of logging and settlement disruptions. Golden Lake, then relatively distant from Montreal, was near relatively viable hunting and trapping grounds. Land-use traditions, originally similar to the TAA's, could be preserved there with adaptations. But the mesh of these traditions with family territories was weaker, and there was no surviving equivalent to the *nastawgan* space of N'Daki Menan.

Until the 1980s, such documentary and anthropological matters had not seemed so important. The Algonquins believed that they had a treaty the Canadian authorities violated. But the Ontario High Court rejected this long-held view in 1981. If no treaty existed, the GLA still had aboriginal title to the Ontario side of the Ottawa River watershed, south of the Mattawa and had to demonstrate continuous use.[48] Petitions in 1983 addressed the Canadian governor-general, apparently to emphasize the Crown's obligations. By 1988, no answer had been given. The GLA requested an end to Crown land patents, where the TAA had sought land cautions.[49] While neither First Nation has contested lands already sold to third parties, parkland covers a far greater portion of game-supporting, forested Crown land remaining on the Algonquin claim area. Most of the rest has been surveyed and sold. The Algonquin proposal of August 1988, backed by the information blockade and hunts, accordingly emphasized the park as a future economic base.[50]

For them, this was entirely understandable, indeed conciliatory, but parks and wilderness activists were shocked. Even those more committed to aboriginal rights either declared neutrality or called on the First Nation to guarantee existing practices.[51] Beginning in the 1930s, Algonquin Park staff had already pioneered spatialization techniques to accommodate multiple uses. But since the 1960s, parks and wilderness lobbies had pushed MNR's parks branch further. Initially focussing on Algonquin and Quetico parks, they had condemned logging and demanded a sophisticated master plan to segregate all park land-uses into discrete zones. The Algonquin Forestry Authority (AFA), a Crown corporation, was the main provincial response in 1974 to the logging debate; a greatly revised master plan, intensifying spatialization, was the wider response. The AFA had unified the provincial regulatory presence over the park's timber while maintaining local industry. It has assumed many forest-related functions undertaken elsewhere by MNR officials and/or licensees; most bush operations are contracted to local firms. Currently the sole commercial logger in an Ontario provincial park, the AFA is subject to increasingly elaborate park master plans.[52]

With the AFA and master plan in place, wilderness lobbyists had shifted to province-wide parks policy, demanding wilderness preservation and systematic park classification. The MNR's 1978 "Blue Book" was a milestone for this lobby, adopted in large measure by the mid-1980s. By then, Algonquin Park was increasingly a tightly interwoven land-use compromise, adjusted at the margin by structured political conflict locally and provincially.[53] Logging, while ecologically better managed, became deeply interwoven in that compromise. The GLA, by contrast, was excluded except in relation to in-park trapping. By the 1980s, the land-use debate returned to logging, but also cottaging, waterskiing, and on-beach parking, activities once relatively well tolerated in Ontario parks.[54] Hunting rights, though valuable for the First Nation, had always been controversial in Algonquin; now in the current climate, it seemed particularly egregious.

But the Algonquin hunting charges of 1990-91 upset such certainties. In the late 1980s and early 1990s (notably the *Sparrow* case[55]), the court had appeared to give aboriginal usufructuary rights primacy on public land, after conservation.[56] Combining these rulings with the 1981 Algonquin case, the NDP feared the courts might authorize Algonquin hunting in the park uncontrolled by the province, and Algonquin control in the long term.[57] These were unexpected enormities to many local residents, as well as equally important NDP supporters, wilderness and parks advocates (see Harries-Jones, this volume). Many environmentalists worried (and worry) about the exercise of aboriginal rights under modern technology. Presumed to prefer nation-to-nation status over multilateral parks politics, GLA members would become in this view another imposition on the threatened wilderness at best. At worst they could undermine the whole parks compromise.

The NDP opened bilateral land talks and dropped hunting charges. They confirmed a right to hunt in eastern Algonquin Park, subject to negotiated conditions. Annual renewals with minor revisions have so far withstood local unpopularity and changes in government (fishing agreements remained elusive). The federal government joined the talks in 1993 and a framework for negotiations was signed in August 1994; work on an agreement-in-principle is progressing slowly as of October 1996.[58]

Conclusions
To sum up, a "struggle to save our Motherland and the non-human life on it"[59] expressed the TAA's struggle in the late 1980s because of links to the land embedded in *nastawgan* space. These had ebbed in importance but had never

finally ruptured. Such discourse also appealed to environmentalists. Some of the latter had experienced and valued *nastawgan* space, albeit on their own cultural terms, and as recreationists had long engaged in meaningful relationships with members of the First Nation. Others knew Temagami's back-country less intimately, but emphasized its overriding provincial and national importance. Solidarity from non-aboriginals seemed helpful in building something new and permanent, namely recognition for N'Daki Menan as an ongoing jurisdictional and ecological unit, a space within which genuine coexistence could be fostered. Similarly, TAA involvement helped the environmental cause. But wanting either spatialized wilderness preserves or N'Daki Menan with fewer compromises, other elements of the non-aboriginal environmental camp and of the aboriginal camp respectively have preferred the cautions as a base to fight from, over any proposed settlements reached to date. While both the First Nation and environmentalists struggled internally and with each other over these issues, the local municipalities have increasingly united to lift the cautions entirely and resume resource activity.

In contrast, the GLA's recent pressure on provincial governments has relied less on direct economic leverage or an alliance with environmental groups, and more on court-proven rights and negotiations with existing state agencies. GLA hunting and potentially control in the park worried and initially antagonized both parks advocates and local industries. Though dialogue has recently been opened through a new group, the Friends of the Algonquins, interested environmentalists have tended not to have the kind of intimate underlying organic links with the GLA's activities and GLA space that similar groups had with the TAA. The GLA's apparent aims seemed more diverse and graduated, and their direct action more legal calculus. Their aim was not fundamentally about revitalizing an entire traditional Algonquin space. It was about acquiring a zoned political-economic base within a complex of zoned spaces on traditional land, in order to sustain distinctive connections with the land.

Any firm conclusions here require cautious interpretation. These First Nations will chart their own path. Effective strategy is always an engagement with a concrete situation. Sharp political reversals have also transformed the general strategic situation. However, the potential for alliances did depend in part on shared social and spatial interactions with the land. This factor of shared socio-ecological space should be taken very seriously indeed. As a result, two strategies for two distinct situations brought two distinct outcomes. The more incremental GLA strategy brought interim results to 1996; in Temagami, something more spectacular and original has at times seemed imminent, but has not yet been realized.

Notes

1. York University's Faculty of Graduate Studies and Political Science Graduate Program provided financial assistance. The paper benefited from several anonymous interviews. Paul Holmes shared archival material on Temagami. Monika Jäggi and Anders Sandberg reviewed earlier drafts, and my spouse Xu Feng provided much support. Fern and Bob Nicholls helped

open a southern relative's eyes. Bruce Hodgins' work and activism have been obvious inspirations. I am responsible for the remaining errors.

2. Peter McFarlane, *Brotherhood to Nationhood* (Toronto: Between the Lines, 1992).

3. David Long, "Culture, Ideology and Militancy: The Movement of Native Indians in Canada, 1969-91," in *Organizing Dissent*, ed. William Carroll (Toronto: Garamond, 1992), 118-134.

4. The First Nation's most broadly based organization, founded in 1978. Treaty and status Indians within the TAA are organized in the Temagami Indian Band (now the Temagami First Nation). The latter retained basic legal responsibilities as a band, and diverged from the TAA leadership during land talks under the NDP. A traditionalist grouping, the Ma-Kominising Anishnabeg, criticizes both.

5. "Algonquins" were first encountered by Europeans at multinational councils on the St. Lawrence in the early seventeenth century. At first contact, many subgroups had homelands along the Ottawa Valley. See text for further details: Joan Holmes and Assoc., *Algonquins of Golden Lake Claim*, Vol. 2, report prepared for Ontario, Oct. 30, 1993, Document Summaries 92-217; M. Jean Black, "Nineteenth-Century Algonquin Culture Change," *Actes du Vingtième Congrès des Algonquinistes*, ed. William Cowan (Ottawa: Carleton, 1989), 62-69.

6. Greg Sarazin, "220 Years of Broken Promises," in *Drumbeat*, ed. Boyce Richardson (Toronto: Summerhill, 1989), 186; Tony Hall, "Where Justice Lies: Aboriginal Rights and Wrongs in Temagami," in *Temagami: A Debate on Wilderness*, eds. Matt Bray and Ashley Thomson (Toronto: Dundurn, 1990), 223-253.

7. TAA, *Teme-Augama Anishnabai*, pamphlet, 1992; Sarazin, op. cit., 195-196.

8. Bruce W. Hodgins and Jamie Benedickson, *The Temagami Experience* (Toronto: University of Toronto Press, 1989), 108-135; Gerald Killan, *Protected Places* (Toronto: Dundurn, 1993), 74-119, 147-151; Township of Temagami, "Old Growth, New Growth," pamphlet, Sept. 1995; Temagami Wilderness Society, *Position-in-Principle* presented to Temagami Council, July 17, 1987, 1.

9. Lawrence Berg et al, "The Role of Aboriginal Peoples in National Park Designation, Planning, and Management in Canada," in *Parks and Protected Places in Canada*, eds. Philip Dearden and Rick Rollins (Toronto: Oxford, 1993), 225-227, 246-248; Madeline Katt Theriault, *Moose to Moccasins* (Toronto: Natural Heritage/Natural History Inc., 1992).

10. The following passage relies on H.V. Nelles, *The Politics of Development* (Toronto: Archon Books, 1974); Richard S. Lambert and Paul Pross, *Renewing Nature's Wealth* (Toronto: Dept. of Lands and Forests, 1967); Sing C. Chew, *Logs for Capital* (Westport, Conn.: Greenwood, 1992); Fiona A. Sampson, *Ontario Aboriginal Policy with an Emphasis on the Teme-Augama Anishnabai*, MA Thesis, Trent University, 1990, 63-65.

11. Killan, op. cit., 14-15, 36-44, 243, 303; Hodgins and Benedickson, op. cit., 76-89, 136-76, 285.

12. Hodgins and Benedickson, op. cit., 245-246; Thomas R. Roach, "Farm Woodlots and Pulpwood Exports from Eastern Canada, 1900-1930," in *History of Sustained Yield Forestry*, ed. Harold K. Steen (Portland, Oregon: Forest History Society, 1984), 202-219; Ian Radforth, *Bushworkers and Bosses* (Toronto: University of Toronto Press, 1987), 13, 20-25.

13. Interviews, Sept. 1995; Gerald Killan, "The Development of a Wilderness Park System in Ontario, 1967-1990: Temagami in Context," in Bray and Thomson, op. cit., 111.

14. Sarazin, op. cit., 196; Killan, op. cit., 1993, 380.

15. Hodgins and Benedickson, op. cit., 251-255, 265; Hall, op. cit., 229.

16. Hodgins in Bray and Thomson, op. cit., 132; Hodgins and Benedickson, op. cit., 244-246, 291.

17. Mary Laronde, "Co-Management of Lands and Resources in n'Daki Menan," *Rebirth*, ed. Anne-Marie Mawhiney (Toronto: Dundurn, 1992), 95, 104; Hodgins and Benedickson, 219, 222; Theriault, op. cit., 116.

18. Frank Speck, "The Family Hunting Band as the Basis of Algonkian Social Organization," in *Cultural Ecology*, ed. Bruce Cox (Toronto: McClelland and Stewart, 1974), 58-75.

19. Hap Wilson, "Deep Water Country," *Seasons* (Summer 1988); Bruce W. Hodgins and Seana Irvine, "Temagami Youth Camping, 1903-1973," in *Using Wilderness*, eds. Bruce W. Hodgins and Bernadine Dodge (Peterborough: Frost Centre, 1992), 143-156.

20. Theriault, op. cit.

21. Theriault, op. cit., 32-33, 54-74, 89-101; Hodgins and Irvine, op. cit., 145-146, 152; Bruce W. Hodgins, *Wanapitei on Temagami* (Peterborough: Wanapitei, 1996); Brian Back, *The Keewaydin Way* (Temagami: Keewaydin, 1983).

22. Hodgins in Bray and Thomson, op. cit., 129.

23. Hodgins and Benedickson, op. cit., 251, 254, 265; Ontario, Ministry of Natural Resources, *Lake Temagami Plan for Land Use and Recreational Development 1973*, 47, 56.

24. Brian Bucknall, "An Overview of the Legislation," in *Registration Revisited,* Continuing Legal Education Conference, Canadian Bar Association—Ontario, Toronto, October 5, 1987.

25. Hall, op. cit., 228-231; Ontario, MNR, Internal Memo, "Re: Claims by Indians to certain lands in Northern Ontario," February 26, 1974, Ontario Native Affairs Secretariat, Toronto.

26. Canadian courts considered aboriginal rights largely in terms of individual renewable resource rights since the late nineteenth century. Hall, op. cit.

27. "Re: Claims by Indians...," op. cit.

28. Bucknall, op. cit.

29. Hodgins and Benedickson, 3-5.

30. Hodgins and Benedickson, 265-266; letter to Alan Pope, Roy McMurtry, Gary Potts, Clovis Demers from E.P. Hartt, April 13, 1982; letter to Gary Potts from John C. Munro, received January 27, 1981.

31. Killan, in Bray and Thomson, 101-102; "Attorney-General for Ontario v. Bear Island Foundation et al., etc.," *Ontario Reports*, 2nd series, 49 (1985): 366; Hodgins and Benedickson, op. cit., 270.

32. Hodgins and Benedickson, op. cit., 264, 278-281.

33. "Attorney General for Ontario (respondent) v. Bear Island Foundation and Gary Potts et al. (appellants)," *Canadian Native Law Reporter* 2 (1989): 73-89; Hodgins and Benedickson, op. cit., 267-289; Kent McNeil, "The Temagami Indian Land Claim," in Bray and Thomson, op. cit., 187.

34. TAA/Ontario, *Memorandum of Understanding* (Apr. 23, 1990).

35. Ontario, MNR, "N[atural] R[esources] Minister Announces Comprehensive Planning Council for Temagami," *News release,* May 23, 1991; Temagami Area CPC, "More Hard Work Ahead for CPC but 'Some Very Good News' Say Co-Chair," *News/Nouvelles,* March 20, 1995; Anthony Usher, et al, *Partnerships for Community Involvement in Forestry* prepared for Ontario, Ministry of Natural Resources, Community Forestry Project, November 1994, Vol. 2, 138-139, 151.

36. Supreme Court of Canada, *Ontario (Attorney General) v. Bear Island Foundation*, Decision, Aug. 15, 1991.

37. *Toronto Star,* October 24, 1991; *Globe & Mail,* February 11, 1992 and April 21, 1993; Ontario, MNR, "An Update From the CPC," *Temagami* June 1995.

38. *Globe and Mail,* March 23, 1993.

39. Usher, op. cit., 137-138, 151; *Sudbury Star,* February 26, 1993; *Toronto Star,* August 19, 1993; *Globe & Mail,* April 21, 1993, November 16, 1993, and March 3, 1994.

40. *Temagami Natives Renounce Treaty Negotiations and Assert their Sovereignty* News Release, Lake Temagami, February 25, 1993; *Sudbury Star,* February 26, 1993; *North Bay Nugget,* September 6, 1995.

41. *Kirkland Lake Gazette,* April 13, 1995; Ontario, MNR, *Lessons Learned 1991—1994* (Sault Ste. Marie: Queen's Printer, 1995), 28-42, appendix.

42. *Temagami Times,* June 1990, 30; Laronde, op. cit., 99.

43. Usher, op. cit., Vol. 1, 145; Ontario, MNR, CPP, *Bulletins* Background Information Series, Revised Mar. 1991; "Draft Land Use Proposal for the Temagami Area," *Temagami,* December 1995.

44. Municipal Advisory Group, Timiskaming, *Presentation Summary,* 1994, esp. 2, 3; *Northern Daily News,* April 3, 1995; *Toronto Sun,* July 28, 1995; *Temiskaming Speaker,* September 6, 1995.

45. Sarazin, op. cit., 191-193

46. Algonquins were among the park's many "poachers." Lambert and Pross, op. cit., 487-489; Sarazin, op. cit., 190. Golden Lake is outside the park and off its main access routes. Only

recently has a GLA AFA director been appointed. Aboriginal history in the fall of 1995 was displayed at the otherwise innovative Visitor's Centre under the heading "The First Visitors." AFA, *Annual Reports* (Toronto: Queen's Printer, 1992, 1993); personal observation.

47. The following relies on G.M. Day and Bruce G. Trigger, "Algonquin," *Handbook of North American Indians*, Vol. 15; *Northeast*, ed. B.G. Trigger (Washington: Smithsonian, 1978), 793-795; Peter Hessel, *The Algonkin Tribe* (Arnprior, Ont.: Kichesipirini Books, 1987); Black, op. cit.

48. Sarazin, op. cit., 193-194; B.H. Wildsmith, "Pre-Confederation Treaties," in *Aboriginal Peoples and the Law*, ed. Bradford W. Morse (Ottawa: Carleton University Press, 1991), 196, n. 1.

49. Perhaps linked to the pending Temagami trial. Sarazin, op. cit., esp. 194-198; Roderick MacKay and William Reynolds, *Algonquin* (Erin, Ont.: Boston Mills, 1993), 111.

50. Peter N. Ward, "Major Flaws in the Golden Lake Land Claim to Algonquin Park," Ad Hoc Committee to Save Algonquin, *Information Bulletin* 1 (June 15, 1991), 16; Sarazin, op. cit., 191-196.

51. Killan, op. cit., 1993, 294-296; Ad Hoc Committee to Save Algonquin Park, op. cit.

52. Usher, 120-121; AFA, *Annual Reports*, op. cit.

53. Killan, *Protected Places*, 170-204, 239-287; George Priddle, "The Ontario Park System," in *Parks and Protected Places*, op. cit., 97-110.

54. Killan, *Protected Places*, op. cit., 74-204.

55. This concerned the right of a band member to fish on traditional lands in the absence of a treaty. Cara L. Clairman, "First Nations and Environmental Groups in Ontario's Parks—Conflict or Cooperation?" *Canadian Native Law Reporter* 1 (1993): 7-9.

56. D.W. Elliott, "Aboriginal Title," in Morse, op. cit., 96-111; McNeil, op. cit., 186, 189-193.

57. ONAS, *Negotiation Bulletin* 1 (May 1992), 5-7.

58. e.g., ONAS, *Fact Sheet*, October 19, 1992; Clairman, op. cit., 12, 15-17; Canada, Department of Indian and Northern Affairs, *Information*, October 1996.

59. Chief Gary Potts, Speech given at Wendaban Line, June 1, 1988, 2.

Chapter Twenty One

MI'KMAQ ENVIRONMENTALISM

Local Incentives and Global Projections[1]

Alf Hornborg

I can think of no other environmental conflict that has been as specifically Swedish-Canadian in scope as that regarding the activities of the Swedish corporation Stora in the Canadian province of Nova Scotia. Of key importance in the public representation of this conflict were the Mi'kmaq people. In this chapter, I would like to discuss the Mi'kmaq involvement in environmental issues as it has developed in the past few decades, how its changing forms relate to national and global processes of identity construction, and the role of the media in these processes. What I ultimately would like to arrive at is a way of understanding Mi'kmaq and other First Nations environmentalism that goes beyond a credulous idealization of indigenous people as somehow essentially "ecological," but *without* turning into a cynical rejection of their stance as strategic and unauthentic.

The Mi'kmaq: A Brief Environmental History

The Mi'kmaq are an Algonquian-speaking people who have inhabited what are now known as the Maritime provinces of Canada for at least three thousand years. Prior to the arrival of Europeans, they were primarily fishermen, hunters and gatherers, spending the warmer half of the year fishing along coasts and rivers and moving inland to hunt moose, beaver and other game in the winter. One of the best sources on Mi'kmaq subsistence practices is a text published in 1672 by the French fur trader Nicolas Denys, who gives us a glimpse of how their daily life was being transformed by the fur trade in the mid-seventeenth century.[2] To be sure, there is nothing in Denys' account to suggest that the aboriginal Mi'kmaq were overexploiting their natural environment. On the contrary, he mentions several taboos and other beliefs which indicate that they perceived human-nature interactions as constrained by a delicate pact. This sense of respect for the game animals and their supernatural masters, however, seems to have been undermined by the very fur trade which Denys himself promoted. It is well known that the natives themselves, spurred by the trade, were the main agents in the depletion of game stocks in much of eastern Canada.

The ambiguity surrounding native hunting ethics has created a lot of controversy all over Canada about the ecological validity of restoring to First Nations their aboriginal hunting rights.[3] The *Mi'kmaq Treaty Handbook*, compiled by the Grand Council of the Mi'kmaq, uses recent court victories to argue for the Mi'kmaq right to rely on their own traditional judgement (*netukulimk*) as the exclusive constraint on native hunting.[4] But when in September 1988 the Grand Council sanctioned a two-week "Treaty Moose Harvest" in the Cape Breton Highlands, some of the hunters were charged with violations of the provincial Wildlife Act.[5] From a European perspective, it is ironic that in November of 1995, a delegation of Canadian Indians and Inuits were compelled to go to Europe in order to convince the European Union to continue to import furs from animals caught in traps found inhumane by the Europeans.

The environmental historian Calvin Martin has tried to explain how the hunting ethics of the Mi'kmaq and other Algonquian peoples could be so rapidly transformed upon European contact.[6] He argues that much of the intensity with which they came to deplete stocks of beaver and other furbearers derived from the aboriginal notion that human disease was inflicted by the animal masters, the "keepers of the game." According to this interpretation, the disastrous epidemics introduced by the Europeans thus unleashed a war of retaliation on the animals, which in turn well served the European fur traders. But Martin comes close to contradicting himself by showing how various other components of the European invasion undermined the very belief system that he holds responsible for the slaughter. The commodity market, new technology, Christianity, and the marginalization of shamanism all contributed to a *secularization* of hunting. This is undoubtedly the more fundamental cause of the demise of aboriginal environmental ethics. The notion of retaliation sounds more like a transitional rationalization than a real incentive. Critics of Martin's work have emphasized how incentives to participate in the fur trade would have been linked to political and economic structures that were already part of native Amerindian societies, although destined to be transformed by it.[7] But on one point Martin and his academic critics tend to agree: they are all very careful to reject the popular notion of the American Indian as what Martin calls "the great high priest of the Ecology Cult."[8] If indigenous resource management was conservationist in practice, its cosmological foundation would have had nothing in common with modern environmentalism.

The European colonization of coasts and rivers in the seventeenth and eighteenth centuries had pushed much of the Mi'kmaq population permanently inland to hunt. Many retreated to the district of Unama'kik, now known as Cape Breton Island, which long remained a wilderness with few European settlers. As game was depleted and the fur trade moved West, the Mi'kmaq resorted to craft production for the European settlements. The raw materials—for baskets, barrels, handles, oars, snowshoes, etc.—were almost exclusively derived from the forest. Nicolas Denys in the 1640s had documented their skill in exploiting forest products, whether marvelling at their birchbark canoes or deploring their cumbersome wooden kettles. Now that neither hunting nor fishing were viable modes of subsistence, history would turn the Mi'kmaq into a nation of basketmakers. Baskets, produced mainly for tourists, are still emblems of their ethnic identity. Thus, when Whycocomagh band chief Ryan Googoo in 1983 charged Stora for the destruction of forests in Cape Breton, it was natural for him to refer to his people's dependency on those forests not so much for game as for fibers for basketry.[9]

The Mi'kmaq-Stora Conflict: A World Systems Perspective

In the days of the fur trade, North America as a whole was reduced to a periphery in an economic "world system" centered on Europe.[10] Today, economic centres and peripheries are somewhat harder to delineate in geographical or political terms. The relationship between industrial "core" areas and their dependent, raw material producing peripheries is a structural one,[11] and though generally speaking a part of the twentieth century "core," both Europe and North America also have their peripheral sectors. Cape Breton Island is definitely such an area. The unemployment rate is among the highest in Canada, and provincial politicians have long invited external, usually American capital to exploit its natural resources. In 1957, the Swedish corporation Stora Kopparberg was persuaded to lease one million acres (520,000 hectares) of Crown lands on Cape Breton and the eastern mainland of Nova Scotia, and five years later it had fulfilled its commitment to build a pulp mill at Port Hawkesbury.[12]

When in the mid-1970s the Cape Breton Highlands were struck by an epidemic of spruce budworm, Stora requested aerial spraying with an organophosphate called *Fenitrothion*, but was stopped through the efforts of an *ad hoc* action group called Cape Bretoners Against the Spray.[13] Among the leaders were highly educated and ambitious U.S. immigrants with activist traditions from, e.g., the Sierra Club and the Friends of the Earth.[14] They played a key role not only in articulating these particular protests and converting them into a political and legal issue, but, more generally, in introducing environmental activism into Nova Scotia as a legitimate form of discourse and social interaction.[15] Most well-known of these was the law student Elizabeth May, who would later be appointed senior policy advisor to the federal Minister of the Environment.

In 1982, Stora was nevertheless issued a license from the Nova Scotia Department of Environment for aerial spraying with phenoxy herbicides in order to control fast growing hardwoods and other weeds in their softwood plantations. These herbicides were diluted relatives of the infamous Agent Orange applied as a defoliant by the Americans in Vietnam. What many activists found particularly disturbing was the fact that Stora pressed to proceed with such measures in Nova Scotia even though all aerial spraying with herbicides had been banned in its home country of Sweden two years earlier. Encouraged by its victory in the "budworm battles,"[16] the nascent Nova Scotia environmental movement in 1982 proceeded by applying to the Nova Scotia Supreme Court for an injunction to stop the spraying. Among the plaintiffs were representatives of two Mi'kmaq bands, former chief Ryan Googoo from Whycocomagh and chief Thomas Francis from Afton. This marked a definitive moment in the emergence of Mi'kmaq environmentalism. Interviewed by Farley Mowat, Elizabeth May recalls, "We now had quite a ground swell going, and it continued to build very fast. It even swept up the Micmac Indians, who had never before become involved in any of the white man's environmental wars."[17]

The application for an injunction, however, was dismissed in September 1983. Two months later, a Swedish coalition called the "Support Committee for Nova Scotia" invited three representatives of the plaintiffs to bring their case to Sweden, including Elizabeth May and Ryan Googoo. May suggests that part of the reason why Swedish environmentalists had been prepared to pay for their travel expenses was that Stora was arguing in Sweden that since Canadian courts were declaring herbicides safe, they should be reintroduced even in Sweden.[18] But, as Dietrich Soyez has noted, it was the engagement of Mi'kmaq Indians that more than anything else aroused media and public opinion in Sweden.[19] An organization called the "Swedish-Indian Association," in particular, here found a cause worthy of intensive activity, but the confrontation was also monitored by the major media. In an interview after a short and unproductive meeting with Stora's president Eric Sundblad, Googoo told the Swedish television audience that he was "the coldest man he had ever met." Elizabeth May seems to underestimate the symbolic significance of the Mi'kmaq involvement when she recalls, in her usual, self-congratulatory style: "We took Sweden by storm. We were on the national news every night. Olof Palme endorsed us. Stora was being vilified in editorials all over the country. People were selling their shares of Stora stock."[20]

There were several things about the Mi'kmaq-Stora conflict which made it exceedingly paradoxical and difficult for most Swedes to digest. Except for brief and very modest experiments in New England and the Caribbean in the seventeenth century, Sweden had never been a colonial power. Throughout most of history, it remained primarily a supplier of raw materials for Britain and continental Europe. In fact, this was how Stora Kopparberg itself came into being in the thirteenth century, three hundred years before the advent of European expansion. Like Canada, Sweden originally industrialized by exploiting the natural resources of its own, national periphery rather than those of other nations. Moreover, in the 1960s and 1970s, leading Swedish politicians such as Olof Palme had seen to it that anti-imperialism had become part of its international image. Finally, the country had been recognized as outstanding in the field of environmental protection, as exemplified by its banning of aerial spraying of herbicides. Yet, all of a sudden, here was the image of an impoverished corner of North America (of all places), whose aboriginal population was complaining that its forests were being pillaged and poisoned (with Agent Orange, of all substances) by Swedish capital. This was deeply disturbing for the self-image of many Swedes. However divorced from the nation state multinational capital may be in practice, it can obviously remain a significant part of national identity.

Every now and then in Canadian debate, the Swedish presence in Nova Scotia continues to be represented as imperialism. A leading, American immigrant environmentalist since long settled in Cape Breton compared Stora's operations in Nova Scotia with the underdevelopment of the third world.[21] In a letter to *The Scotia Sun*, a Buffalo University professor born in Montreal and summer resident of Nova Scotia similarly complained that "Stora is using Canada as a third world country where environmental damage that would not be tolerated in Sweden can be inflicted at will."[22]

Enclosing the ecological and economic realities we thus find a subtle issue of contested, moral identities. Where was the periphery and where the centre? Whose periphery was it, the central provinces', the Americans' or the Swedes'? In this moral identity contest, the Mi'kmaq involvement emerged as a trump card for the environmentalists: they obviously represented the ultimate periphery. Irrespective of any court decision, public opinion in Sweden was strongly on the side of the Mi'kmaq. Soyez somewhat naively calls this trump card "the deliberate utilization of specific Swedish sensitivities,"[23] as if their involvement was somehow unfair to Stora, and as if Stora had not deliberately utilized "specific sensitivities" when it explicitly threatened the Cape Bretoners with unemployment. The point is rather that environmental conflicts will always be framed in terms of culturally more or less potent metaphors, and their outcome geared to the persuasiveness of the conjured images. "Nova Scotia is sick," Stora president Eric Sundblad had ominously and rather insensitively told the province in 1976, it "must take the medicine."[24] But rather than the benevolent doctor, Stora to many people emerged as a grinning wolf turning a forest into a cemetery.[25]

Elizabeth May's concluding reflection in Mowat's interview in turn suggests an insensitivity of another magnitude. "There is a strange epilogue," she tells him,

> We lost our case in Canada, but won it in Sweden. The stockholders and board of Stora got so much flak that they decided to dispense with Eric Sundblad, who had been their chief executive since 1975. While driving to the meeting at which he was going to be ousted, he pulled his car to the side of the road and shot himself.[26]

Mi'kmaq in the Media: The Political Economy of Signs
In 1984 Stora began to spray about 3,000 hectares of Nova Scotia forest annually, but with Roundup, a less lethal chemical than was originally planned. Environmentalists continued to be concerned. There was also a growing alarm about the clearcutting of vast areas in the Cape Breton Highlands. In October 1987, Whycocomagh band chief Rod Googoo complained in an interview, "Not only is Stora picking the apple tree, but they're cutting down the whole orchard and shipping it to Sweden."[27] In June 1988, as Stora was celebrating its 700th anniversary in the city of Falun, a new delegation of Nova Scotia activists made the Swedish headlines. Once again, one of them was a U.S. immigrant to Cape Breton complaining over Swedish imperialism[28] and another a Mi'kmaq from Whycocomagh. A third was a Jewish filmmaker originally from Toronto. To some Swedish newspapers, however, they were all Mi'kmaq.[29]

Charles Joseph (Junior) Bernard, 25 years old, represented a new generation of Mi'kmaq activists, reflecting the surge of pan-Indian "traditionalism" in the Nova Scotia reserves in the 1980s. During the previous Mi'kmaq visit, Eva Bjärlund, editor of the bulletin of the Swedish-Indian Association, had congratulated Ryan Googoo for *not* appearing in feathers, long hair or "traditional" dress. She concludes an editorial,

> *Thank you, Stora Kopparberg for having mass media and people backing up an Indian with short hair. A normal, concerned human being. From 1983. This is something the Swedish-Indian Association has not succeeded with in all its fifteen years. The Hollywood Indian packs his colourful feathers and headband and machine-made moccasins and leaves the stage. Reality can begin.*[30]

Five years later, however, Bernard posed for the press with a headband and a drum he had borrowed from some acquaintance in Falun.[31] In these media images, we can detect a postmodern conflation of attribute and essence that brings to mind Jean Baudrillard's theory of the political economy of signs. And this time, the new Stora president Bo Berggren had joined the game. He had showed up dressed in a traditional Swedish folk costume and managed, as the cameras were clicking, to lure Bernard into a joyous embrace. The startling photograph[32] was a political disaster for the delegation of Nova Scotia environmentalists. One newspaper headline translates, "The Indian war is over. Winner: Bo Berggren." Dismayed, Bernard went on a hunger strike outside Stora's office for the remainder of his stay in Falun, but the confrontation had undeniably lost most of its momentum.

Nevertheless, contrary to Eva Bjärlund's expectations in 1983, the political significance of conspicuous ethnic markers and pan-Indian "traditionalism" increased around the turn of the decade, not only in Sweden, with its allegedly "specific sensitivities,"[33] but in Canada as well. By then, it had become politically correct in Nova Scotia to invite Mi'kmaq traditionalists to environmentalist protest meetings. In May 1990, for instance, at a meeting arranged by the Eastern Shore Wilderness Association, "Noel Knockwood, spiritual leader of the Micmac Indians, performed a special sacred ceremony during the protest. He said the land is sacred to the Indian people and should be to everyone."[34]

By 1990, however, the focus of such "traditionalist" Mi'kmaq environmentalism had to a large extent shifted from the protection of forests to the protection of a sacred mountain.[35] This shift, I believe, marks an important point of transition in that Mi'kmaq involvement is no longer a rhetorical supplement to mainstream environmentalism but increasingly propelled by its own, ethnic initiative. At the same time, other, more specifically Mi'kmaq concerns about the environment have been increasingly "traditionalized." One such issue is the industrial waste treatment facility at Boat Harbour, the inadequacy of which has plagued the Mi'kmaq band at Pictou Landing since the early 1970s, but which was drawn into the orbit of traditionalist protest as late as 1992. Drums, sweetgrass and eagle feathers are henceforth appropriate elements of any such negotiations.

It would be impossible to conclude an account of Mi'kmaqs in Sweden without mentioning that in 1992 a group of forest-dwelling, European hippies calling themselves "Mi'kmaq" captured the Swedish headlines. They stayed for several months in the forest in the north of Sweden, convincing a number of journalists and citizens of their Amerindian heritage and enjoying the good will of credulous Swedes. One of their more remarkable claims was that their "Mi'kmaq" ancestors were vegetarians. The Swedish-Indian Association tried in vain to expose the impostors by publishing an infuriated letter from Alex Denny of the Mi'kmaq Grand Council.[36] I mention this episode here because I am convinced that the Swedish willingness to adopt their very own tribe of ecological "Mi'kmaq Indians" was in part preconditioned by the Stora-Mi'kmaq conflict. In fact, in the course of fieldwork in Nova Scotia in 1992-93, I was amused to hear Mi'kmaq jokingly refer to the hippie group in Sweden as "Junior's tribe."

First Nations' Environmentalism: Traditionalism and Authenticity

As mentioned, the Mi'kmaq have been involved in several environmental conflicts in addition to that over Stora's forestry. I have elsewhere traced the development of the conflict over Kelly's Mountain, also on Cape Breton Island, which represents the consolidation of a more militant, ethnic activism among the Nova Scotia Mi'kmaq.[37] Some of the leading figures in the struggle to save Kluskap's sacred mountain from being turned into a granite quarry had in fact participated in the dramatic Mohawk Warrior blockade at Oka, Quebec, in the summer of 1990. By the fall of 1990, they had founded a Mi'kmaq Warrior Society and declared that they would stop the proposed quarry at any cost. Blockades had also been used in Whycocomagh to protest against the hauling of pulpwood to Stora's mill in Port Hawkesbury.

This hardening of attitudes is linked to a noteworthy shift from pragmatic to cultural and spiritual arguments. The argument that a mountain is sacred and crucial to a people's identity is not amenable to bureaucratic negotiation in the same way as concerns over dwindling resources. The growing success of such arguments, as illustrated by Oka as well as Kelly's Mountain, suggests that they represent an increasingly viable means of confronting the hegemony of modernist rationality. In being more self-reflexive about the existential undercurrents of environmental concern, they may signify the articulation of a discourse through which modernity might finally transcend itself. The current "ethnification" of the world may thus be more than the completion of another civilizational cycle.[38] Ethnicity and sanctity have both been irreversibly transformed by the experience of modernity. To so self-reflexively evoke sanctity and identity is to consciously reject the interchangeability of values on which modernity rests.

Environmentalism has for several decades been an arena for political careers, in native contexts as well as non-native. Not very surprisingly, frustrated industrialists like Kelly Rock's president will tend to dismiss ethnic environmentalism as mere political strategy.[39] Granted, if presenting themselves as protectors of Mother Earth is yet another emblem of a First Nation's "opposition ideology,"[40] it is obvious that the choice of this emblem is not entirely their own. It is probably in large measure a response to what the media are interested in hearing. Only a very superficial glance, however, could fail to see the profound, existential issues at stake for many First Nations traditionalists. Their new-found identities are no less worthy of respect because their cultural creativity is so obviously geared to the White Man's own, Jungian projections. I have elsewhere argued that in being encouraged to say the things that mainstream North Americans cannot say themselves, the First Nations are being assigned a crucial, historical mission.[41]

The ethnic creativity characteristic of recent world processes has kept anthropologists busy redefining the concept of "culture." It has become conspicuously evident that cultural identity to some extent is continuously being "constructed," or even "invented," but opinions have varied as to what the implications of this discovery might be. Perhaps most important in these deliberations is an emergent reassessment of the concept of "authenticity."[42]

Some researchers have kept focusing on the degree of faithfulness with which historically documented cultural forms are being reproduced.[43] An alternative would be to look *beyond* the partly arbitrary *bricolage* of cultural accessories, such as drums or sweetgrass, in order to acknowledge the human essence trying to express itself through them. Do the Mi'kmaq traditionalists, as the rhetoric goes, "speak from the heart?" Using this, more reasonable criterion, I will conclude by submitting that they tend to be more deeply concerned with maintaining their authenticity than most of us. Ultimately, Mi'kmaq and other indigenous environmentalists give voice to universal, human concerns. The rest of us might listen to them as to a suppressed substratum of our own consciousness. To be sure, the self-conscious "traditionalist" is as much a projection of modernity as was ever the "environmentalist," or, for that matter, any other category of modern identity. But this does not detract from the earnestness with which they, or anyone else, may experience the fulfilment of their selves as such. To deny them the same measure of self-reflexivity as is essential to other modern identities (including those of anthropologists) is, to quote Marshall Sahlins, to "do in theory just what imperialism attempts in practice."[44]

Notes

1. I would like to thank the Bank of Sweden Tercentenary Foundation for funding my fieldwork in Nova Scotia in May-June 1991, from August 1992 to April 1993, and in July-August 1996.

2. Nicolas Denys, *Concerning the Ways of the Indians: Their Customs, Dress, Methods of Hunting and Fishing, and Their Amusements* (Halifax: The Nova Scotia Museum, 1672/1908).

3. Cf. Yngve George Lithman, "Ideologizing About Indian Attitudes to Wildlife: The Provincial-First Nation Interplay," paper presented at the symposium *Indian Conservation of Game: Ideological Bias or Cultural and Historical Variation* (Vancouver: CASCA, 1994).

4. Grand Council of Mi'kmaqs et al., *The Mi'kmaq Treaty Handbook* (Sydney: Native Communications Society of Nova Scotia, 1987).

5. Donald Marshall, Alex Denny and Simon Marshall 1989, "The Mi'kmaq: The Covenant Chain," in *Drumbeat: Anger and Renewal in Indian country,* ed. Boyce Richardson (Toronto: Summerhill Press/The Assembly of First Nations, 1989), 71-104.

6. Calvin Martin, *Keepers of the Game: Indian-Animal Relationships and the Fur Trade* (Berkeley: University of California Press, 1978).

7. Cf. J. Kay, "Native Americans in the Fur Trade and Wildlife Depletion," *Environmental Review* 9 (1985), 118-130; Shepard Krech, ed., *Indians, Animals and the Fur Trade* (Athens: University of Georgia Press, 1981).

8. Martin, op. cit., 157.

9. *Indianbulletinen* 4 (1983), 4.

10. Immanuel Wallerstein, "The Rise and Future Demise of the World Capitalist System: Concepts for Comparative Analysis," *Comparative Studies in Society and History* 16 (1974), 387-415.

11. Andre Gunder Frank, "The Development of Underdevelopment," *Monthly Review* 18 (1966), 17-31.

12. L. Anders Sandberg, "Forest Policy in Nova Scotia: The Big Lease, Cape Breton Island, 1899-1960," in *Trouble in the Woods: Forest Policy and Social Conflict in Nova Scotia and New Brunswick,* ed. L. Anders Sandberg (Fredericton: Acadiensis Press, 1992), 65-89.

13. Elizabeth May, *Budworm Battles: The Fight to Stop the Aerial Insecticide Spraying of the Forests of Eastern Canada* (Halifax: Four East Publications, 1982); Farley Mowat, "Grass-roots Crusader: Elizabeth May and the Budworm Battle," in *Rescue the Earth!Conversations with the Green Crusaders* (Toronto: McClelland and Stewart, 1990).

14. Dietrich Soyez, "The Internationalization of Environmental Conflict: The Herbicide Issue in Nova Scotia's Forests and its Links with Sweden," in *Canada and the Nordic Countries: Proceedings from the Second International Conference of the Nordic Association for Canadian Studies,* eds. Jørn Carlsen and Bengt Streijffert (Lund: Lund University Press, 1987), 309-320.

15. Alf Hornborg, "Environmentalism and Identity on Cape Breton: On the Social and Existential Conditions for Criticism," in *Green Arguments and Local Subsistence,* ed. Gudrun Dahl (Stockholm: Almqvist and Wiksell International, 1993), 128-161.

16. May, op. cit.

17. Mowat, op. cit., 200.

18. Ibid., 203.

19. Soyez, op. cit., 316-317.

20. Mowat, op. cit., 203.

21. Aaron Schneider, "Underdeveloping Nova Scotia's Forests and the Role of Corporate Counterintelligence," in *Deforestation and "Development" in Canada and the Tropics: The Impact on People and the Environment,* ed. Aaron Schneider (Sydney: Centre for International Studies, University College of Cape Breton, 1989), 181-183.

22. *The Scotia Sun,* August 18, 1992.

23. Soyez, op. cit., 316.

24. May, op. cit., 31; Mowat, op. cit., 195.

25. Cartoon circulated by the Support Committee for Nova Scotia.

26. Mowat, op. cit., 204.

27. *The Scotia Sun,* October 21, 1987.

28. *Borlänge Tidning,* June 18, 1988.

29. E.g., *Dala-Demokraten,* June 21, 1988.

30. *Indianbulletinen* 4 (1983).

31. *Dala-Demokraten,* June 21, 1988.

32. *Expressen,* June 19, 1988.

33. Soyez, op. cit., 316.

34. *Chronicle-Herald,* May 2, 1990.

35. Alf Hornborg, "Environmentalism, Ethnicity and Sacred Places: Reflections on Modernity, Discourse and Power," *Canadian Review of Sociology and Anthropology* 31 (1994), 245-267.

36. E.g., *Miljötidningen* (1993), 1.

37. Hornborg, 1994, op. cit.

38. Jonathan Friedman, *Cultural Identity and Global Process* (London: Sage Publications, 1994).

39. *Inverness Oran,* February 1991.

40. Tord Larsen, "Negotiating Identity: The Micmac of Nova Scotia," in *The Politics of Indianness: Case Studies of Native Ethnopolitics in Canada,* ed. Adrian Tanner (St. John's: Memorial University of Newfoundland, 1983), 37-136.

41. Hornborg, 1994, op. cit., 252-253.

42. E.g., Jean Jackson, "Is There a Way to Talk About Making Culture Without Making Enemies?" *Dialectical Anthropology* 14 (1989), 127-143; Jean Jackson, "Culture, Genuine and Spurious: The Politics of Indianness in the Vaupés, Colombia," *American Ethnologist* 22 (1995), 3-27; Friedman, op. cit.

43. Jocelyn Linnekin, "Defining Tradition: Variations on the Hawaiian Identity," *American Ethnologist* 10 (1983), 241-52; F. Allan Hanson, "The Making of the Maori: Culture Invention and Its Logic," *American Anthropologist* 91 (1989), 890-902.

44. Marshall Sahlins, "Goodbye to Tristes Tropes: Ethnography in the Context of Modern World History," in *Assessing Cultural Anthropology,* ed. Robert Borofsky (New York: McGraw-Hill, 1994), 381.

Index